THE COGNITIVE SYSTEM OF THE FRENCH VERB

JOHN HEWSON
Memorial University of Newfoundland

JOHN BENJAMINS PUBLISHING COMPANY
AMSTERDAM/PHILADELPHIA

The paper used in this publication meets the minimum requirements of American National Standard for Information Sciences — Permanence of Paper for Printed Library Materials, ANSI Z39.48-1984.

Library of Congress Cataloging-in-Publication Data

Hewson, John. 1930-
 The cognitive system of the French verb / John Hewson.
  p.   cm. -- (Amsterdam studies in the theory and history of linguistic science. Series IV, Current issues in linguistic theory, ISSN 0304-0763 ; v. 147)
 Includes bibliographical references and index.
 1. French language--Verb. 2. Cognitive grammar. I. Title. II. Series.
PC2271.H49   1997
445--dc21   97-6144
ISBN 90 272 3651 8 (Eur.) / 1-55619-862-0 (US) (alk. paper)   CIP

© Copyright 1997 - John Benjamins B.V.
No part of this book may be reproduced in any form, by print, photoprint, microfilm, or any other means, without written permission from the publisher.

John Benjamins Publishing Co. • P.O.Box 75577 • 1070 AN Amsterdam • The Netherlands
John Benjamins North America • P.O.Box 27519 • Philadelphia PA 19118-0519 • USA

THE COGNITIVE SYSTEM OF THE FRENCH VERB

AMSTERDAM STUDIES IN THE THEORY AND HISTORY OF LINGUISTIC SCIENCE

General Editor
E. F. KONRAD KOERNER
(University of Ottawa)

Series IV – CURRENT ISSUES IN LINGUISTIC THEORY

Advisory Editorial Board

Henning Andersen (Los Angeles); Raimo Anttila (Los Angeles)
Thomas V. Gamkrelidze (Tbilisi); John E. Joseph (Edinburgh)
Hans-Heinrich Lieb (Berlin); Ernst Pulgram (Ann Arbor, Mich.)
E. Wyn Roberts (Vancouver, B.C.); Danny Steinberg (Tokyo)

Volume 147

John Hewson

The Cognitive System of the French Verb

À MON MAÎTRE

ROCH VALIN

A L'OCCASION
DES VINGT-CINQ ANS ÉCOULÉS DEPUIS LA PUBLICATION DU
PREMIER VOLUME DES *LEÇONS DE LINGUISTIQUE*
DE GUSTAVE GUILLAUME

(1971-1996)

PREFACE

Such terms as *system, structure, function*, have been understood in many different ways in twentieth century work in linguistics. In the title of this work, *system* means the *content system* of the French verb, the meaningful system of contrasts, the underlying system of *invariants*, to use the familiar term of Jakobson, that permits the range of surface meanings, of surface usage. This notion of a grammatical system as fundamentally a content system is central to the work of such linguists as Hjelmslev, Jakobson and Gustave Guillaume.

Some of the subject matter of this book has been taught, in one form or another, for over half a century, and I myself have taught it for more than a quarter of a century: the original course was initiated by Roch Valin at Université Laval in Quebec City in the early 1950's. The basic elements may be found as early as 1929, in Gustave Guillaume's *Temps et verbe*, in later articles collected in his posthumous *Langage et science du langage* (1964), and in several of the volumes of his posthumous *Leçons de linguistique* (1971 onwards, thirteen volumes so far published). Nevertheless, there exists no single comprehensive volume, in either French or English, that presents a coherent overview of this material.

When students perceive how this analysis reduces the complexity of the French verb to certain fundamental simple principles, of a kind that could be easily mastered by a child, their response is often "Why wasn't it taught to us like this in the first case?" The answer must be given in three stages. First, one has to know the data before being able to make an analysis of it. Second, a point of view as revolutionary as that presented in Guillaume's *Temps et verbe* and in the later *Leçons de linguistique* takes time to percolate through the educational establishment, although much of it - the analysis of the French aspect system, for example - has now become a commonplace of French grammars, even those used in elementary schools in France. Thirdly, the students taking this course were themselves the first generation of new teachers to have this knowledge. Many have now made use of it in their own language teaching, giving their students sound instruction in such matters as tense, aspect, mood, and voice.

The time has come, therefore, to make this material more easily accessible to the scholarly public, for two reasons. The first of these is that much work has been done, and needs to be reported on, since the development of the original course. The second reason is the steadily growing interest in what has been called

PREFACE

Cognitive Linguistics: Guillaume's endless search for mental mechanisms (hence the name *Psychomechanics* that he gave to his work) is very much a form of cognitive linguistics. The whole of his scolarly life, from his earliest book *Le Problème de l'article* (1919), to his death in 1960, was devoted to the principle that language involves mental processing, and that the operations involved can be discerned through the results that they produce in discourse, a method that parallels historical reconstruction of unobservable protolanguages from their observable daughter languages, as he points out from the very beginning (1919:11-13). Guillaume's ability at this work was much admired by his mentor Meillet, and the French comparativist Louis Havet notes, in his review of *Le Problème de l'article* in the *Bulletin de la Société Linguistique de Paris*, that such work requires "un incroyable don de discerner l'invisible" (1919:158).

There are, consequently, four interwoven threads in the text that follows. The first is the original course as conceived and presented by Valin. The second is the accumulation of ideas and insights from almost thirty years of presenting and explaining the material. The third is composed of references to the thirteen volumes of the *Leçons de linguistique*, Guillaume's lectures at the Ecole des Hautes Etudes in Paris. The fourth is the attempt to relate the work done in the Guillaumian school to work done in recent years in Cognitive Linguistics, and to make explicit the cognitive basis of Psychomechanics.

The intended audience is therefore twofold. It includes, first of all, students of the French language, including language teachers, in search of a better understanding of the way that the verbal system operates. It also includes linguists with an interest in the cognitive operations and cognitive systems of languages. To make the task easier for both groups, for an audience confronted with such a novel approach, Chapter Two presents a brief description of the English verbal system, to give an idea of what the method does for English, and to present the fundamental elements from which verbal systems are constructed. Chapter One, on the other hand, has been included to justify the historical and methodological rationale behind the approach: this chapter may be bypassed by students of French who are not interested in the convolutions of twentieth century linguistics.

The ideas in some of these chapters have been previously presented at a variety of scholarly conferences, and published in the proceedings of those conferences. The seven relevant publications are in the Bibliography: Hewson 1976, 1988a, 1988b, 1989, 1990b, 1990c, 1990d.

November 1996
St. John's, Newfoundland   John Hewson

CONTENTS

Preface vii

Chapter One	**The Nature of Content Systems**	**1**
1.	Introduction	1
1.1	Origin of the idea	1
1.2	System in phonology	2
1.3	System and grammatical structure	4
1.4	System in language	7
1.5	Tongue and discourse	8
1.6	Systems and rules	10
1.7	Content systems and referential meaning	11
1.8	Prior studies with Guillaumian influence	14
1.9	Conclusion	15

Chapter Two	**Verbal Paradigms and their Content**	**17**
2.	Introduction	17
2.1	The paradigm of tense	17
2.1.1	Incidence and decadence	19
2.1.2	Time spheres	19
2.1.3	The problem of the threshold	21
2.2	Mood	23
2.2.1	The subjunctive	23
2.2.2	Infinitive and participles	25
2.3	Aspect	27
2.3.1	The modal auxiliaries	28
2.3.2	The grammatical auxiliaries	29
2.4	Voice	33
2.5	The verbal paradigms of French	34

Chapter Three	**Chronogenesis**	**35**
3.	Introduction	35
3.1	Three morphosyntactic types	35
3.1.1	Three chronogenetic stages	36
3.2	Stage I: the quasi-nominal mood	37
3.2.1	A simpler view of the quasi-nominal forms	38

3.2.2	Functions of the quasi-nominal forms	39
3.3	Stage II: subjunctive mood	41
3.4	Stage III: indicative mood	43
3.5	Conclusion	46
Chapter Four	**Aspect**	**48**
4.	Introduction	48
4.1	Distinguishing tense from aspect	49
4.1.1	The surcomposé in student grammars	50
4.1.2	The mechanism underlying the aspectual system	50
4.1.3	Simple forms	51
4.1.4	Compound forms	52
4.1.5	Double compound forms	52
4.1.6	Usage of French aspectual forms	54
4.1.7	Modern use of the composé as a preterit	55
4.1.8	Expressing anteriority	56
4.2	Sequence of tenses in English	59
4.3	Use of the surcomposé in main clauses	60
4.4	Conclusion	61
Chapter Five	**Voice**	**63**
5.	Introduction	63
5.1	The grammatical representation of agent and patient	64
5.2	Passive voice in French	66
5.2.1	The role of the subject	67
5.3	The pronominal verbs	69
5.4	The verbs of resultant state	71
5.4.1	Resultative verbs as a morphosyntactic category	74
5.4.2	Change of auxiliary with transitive verbs	75
5.5	Middle voice	76
5.5.1	Morphosyntax of middle voice	77
5.5.2	Agentive and patientive senses of middle voice	78
5.5.3	Reflexive and reciprocal senses of middle voice	79
5.5.4	Middle voice with pure intransitives	81
5.6	Active and middle with inanimate objects	82
5.7	Conclusion	83
Chapter Six	**Tense**	**85**
6.	Introduction: tense and aspect	85

6.1	Defining tense and aspect in cognitive terms	86
6.2	Tense in cognitive terms	88
6.3	Tense and the experience of time	89
6.4	The parameters of tense in French	92
6.4.1	The verticality of the present in French	92
6.4.2	The breadth of the French present	94
6.5	Past tenses	96
6.5.1	Imperfect and Passé simple: tenses or aspects?	98
6.5.2	The Imperfect	100
6.5.2.1	Imperfects of Type 1	101
6.5.2.2	Imperfects of Type 2	103
6.5.2.3	Imperfects of Type 3	104
6.6	Future and conditional	105
6.6.1	The future in the past	107
6.6.2	Conditional clauses	108
6.6.3	The conditional of probability	109
6.7	Conclusion	110
Chapter Seven	**Mood**	**111**
7.	Introduction	111
7.1	A simple cognitive contrast	111
7.2	The subjunctive as a position in the system	112
7.2.1	Quasi-nominal mood	113
7.2.2	Subjunctive mood	113
7.2.3	Indicative mood	114
7.3	The indicative/subjunctive contrast	114
7.3.1	Possible vs. probable	115
7.3.2	Affirmative vs. negative	116
7.3.3	Relative clauses	116
7.3.4	Conjunctions	117
7.3.4.1	The subjunctive with *après que*	118
7.3.5	Value judgements	120
7.3.6	Variable usage	122
7.4	Facing the problems of subjunctive usage	123
7.5	Conclusion	124
Chapter Eight	**Present and Present Perfect**	**129**
8.	Introduction	129
8.1	Concrete cognitive activity	129

8.2	The nature of a threshold	130
8.3	Cognitive contrasts, lexical and grammatical	131
8.3.1	Contrastive usage: past versus present	132
8.3.2	Contrastive usage: present perfect versus present	133
8.3.3	Contrastive usage: the first time	134
8.3.4	Contrastive usage: immediate physical realizations	135
8.3.5	Contrastive usage: passé composé versus preterit	136
8.4	Conclusion	138
Chapter Nine	**Semiology, the System of Signs**	**139**
9.	Introduction	139
9.1	The arbitrary nature of the sign	139
9.2	Arbitrariness and the law of coherence	141
9.3	Allomorphs of *aller*	144
9.4	The '*verbes de puissance*'	144
9.5	The morphology of the imperative	145
9.6	Conclusion	146
Chapter Ten	**Verbal Paradigms**	**148**
10.	Introduction: regular and irregular verbs	148
10.1	Verbal paradigms of French	148
10.2	Derivational verb suffixes of Latin	149
10.3	The French suffix /-i(s)-/	150
10.4	The axial consonant	151
10.5	Other correspondences in the paradigms	152
10.6	The forms of the Latin perfect	154
10.7	The past participle	155
10.8	Conclusion	155
Bibliography		**158**
General Index		**170**
Index of Verb Forms		**182**

CHAPTER ONE
THE NATURE OF CONTENT SYSTEMS

1. *Introduction*
Linguists would almost universally assent to the proposition that there is system in language. Where system is to be found, and the form that it takes, however, are matters of considerable controversy. There has been, for example, much impassioned discussion of Meillet's famous dictum "Une langue est un système où tout se tient et a un plan d'une merveilleuse rigueur" (1903/1937:475). Even the origin of the phrase *un système où tout se tient* has been much discussed (Brogyanyi 1983, Toman 1987, Hewson 1990d, Peeters 1991). It has often been wrongly attributed to Saussure (e.g., Hockett 1967:937), for example. The principle thus stated has often been criticised and rejected, but it can nevertheless be demonstrated to be valid, and to be necessary for a proper representation of the functioning of language. The remarkable linguistic insights of Jakobson, who praises the Prague School view of a language as 'a system of systems' (1990:59), a point of view also promoted by Gustave Guillaume (1952, 1964:220–240), the first to present a systemic view (1929) of the French verbal system, led to Jakobson's untiring quest to find the simple systemic elements that make sense of complex data, such as the universal features that are the basis of phonemic systems.

1.1 *Origin of the idea*
It is not totally incongruous, in fact, to attribute this well-known comment to Saussure: Meillet was directly influenced by Saussure (see Koerner 1984:31), and indeed, as Stefanini (1973:322) has stated: "L'idée que la langue est un système a toujours été considérée par toute l'école de Paris, de Meillet à Benveniste, comme l'apport fondamental de Saussure." The notion of system is fundamental to all of Saussure's work, both synchronic and diachronic: in fact, as Gustave Guillaume points out, it is fundamental to the whole comparativist enterprise (1986:10). It is not surprising, therefore, that the centrality of the notion of system in Saussure's work is to be found as early as his 1879 *Mémoire sur les voyelles*: in that work he proposed a system of three laryngeals based entirely on regular correspondences in the IndoEuropean languages.

Implicit in this approach is the conclusion that a certain kind of sound change is regular because it is the product of systemic change: change a letter on a typewriter (change in the system) and the text will be affected in regular fashion. If one replaces *s* by a dollar sign, for example, a word such as *stress* would appear as *$tre$$*. In fact Saussure made no attempt to delineate the phonetic reality of these three phonemes: he simply labelled them as indeterminate vowels numbered 1,2,3, and treated them as systemic not phonic elements. This immediately raises a fundamentally important question: what is the nature of a linguistic system? Is a phonemic system a system of sounds or not?

1.2 *System in phonology*

This question has, in fact, been given categorically different answers during the twentieth century. It is clear, for example, that the Bloomfieldian phoneme, which is determined by its allophones, is essentially phonic, so that the [ŋ] of *ink* and the [ŋ] of *sing* are two different exponents of the same phoneme for Bloomfield (1933:133). Such a view makes phonemic overlapping impossible, because what one *hears* is the final and ultimate determiner of the phoneme. Here we have an outstanding example of the interference of metaphysics with science, where a scientific stance is based upon a commitment to positivism and behaviourism. And, as always in science, confusion and distortion result when one attempts to sort data into a preconceived mold, when one forces data into categories that do not fit.

In direct contrast is the view of Sapir (1933), who criticises the Bloomfieldian view, for all its emphasis upon the directly observable, as being "the reverse of realistic" (1933/1949:46). For Sapir it is the phoneme that determines the allophones, and it is therefore perfectly conceivable that the [ŋ] of *ink* is a velar allophone of /n/, an assimilation that may be expected to occur on a regular basis before a following velar consonant. This is clearly the correct approach, since it can justify the [s] and [z] of the plural marker in *cats and dogs*, which in the Bloomfieldian view are two different phonemes whereas from Sapir's point of view they are both allophones of /z/, the devoicing that produces [s] in *cats* being the product of a simple assimilation. To make the allophones determine the phoneme, in short, is cart-before-the-horse thinking, a confusion of cause and effect.

The priority of the phoneme in the act of language should, in fact, be obvious. The phoneme is the permanent entity without which the allophones, the sounds that vibrate on the airwaves in temporary fashion only to dissipate and be lost, could not be created. In the printing process the printed page can not be produced without the permanent fount of type, a small and finite set from which myriads of printed pages can be produced. If the pages are all destroyed, the process may still continue: if the fount of type is lost or destroyed, printing comes to a halt. Common sense leads to the conclusion that in the act of language a phoneme necessarily determines its allophones.

If, therefore, it is the phoneme that determines the allophones, the phoneme is the mental entity that triggers the motor mechanisms of speech. To speak in this way would have caused an uproar in the middle years of this century, in spite of the fact that it was at that very time that Wilder Penfield was conducting experiments on the cortex of the brain during brain surgery, and demonstrating that one could trigger the motor mechanisms of vowel sounds by application of an electrode to certain areas of the cortex. When the electrode is applied, the patient utters a spastic vowel sound, which is continued as long as the patient has breath. "Then, after he has taken a breath, he continues helplessly as before" (Penfield & Roberts 1959:199). In this demonstration we see the role of the phoneme as a mental entity with a physical correlate that can be activated by the intervention of a slight electric current. Such a phoneme is a mental trace that plays the fundamental determining role in the production of a speech sound.

Our analysis of phonological systems also shows us that these systems are creations of nature, with patterns and regularities that remind us of the crystalline structure of the snowflake. Vowel systems, for example, run all the way from a more or less basic three vowel system to the eight vowels of the so-called cardinal system, and there are sub-systems of diphthongs and long vowels, and regular allophonic patterning for closed and open syllables, stressed and unstressed syllables, and so forth. The universality of some of these patterns is itself significant. As Jakobson notes, the triangular vowel system (a-u-i) based on the two distinctive contrasts compact-diffuse and grave-acute "is nearly universal in three vowel systems and is fully universal in languages with a higher number of vowel phonemes" (1979/1990:286).

An important systemic fact emerges from comparison of such systems: the high front vowel in a three vowel system is appreciably different from the high front vowel in a five vowel or a seven vowel system. Such a phoneme in a three vowel system will trigger allophones that would be mid-vowels in a five vowel system, and high-mid (but not low-mid) vowels in a seven vowel system. A phoneme therefore is not a sound, since no one could utter, as a single sound, the range of sounds covered by the high front vowel of a three vowel system. One may, admittedly, choose to define a phoneme as a range of sounds, but ultimately such a range of sounds is still a mental entity, a diversity of experiences that the mind groups together and recognizes as belonging to a unit. Inuktitut (Eskimo), for example, has a three vowel system in which the high front vowel /i/ has an allophone [e]. In French or English this [e] would be identified as belonging to

/e/, not /i/, since these languages have mid-front vowel phonemes, which Inuktitut does not.

Defining a phoneme as sound, in fact, is still putting the cart before the horse, and can lead to making erroneous judgments on the basis of appearances, as happened in the case of the famous vowel grid of Bloch & Trager (1951), which is an attempt to find system, as good structuralists should, but in the wrong place: in the surface appearances, rather than in the underlying causation. We learned long ago in historical linguistics that what appears to be related on the surface is often not related at all: that Germanic /p,t,k/ do not correspond to Romance /p,t,k/, Slavic /p,t,k/ or Indic /p,t,k/. The same is true of synchronic linguistics: the American pronunciation of *cod* and the British pronunciation of *card* are frequently indistinguishable. The vowels of these syllables are systemically different; to allocate them to the same phoneme on the Bloch & Trager grid consequently creates a gross confusion that brings the whole structuralist enterprise into disrepute.

1.3 *System and grammatical structure*

The properties of linguistic systems are nowhere better illustrated than in Saussure's analogy of the game of chess. Each of the chess pieces moves differently, and the system of the whole game, which determines both the way it is played and the outcome, lies in the moves each piece can make and the possibilities thereby created. The system does not lie in the pieces: if a rook is lost, for example, it can be replaced by a spice bottle or "any conceivable object of a suitable size" (Hjelmslev 1959:28) without altering in any way the system of the game. The pieces are merely markers, just like the linguistic morphology that marks meanings and functions.

In linguistic terms the chess pieces are elements of 'expression', and their systematic moves elements of 'content', to use Hjelmslev's well known terms. We may also make the following partial correspondences with other current terminology.

Hjelmslev:	expression	content
Saussure:	signifiant	signifié
word grammar:	morpheme	sememe
sentence grammar:	morphosyntax	semantics
game of chess:	chess pieces	chess moves

It is important to note that Saussure was attempting, in the analogy of chess, to drive home the point that the grammatical system is not to be found in the directly observable morphosyntax, but in the meaning relationships that are not directly observable. This was also the point of view adopted by such post-Saussurians as Jakobson (1936), Hjelmslev (1935), and Gustave Guillaume (1929). We find the following in Hjelmslev (1935:20,84), for example:

> Tout fait linguistique est un fait de valeur et ne peut être défini que par sa valeur (1935:20). La grammaire est la théorie des significations fondamentales ou des valeurs et des systèmes constitués par elles ... (1935:84). " Every linguistic fact is a fact of value [i.e a meaningful position in a system] and can only be defined by its value... Grammar is the theory of basic meanings or values and of the systems of which they are a part".

A similar point of view has more recently been asserted as a basic tenet of Cognitive Linguistics:

> Grammatical structures do not constitute an autonomous formal system or level of representation: They are claimed instead to be inherently symbolic, providing for the structuring and conventional symbolization of conceptual content (Langacker 1986:2).

In the generation immediately following Saussure, in fact, we find the attempt among European linguists such as Hjelmslev (1935) and Jakobson (1936) to treat the nominal case systems as *systèmes de valeurs*, systems of meaning where each case draws its meaning from its position in the system and the contrasts that it generates with the rest of the system. This practice of delineating the overall structure of the system in order to distinguish the meaning of the parts is, of course, a fundamentally structuralist approach. The same approach is taken even further by Gustave Guillaume in *Temps et verbe* (1929) where verbal systems are seen as not only having systemic contrasts, but also contrasts of staging within the system, whereby Stage Two is a further development of Stage One, and Stage Three is the most complete representation of verbal events because it is a further reworking of the basis established in Stages One and Two, as will be shown in Chapter Three.

At the same time in North America, however, there was the attempt, especially under the influence of Bloomfield (1926) to find system in the directly observable morphology itself. This again is a fundamentally misguided orientation: in Saussure's game of chess it would be like trying to find the system of the game of chess in the directly observable chess pieces rather than in the moves that the chess pieces can make. This point of view is still maintained today in the doctrinal separation of syntax and semantics, where the grammatical system is supposed to lie in a syntax that is independent of meaning.

In the generation immediately following Saussure, therefore, we again find modern linguistics diverging in two different directions, one seeking to find grammatical system in the content side of language (Hjelmslev, Jakobson,

Guillaume), the the other in the expression side (the Bloomfieldians). The early attempts by Hjelmslev and Jakobson to describe case systems failed to provide totally convincing analyses of the underlying content systems of paradigms, thereby fuelling the prejudice that morphosyntax is meaningless, and the attempt to find meaning in it a waste of time. The work of Guillaume, seeking for mental mechanisms, was rejected by the anti-mentalist temper of the times, and has remained in obscurity until recent years.

The Bloomfieldians, on the other hand, found system in the morphology by fudging, by regularising it where it was irregular, as when Bloch (1947) gave to the past tense of the English strong verbs, such as *took*, a zero suffix (to parallel the *-ed* suffix found on the weak verbs) and indicated that the ablaut difference between *take* and *took* was meaningless: *took* was simply the base of the verb *take* to which the past tense inflection was added, "the only difference being that after this particular base the preterit suffix has the phonemic shape zero, as it has also after the base *put*" (1947/1957:245). It is true that past tense forms like *took* and *talked* do have something in common, but what they have in common is a meaning, not a morphology, as Bloch would have us believe. The meaning stems from a simple binary system: a notional contrast of past vs. non-past that is absolutely regular, available to every normal verb in the language. The morphology that conveys this contrast is also for the most part regular, but there is no requirement that the morphology should be as regular as the content system.

It was left to Gustave Guillaume to point out that it *is* possible to find system in the expression side of language, in the directly observable morphology, which is what enticed the Bloomfieldians to think that they were making an interesting discovery. In the game of chess, for example, all the pawns *look* alike, and all the pawns *move* alike. There is system at the level of what is perceivable, what is directly observable, (the shape of the chess pieces themselves), and system at the level of what is conceivable, of what is only indirectly observable: the moves that belong to each chess piece, the meaningful function that belongs to each piece.

But, Guillaume points out (1984:73–74), whatever is systematic in the morphology is only a reflection of the real system, which is a *système de valeurs* in the content side of language. The morphology, at the level of perceivability, is only a sometimes incomplete reflection of the grammatical system, the system of conceivability. The morphology, consequently, is often incoherent and irregular, whereas the grammatical system is coherent and regular. The English nouns *mice*, *men*, *teeth*, for example, are just as regular in their plural meanings as are the 'regular' nouns *cats*, *dogs*, *horses*. This difference leads Guillaume to posit two laws, the *loi de cohérence* which states that systemic coherence is the norm for content systems, and the *loi de simple suffisance*, which states that an expression system may contain irregularities, and only contains sufficient coherence to maintain an adequate reflection of the underlying and conditioning content system (1984:73-74, 1971:70–71). Content, in short, is where the real system lies, and is consequently completely maximally coherent. It is content that conditions and determines expression, which may be only minimally coherent. *The role of the morphosyntax is an intermediary one of making the content perceivable.*

It should also be noted that Guillaume's *loi de simple suffisance* is also a reaffirmation of the Saussurian doctrine of *l'arbitraire du signe* which simply states that no matter what sign is used, it could be different, it could be replaced: the spice bottle replacing the rook. There is no requirement that morphosyntax should be completely coherent, no requirement that the past tense of *take*, a regular systemic element, should be marked by *taked*. The relationship between content and expression, however, is also an important study, which will be briefly surveyed in Chapter 9.

1.4 *System in language*

If we wish to survey the whole question of system in language there is another important fact that has to be taken into consideration. Hockett, for example, is critical of those who talk of system, and claims that "the search for system in language is a wild goose chase" (1967:910). Curiously, Hockett is absolutely right, and even the most dyed-in-the-wool Saussurean would have to agree with him, since Saussure himself observed (1916:38) that "Le tout global du langage est inconnaissable." The search for system in the unknowable is quite clearly a wild goose chase.

The search for system in what Saussure called *langage* is indeed a waste of time, because that is the wrong place to look for system. System is only to be found in tongue (normally the mother tongue of the speaker), in what Saussure called *langue*. If we use the analogy of a child's construction toy, such as a Meccano or Erector set, consisting of sets of girders, sets of plates, sets of axles, sets of wheels, nut and bolts, and so forth, we can see that the set itself is a system of sorts, with paradigms of girders, plates, axles, wheels. But the models that the child makes from the kit: cranes, trucks, helicopters, do not form a system; here we have an analogy for the free enterprise of discourse, where we can discern that the parts that are used for these constructions belong to systems, but that the constructions themselves do not.

A word, for example, is certainly a phonological structure, but it is not a phonological system. Phonological systems, being fundamentally cognitive, belong to the subconscious mind and are not directly observable; they can only be discovered by observation and analysis of data. The words that vibrate on the air waves are made up from systemic elements, but are not themselves systems. The sentence likewise is made up from systemic elements, but is a structure, not a system. To look for system in the sentence is indeed a wild goose chase: to find system we need to do comparative work on the sentence elements. Guillaume at the beginning of his career (1919:27) compared his procedures to the operation of the comparative method, and Valin (1964) has made a detailed study of the parallels between the two procedures. In phonology, observation and analysis allow us to reconstruct the cognitive contrasts of the phonological system: Jakobson's simple binary features that underlie the quasi universal organisation of triangular vowel systems. The same procedures in grammar allow us to reconstruct the simple and fundamental cognitive contrasts of grammatical systems.

1.5 *Tongue and discourse*

Guillaume's posthumous *Leçons de linguistique* show us that when he began a new academic year with newcomers intermingled with his regular audience, he would spend the first lecture making sure that the newcomers had the necessary tools to follow the presentations that his regular audience were prepared for (1991:1–6). His insistence was first of all on the importance of making a clear distinction between *langue* and *discours*, which is essentially an operational view of *langue* and *parole* in the Saussurian scheme; above we have used the English words 'tongue' and 'discourse', a choice of words which has its own explicit justification (Hewson 1984, 1987): the term *language* is hopelessly ambiguous, and if the French word *langue* is used, it is normally explained as meaning "language", which simply returns us to square one. The term 'tongue', as in 'the mother tongue' (never 'the mother language'), or "The tongue of one nation as distinct from others", to borrow a definition from Dr. Johnson, represents a learned, acquired mental faculty in the same way that *memory* represents an inherent mental faculty.

Guillaume was one of the first to insist that language is an activity, not a thing, and that this observation has important repercussions for the science of linguistics. Tongue and discourse are not analytic abstractions, they are different mental moments in the activity of language. Tongue, like the fount of type, necessarily is a prior moment in the act of language, and discourse, like the printed page, is a conclusion, a product of the activity. Tongue is also permanent, once it has been acquired by the child, whereas discourse, apart from those rare occasions that it is recorded, is ephemeral: it vibrates on the airwaves and

THE NATURE OF CONTENT SYSTEMS

disappears. Tongue, like the fount of type, is finite, and discourse, like the printed page, has no bounds, is limitless, infinite. We may present these contrasts in tabular form, and add others:

TONGUE	DISCOURSE
condition	consequence
permanent	ephemeral
finite	infinite
subconscious	conscious
system	use of system
word	sentence
collective	individual

Speakers are aware of what they are saying, since they may repeat it or correct it, or translate it: consequently we may state that discourse is conscious. But they are not aware of their mother tongue, which is why they study the parts of speech in elementary school, or phonetics and phonology in linguistics courses: the mother tongue is stored out of awareness, accessible through a cognitive 'filing system'. And finally we notice that children learn and store words, they do not learn and store sentences, so that the fundamental unit of the mother tongue is the word, whereas the fundamental unit of discourse is the sentence.

To demonstrate the interactive relationship of tongue and discourse we may once more use the analogy of the child's construction kit, and imagine the child using the kit to make a model of a crane, or a truck. The creation of models from such a kit is a two-stage process:

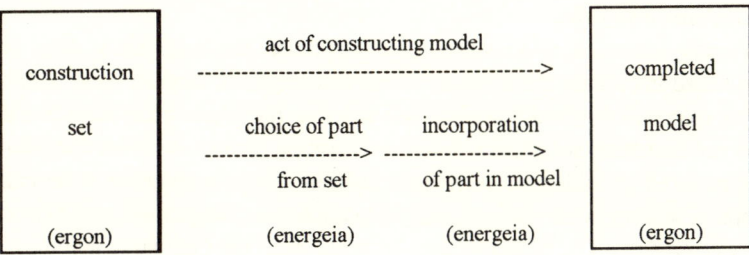

To make the analogy clear, we can replace every single item with linguistic terms:

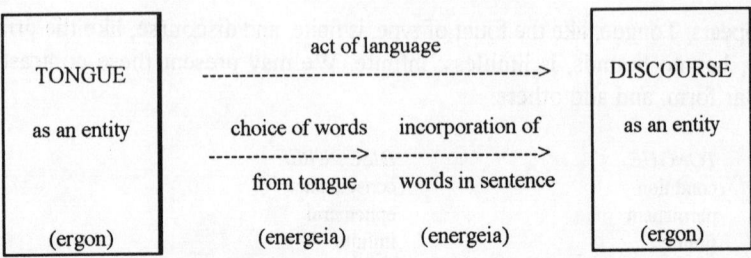

This deliberate oversimplification ignores (1) the fact that the choice of words also involves the grammatical adaptation of words to make them suitable for their syntactic function, and (2) that the incorporation of words into the sentence necessarily involves having a syntactic ground plan (called a *visée de discours* by Guillaume, e.g. 1991:2) in much the same way that the child has a pre-conceived idea of what his crane or truck should look like. These issues have been discussed in detail by Valin (1981:7ff), who points out the necessity not only of a *visée de discours* (communicative goal or intended message) but also of a *visée phrastique* (strategic goal or sentence planning), both of which must be operational for the actual construction of the sentence to begin: they are both necessary cognitive preliminaries to any act of language. There is evidence for these two operations in the use of sentence adverbs: as Claude Guimier (1985:239) has pointed out, adverbs such as *obviously* are predicated of the intended message, and adverbs such as *briefly* are predicated of the sentence planning, rather than of the sentence itself.

1.6 *Systems and rules*

Finally, let us ask what is meant by the phrase 'the linguistic system' that is often heard in current discussions. When challenged to explain what they mean by this expression, many linguists will say that the linguistic system is a set of rules. An unordered set of rules, however, is simply a random collection, that can be re-ordered or added to in random fashion; in no way could it be called a system. A system is normally closed and cannot be changed without destroying and revamping it. The binary system of tense in all the Germanic languages has not changed, for example, since the earliest Germanic documents, although the different languages have come to exploit this common system in different ways, so that the usage in English is now quite different from that in German (stemming at least in part from different aspectual contrasts; e.g., simple vs. progressive in English, a contrast non-existent in German). The indicative system of five tenses, common to most Romance languages, on the other hand, is a significant revamping of the original Latin system of six forms, three imperfective and three perfective (this too being a revamping of tense vs. aspect, since the *perfectum/ infectum* contrast in Latin was aspectual).

Latin, in short had only three tenses: past, present and future. The *infectum* forms of these three tenses were *amabam, amo, amabo*; in the *perfectum* the forms were *amaveram, amavi, amavero*. Modern Romance languages mostly show a totally reshaped system of five tenses (e.g. French *aimai, aimais, aime, aimerai, aimerais*) and the corresponding perfect forms all have auxiliaries (e.g. French *eus aimé, avais aimé, ai aimé, aurai aimé, aurais aimé)*. Such total reshaping is normal in systemic change, for change in the system; it is a change in the set of contrasts, and has nothing whatever to do with rules.

1.7 *Content systems and referential meaning*

When we examine the meaning of grammatical forms we must be aware that there is the permanent meaning (Jakobson's 'invariant') that is a part of the permanent content system and also the varying temporary, surface meanings that are found in sentences. The same is, of course, true of phonology, where a given phoneme must be considered as a permanent acquisition, whereas the endless allophones are purely temporary; they vibrate on the airwaves and are lost.

This distinction between permanent underlying meanings and varying surface meanings is vital for an understanding of the operation of the kind of permanent content systems sketched by Jakobson (1932, 1936) and Guillaume (1929, 1945, 1964, 1971). The speaker opting for a grammatical form of a verb adopts a representation that will be suitable for the sentence; this underlying representation will be affected not only by the linguistic context (as also happens to allophones) but also by the context of situation to give a surface meaning. These different surface meanings can vary widely from one context to another. In much (but not all) linguistic usage, these verb forms also refer to real events in the experiential world, and there is a temptation to reduce the role of language from that of an intermediary representation to that of direct reference, whereby the meaning of a verb is the experiential event which is referred to. In this view a language is nothing but a nomenclature, an onomasiology (Vassant 1981:287–288), for events in the real world. *If this were really the case, of course, fiction would be impossible.*

Nevertheless, because a language can only be learned by observing the way that it is used to represent experience, it is normal to create descriptive categories for verb usage in terms of non-linguistic categories. The most influential of these descriptive systems has been that of Reichenbach 1947, which deals with verb forms in terms of the following non-linguistic categories:

S = point of speech on the line of time
E = point of the event on the line of time
R = point of reference on the line of time

While these reference points are useful for purely surface description, any attempt to map such parameters directly onto verb forms fails to recognise the linguistic meaning of these verb forms, and in particular fails to distinguish how both tense and aspect can be used to represent an event as past or future, fails in short to distinguish overlapping categories. In this respect we may make a comparison with the Bloomfieldian phoneme, which, in staying too close to the directly observable sound, remained purely phonetic and descriptive, and was consequently quite incapable of dealing with phonemic overlapping, whereby two different phonemes could result in the same phonetic result (see 1.2 above).

Just as we have gone on beyond the Bloomfieldian phoneme, a necessary stage in the evolution of linguistic method, we also need to to go beyond Reichenbach's empirical, non-linguistic categories, and reconstruct the underlying verbal system using not just the empirical reference points, but also such language internal evidence as (1) the paradigmatic morphology, (2) the morphosyntactic shape of the verb phrase or verbal piece, (3) contrastive values in the usage of one and the same language, and (4) contrastive usage between different languages. What is of interest to the linguist is not just what is referred to, but even more how the reference is made by different languages, and what different systems of representation languages have for making such references. Such sentences as

(1) I have seen that film
(2) I saw that film last week,

in fact from Reichenbach's point of view are both past tenses because they both represent the same R on the line of time. The only tense mark in (1), however, is the present tense of the auxiliary. To call this verb a past tense gives too much emphasis to what is represented and ignores the value of the representation within the representational system. As with the Bloomfieldian phoneme, too much emphasis on the surface appearances leads to analyses that are, in Sapir's words, 'the reverse of realistic'.

In short, while keeping firmly in mind the importance of what is represented, we have shifted the emphasis, in this work, to the 'means of representation'. It is this shift of emphasis to an underlying system that distinguishes the work of Jakobson and Guillaume from that of other writers on the meaning of verbal morphology, such as Bull (1963), Comrie (1976, 1985), Dahl (1985), Binnick

(1991), who in their work make comparative studies of a variety of languages, and the verbal morphology that these languages use to express various common features of tense and aspect. The attempt to find the underlying system necessarily goes much further and deeper than an examination of the morphosyntax and what it represents, and requires us to concentrate on one system only, referring to others only for contrastive purposes. The intent of this study, therefore, is to concentrate on one system only, and to attempt to discern its fundamental features, in the style of Jakobson's phonology.

There are also other prior studies of the French verb which, in dealing only with the verbal morphology and what it is able to express, may be compared with the kind of phonology that concentrates on physiology: point of articulation, and so on, rather than on Jakobsonian distinctive features. Such, for example, are the studies by Schogt (1968), Fuchs (1979), Vet (1980), Golian (1979), who, while following other schools of thought (Martinet, Benveniste, Dik), occasionally indicate their own view of the work of Guillaume, e.g., Fuchs (1979:51) has this to say:

> La fréquence des références que nous faisons à G. Guillaume ne doit pas laisser penser que nous reprenons à notre compte l'ensemble de la démarche guillaumienne [...] Par ailleurs, le fréquent rapprochement que nous opérons entre G. Guillaume et E. Benveniste peut paraître surprenant; toutefois il nous semble justifié par un certain nombre de convergences sur des points à nos yeux capitaux: critique du positivisme, études des catégories linguistiques considérées en tant que telles, intérêt pour les problèmes de signification, refus d'une conception de la langue comme un inventaire au profit de systèmes d'opérations dynamiques, approche du langage comme une activité plus ou moins reliée au sujet.
> (One should not deduce, from the frequent references we make to Guillaume, that we are adopting the Guillaumian approach in its entirety [...] The parallelisms that we find between Guillaume and Benveniste may also appear surprising; however, we feel they are justified by agreement on certain fundamental principles: disapproval of positivism, study of linguistic categories in and for themselves, interest in problems of meaning, view of a language not as a static inventory but as a system of operational systems, view of language as basically an activity requiring a speaker.)

The following commentary by Golian (1979:2,4) was originally written as part of a doctoral thesis in the functional school of André Martinet. Here 'functional' means emphasis upon how the linguistic element functions, rather than upon the nature of the element, so that again there is no possibility of distinguishing where the usages of tense and aspect overlap (cf. the comments on Reichenbach above).

> En 1929, Gustave Guillaume publie sa théorie sur le système verbal du français dont les influences se font sentir jusqu'à nos jours. Il s'agit d'un ouvrage qui sort de l'ordinaire tant par la démarche mise en oeuvre pour aboutir à une analyse du système verbal français que

par les résultats de cette analyse. [...] Gustave Guillaume a eu ses adeptes en France et ailleurs, et sa théorie, si ce n'est pas par sa méthode, au moins par ses résultats, a sans aucun doute influencé toute une génération de grammairiens et de linguistes français jusqu'à l'époque actuelle.
(In 1929, Guillaume published his theory on the French verbal system, a work whose influence is still operative. It is a work that is out of the ordinary both by its method and its results. ... Guillaume has had his followers in France and elsewhere, and his theory, at least by its results if not by its method, has without doubt influenced a whole generation of French grammarians and linguists right up to the present.)

Golian is critical of the method, repeating Martinet's criticisms of Guillaume's mentalism, a charge that was frequently made against Guillaume in the days when anti-mentalism was the fashion, and Guillaume, the unrepentant researcher of mental mechanisms, refused to go along with the fashion, and was critical of the positivism that lay behind it (as Fuchs points out above). The reader of Golian's comments is left to wonder how one who is guilty of such flawed methods is capable of such outstanding results.

Guillaume in the *Leçons* is repeatedly critical of heavy handed empiricism, and he was always insistent that a mature science must be theoretical. For him the purpose of theory is not to propose abstractions, but to make an attempt to reconstruct the underlying reality that is not directly observable, but is only inferrable from the results observed in the empirical data. For him these underlying systems were simple, construed of elements that small children could easily master, cognitive units with simple binary contrasts; and the more complex forms, as in Jakobson's phonology, were necessarily built upon forms that were less complex.

Consequently it is not just WHAT is represented in language that is important; even more important is HOW such representation takes place. The observation that there are clearly systemic elements in languages leads to the attempt to reconstruct the elements of these systems, which, existing only in the storage of the subconscious mind, are not amenable to direct observation and may only be approached by a theoretical method well supported by coherent evidence. It is fundamentally the same method as that used for the comparative reconstruction of protolanguages, a method with a long and productive history in linguistics.

1.8 *Prior studies with Guillaumian influence*
There are several previous studies of the French verb that pay tribute to Guillaume and admit extensive influence of his ideas, such as Paul Imbs' *L'emploi des temps verbaux en français moderne*. Much of the book deals with usage, but for the theoretical basis Imbs (1960:vii) states "La perspective

générale de notre partie systématique est celle de M. Guillaume". There are, however, significant differences, such as two different systemic futures that share the same morphology (a questionable procedure), and the difference between *passé simple* and *imparfait* becoming part of the aspect system, rather than the tense system, a view that is also shared by Robert Martin (1971:71), in his book on tense and aspect in Middle French. This latter view is not a serious disagreement, since one can argue the case from both points of view, as we shall show (6.5.1). The systemic evidence, however, is ultimately against it.

There are also other studies that present Guillaumian sketches of the French verbal system in certain chapters or sections, such as Wilmet (1970), Barral (1980), Moignet (1981), and Garnier (1985). Another more recent, and more extensive volume, is by Hervé Curat (1991), *Morphologie verbale et référence temporelle en français moderne*, who admits in his *Avant-propos* to some ambivalence: on the one hand to a sense of overwhelming admiration at a theory which so coherently explains so much; on the other hand to a frustration at the complexity of some notions. He consequently makes considerable changes, the result being not always what Guillaume taught, but an idiosyncratic view. Sometimes this is enormously successful, so that the section on the Imperative is the best account that has so far been written by anyone on the French Imperative. At other times the author has drifted a long way from the Guillaumian point of view, as when he wishes to introduce cart-before-the-horse Reichenbach style features into the Guillaumian scheme. The book is notable, however, for the breadth of its scope, and for the outstanding quality of its examples. It has valuable insights that will be incorporated into our own account.

1.9 *Conclusion*

We conclude that the notion of *system* has had a checkered history in twentieth century linguistics. There have been those who have sought for system in the wrong place, thereby creating confusion; those who have chosen to ignore or deny the existence of systems, perpetuating a myth that language is merely atomistic; those who pay lip service to system, and then produce grammatical analyses in which there is no consideration of system. Even among those who insist on the systemic nature of grammatical elements, there can be considerable disagreement, which must be looked upon as a positive force: without a dialectic, without the push and pull of differing opinions, there would be little, if any progress towards a better understanding of difficult linguistic questions. It is important, therefore, to present any case with as much coherence and clarity as possible, and with a recognition of cognate or differing views.

In the chapters that follow grammatical mechanisms will be presented as elements of simple but rigorous cognitive systems, involving the kind of fundamental mental contrasts that are within the cognitive capacities of small children, the learners of languages. Out of these simple cognitive contrasts are built our verbal systems, with subsystems, in Indo-European languages, of tense, aspect, mood, and voice.

CHAPTER TWO
VERBAL PARADIGMS AND THEIR CONTENT

2. Introduction

The verbal system of a language is a content system, with a restricted number of permanent, potential meanings giving rise to a finite number of meaningful contrasts. Each of the meanings so produced will normally be marked by a separate morphological form, and the whole set of morphological forms may be set out in a paradigm. The contrasts to be found in the paradigm, and the differing functions in discourse of the different paradigmatic forms are the clues and the evidence that are needed for deciphering the underlying content system, which, like other forms of underlying meaning, is not directly observable, but only observable indirectly, through its use, like the moves of Saussure's chess pieces. The verbal paradigms of English and French are very different, as we shall see. It follows that the verbal content systems of French and English are also very different, and in fact, the differences that arise in translation are further clues and evidence as to the nature of those systems. Before proceeding to examine the French system, it is useful to make a brief survey of the morphology and meaningful contrasts of the English verbal system.

2.1 *The paradigm of tense*

The grammarians of English have long insisted that the English indicative has only two tenses (e.g. Quirk et al 1972:84): a past and a non-past, to use the now classical terminology. If we take a simple verb such as *to talk*, the past tense is marked in the morphology by the spelling *-ed*, whereas the non-past is unmarked: *I talked, I talk*. The justification for this analysis is a morphological one: there are no other simple forms of the indicative. Admittedly an *-s* is added in *he talks*, but this marks third person singular, not a new tense. And admittedly, many other finite forms of the indicative may be found, but none of them are expressed in a single word; all are compound forms, as in the following examples:

(1)	I do talk	(6)	I will be talking
(2)	I am talking	(7)	I should talk
(3)	I have talked	(8)	I should be talking
(4)	I have been talking	(9)	I may have talked
(5)	I will talk	(10)	I may have been talking

We shall treat the contrast between the simple forms *I talk/I talked* as one of *tense*, and the compound forms exemplified in (1) to (10) as examples of these same two tenses (marked in the auxiliaries) with the secondary development of 'different aspects' giving rise to the compounding. The system of aspects is, as indicated in Guillaume (1992:19), "complementary to the system of tenses". The tense of all compound aspectual forms is to be found in the tense marking of the auxiliary. The nature of the category of aspect will be analysed in detail in Section 2.3.

The terminology 'past/non-past' is used to describe the underlying contrast of the English tense system because the simple unmarked form *I talk* that is popularly called the present tense represents a tense value quite different from the present tense of other languages. When we observe such a pair as

(11)   I talk too much
(12)   I am talking too much

we may note, as native speakers, that (11) has overtones of permanency that are not found in (12), which would normally refer to the immediate here and now. This element of permanency arises from the fact that in the English tense system a simple binary contrast is made of the whole of imaginary (or universe) time:

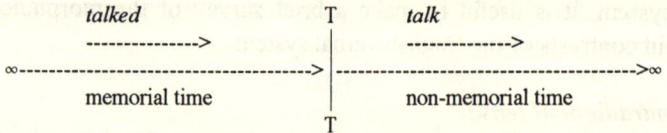

The whole of time is divided, in short, between the approach to a limit and the departure from that limit. The limit, the threshold (T) that is thus represented, is the experiential present, the here and now of the speaker. The past tense consequently represents memorial time, which in cognitive terms is the time that lies within the memory, and beyond, into the infinite past. The non-past tense represents the time which is not yet part of the memory: immediate experience, and beyond, into the infinite future.

To justify such an analysis, it will be necessary to analyse the various ways of representing the passage of time, and to note that different languages make use of different contrastive elements.

2.1.1 Incidence and decadence

Time is movement, and may, therefore, be represented as movement *to* or movement *from*. A useful analogy is that of the hour glass, where sand drips from the upper chamber into the lower. As the sand drops, it may be seen as descending, as it accumulates in the lower chamber, it may be seen as rising; as the sand descends in the upper chamber, it rises in the lower; both of these are aspects of one and the same movement. Guillaume states (1971:98) that the immanent view of time, of universe time by which we are confronted, is that of time flowing from the future into the past: he supports this claim by observing that tomorrow becomes today; yesterday never becomes today. Tomorrow arrives and confronts us with the future that it brings.

Events that occur in time, however, accumulate in the memory of the observer as does the sand in the lower chamber, with one moment added to the next until the event be complete. An event that is started today may well be carried over into tomorrow and be completed some time in the future.

Guillaume uses the terms 'decadence' for the downward flow of time and 'incidence' for the upward development of an event:

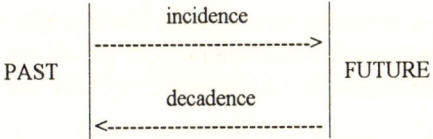

From the point of view of 'descending time', we are obviously bound, since we must accept whatever circumstances the morrow may bring: it may rain, or it may snow. However, from the point of view of 'ascending time', we are also free to initiate action that will carry on into tomorrow.

Such a simple and fundamental representation of time, however, leaves several ambiguities unresolved because there is no representation of time spheres, no clearly delimited zones, such as the past and the future. The representation of Descending Time (capitals indicate the linguistic representation), because of its orientation toward the past, may be used to express the past, and likewise the representation of Ascending Time may be used to express the future, but what of the present, the dividing line between past time and future time?

2.1.2 Time spheres

There are several possible solutions to this situation, and the solution found in the English indicative is to represent the present as the threshold between time that is memorial, already a part of memory, and time that is non-memorial:

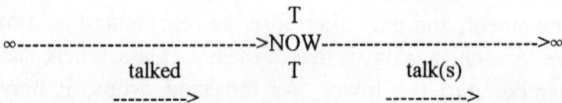

According to this scheme, the two time spheres are represented in the English tense system as being in Ascending Time, not Descending Time. Consequently, events expressed through the medium of the two tenses are seen as unfolding toward their conclusion: They represent a complete event, a typical representation of Ascending Time, which offers a view toward the future, toward the completion of the event.

As a result, the English simple past is a preterit, used to express a complete event. Likewise the simple non-past is used to represent a complete event, as when the commentator on an ice hockey game exclaims

(13)   He shoots, he scores!

(Example from Hirtle 1967:36). It would be absurd in (13) to say *he is scoring*, since the semantic content of this particular verb requires that a simple instance of such an event must be complete in itself before the verb can be used: the puck must be in the net, and an immediate, automatic and complete consequence is that a score is registered.

We may conclude, therefore, that the two simple tenses of English represent Ascending Time and consequently represent enduring states or complete performances. In fact, as a balance towards this emphasis on Ascending Time and complete performance it will be found, when we come to examine aspect in 2.3 that the two most persistent aspects (as opposed to tenses) in English are (a) the progressive, which presents an imperfective view of the event

(14)   He is shooting

and (b) the transcendent aspect which makes use of the past participle, a verbal element that features the perfective in Descending Time:

(15)   He has worked here for three years

The transcendent aspect, in other words, gives a view from the moment of the present back into the past (i.e. the orientation of Descending Time). By way of contrast if we say

(16)   He works here for three years

the time reference (3 years) no longer represents past time, but, because of the orientation (in Ascending Time) of the simple tense form, it is obliged to represent future time, and one would expect the sentence to run on:

(17)   ... and then he goes on a new posting.

We may represent the contrast of (15) and (16) in diagram form as follows:

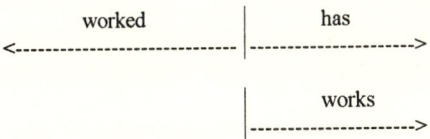

In English, therefore, the simple non-past (the so-called present) is incapable of representing a retrospective view from the present into the past, such as may be done, by contrast, with the present tense in French,

(18)   Il travaille ici depuis trois ans

where the sentence gives a translation of (15), not of (16). The reason for this difference between English and French will be examined in detail in Chapter Eight.

2.1.3 *The problem of the threshold*
A threshold is a line that marks the boundary or limit between one space and another. Ideally, such a boundary should itself occupy no space; but if it did not, it would be zero, or non-existent. As every carpenter knows, when an 8 foot length of plywood is cut in half, each half is just a shade less than 4 feet. The sawdust on the floor is mute testimony to the dimension of the cut that has become the new threshold between the two halves.

A geometrical line, therefore, has dimension, since if it was so thin that it had no dimension it would not exist. Similarly a threshold, even an imaginary one, must occupy some part of the spaces that lie on either side of it, the spaces that it is intended to separate. In short, if there is no space between the two spaces in question, they are not separated and there is no limit or threshold.

Consequently, the representation of the present as the threshold between the past and the future necessitates that we represent it as occupying the last quantum of the past, or omega chronotype in Guillaume's terminology (1964:60–61), and the first moment of the future (or alpha chronotype):

$$\begin{array}{c} T \\ \text{Past} \text{-----------}\!\!> \text{Now}_1 \;\Big|\; \text{Now}_2 \text{-----------}\!\!> \text{Future} \\ \text{(omega)} \;\;\; \text{(alpha)} \\ T \end{array}$$

Immediately we may observe another systemic factor that has significant consequences in the use of tenses in English: the omega moment of the present is represented as belonging to memorial time, i.e. to the past. Consequently, we find instances in English usage where a past tense form is used to represent the experiential present, although the transcendent non-past (i.e. present perfect) may also be used:

(19) This is the first time I ever ate caviar.
(20) This is the first time I have ever eaten caviar.

In these examples the simple non-past is not suitable for representing the event that is actually in progress: the eating of caviar. The present perfect may, of course, be used because of the element of decadence that is a feature of the past participle. Similarly, we express events that are very recent by means of the simple past:

(21) He just left
(22) I came to buy some milk
(23) I came to tell you you left your car lights on.

The present perfect may also be used in most situations where (21), (22) and (23) might be used. In all these cases, the sentences would be translated into French by a present tense, e.g.:

(24) Il vient de partir
(25) Je viens acheter du lait

One may, furthermore, visualize (22) or (25) being said by a child (sent on an errand) at the precise moment he arrives in the store or at the counter to make his purchase. This moment, the experiential omega moment, is included in the representation of the English past tense, whereas in French, which makes use of the aspect of decadence in the tense system, it is included in the representation of the present tense. (For details see Chapter Six).

Much could be written on the complexity of usage that results from the problem of representing the experiential present as a threshold between past and future. Many such instances of usage require to be analysed and discussed at great length in order to relate them to the representational mechanisms that underly them, and an important series of such usages will be so analysed in Chapter Eight. Our purpose here, however, is to delineate the mechanisms rather than to discuss usage.

2.2 *Mood*

Time itself has no past, present or future, which are relative only to the consciousness of the individual. From the Einsteinian model of the universe, we come to realize that each individual has his own personal present of consciousness in time just as he has his own personal place in space. In short, only individuals can distinguish *here* from *there*, or *now* from *then*. Such items as *here* and *now* were labelled 'shifters' by Jespersen (1922:123) because they change from speaker to speaker, and from situation to situation. The whole category of shifters was extensively discussed by Jakobson (e.g. 1957/1992:386–392)

We may, therefore, represent an event as occurring in time, without relating it to any time sphere. In the English verbal system, such an event is consequently not represented as being related in any way to our own personal empirical experience of time, and remains a potential, theoretical, unallocated event. Such is the common simple subjunctive of English, which thereby contrasts with the tense representations of the indicative, which are shifters determined by the here and now of the speaker (2.2.1 below).

There are also what we shall call the quasi-nominal forms of the verb: the infinitive, present participle, and past participle. These are not only not unallocated to any time sphere, but are not required to be syntactically supported by a subject (nominal or pronominal, internal or external).

English, therefore, has three fundamental moods: quasi-nominal, subjunctive, and indicative. There is no need to consider imperatives as a separate mood since morphologically they do not differ from subjunctives, and although they require no syntactic subject, they are predicated directly of the person addressed.

2.2.1 *The subjunctive*

The subjunctive forms of all verbs are identical to the infinitive, and are, therefore, also identical to indicative forms except for (a) the verb *to be*, and (b) the third person singular form (which has -*s* in the indicative, but is unmarked in the subjunctive):

(26) I move that the meeting *be* adjourned
(27) I insist that he *withdraw* the comment
(28) If he *withdraws* the comment ... (indicative)

But the subjunctive is also distinguished by certain syntactic peculiarities as Hirtle (1964) has pointed out: (a) it does not use the auxiliary *do* in the negative as do the simple indicative tenses, and (b) it is not subject to the normal sequence of tenses that operates with indicatives:

(29) I propose that we not do anything
(30) Decency required that I go to see him.

A verb such as *suggest*, with its common variant meanings *hint* and *propose* will, therefore, yield minimal pairs of sentences, depending on whether hint (+ indicative) is intended as in (31) and (33) below, or propose (+ subjunctive) as in (32) and (34):

(31) I suggest that we don't have any agreement
(32) I suggest that we not have any agreement
(33) I suggested that we didn't have any agreement
(34) I suggested that we not have any agreement.

The frequency (and even acceptability) of these syntactic sequences varies according to regional norms, but their frequency in North American English is well documented by Hirtle, who records citations from writers, from prominent public figures, and also from the business meetings of linguists.

The subjunctive is a representation of an event that is in all ways equivalent to the indicative except that it is not allocated to any time sphere, and, therefore, is not represented as taking place in any defined time. Consequently, it is used to represent intended events, possible events, and other purely notional or potential events.

Two systemic details, therefore, emerge which yield clues as to the role played by the subjunctive in the mechanical content system that underlies the simple verbal paradigm:

(i) It is independent of the mechanism of time-spheres, since it is not subject to syntactic sequence of tense,

(ii) It represents a purely formal, potential event, and not a material (or realized) event.

Historically, there was also a second subjunctive, of which the only morphological contrast remaining today is in the singular of the verb *to be* (and even that not found with all speakers):

Indicative	Subjunctive$_2$
I was	I were
He was	He were

Some would conclude from this evidence that Modern English still has a fully operant second subjunctive. It is more probable, however, that the second subjunctive has disappeared, and that the use of the past tense forms with non-past reference is the means of expression that has been utilized to replace it. It would be hard to justify the form *went*, for example, as the subjunctive of the verb *to go*:

(35)   It's time we went.

Went is the irregular, suppletive preterit (past tense) of the verb, not the subjunctive.

In this case, *was/were* would today be alternate indicative forms (in similar fashion (see 9.2) to French *peux/puis*), and speakers would be free to utilize this alternance for the purposes of finesse of expression, a proposal supported by the variation in the usage.

The interesting question of the use of past indicatives in a modal sense must await a later study. The exploration of the French imperfect in such usage is examined in 6.5.2.1.

2.2.2 *Infinitive and participles*

If the subjunctive and indicative in English represent events that are contained in Universe Time, the infinitive and participles represent events that are self-contained, and therefore, in a sense, independent of Universe Time. Their normal predication is consequently either in the mode of an adjectival relationship, or that of a dependent clause:

(36)   We watched the setting sun
(37)   We watched the sun setting
(38)   We found the broken bottle

(39) We found the bottle broken
(40) We saw the bottle break.

We note, also, that the infinitive in (40) cannot be placed before the noun, and that if we make (40) into a passive sentence, the infinitive requires *to*:

(41) The bottle was seen to break.

Of these three forms the infinitive presents a view of the event as a total performance; the present participle represents a view of the event in progress, and the past participle presents a retrospective view of the material completion of the event.

The two participles, perfective (*talked*) and imperfective (*talking*) indicate by the addition of -*ed* and -*ing* that a morphological predication has taken place, that is, a further stage of grammaticalisation beyond the (unmarked) infinitive. We are entitled, from the evidence of the three quasi-nominal forms, to propose a double binary contrast first between the unmarked (infinitive) and the marked forms, then with a second binary contrast between the internal view (breaking) and the external view (broken) of the content:

CONTAINER	CONTENT 1	CONTENT 2
break	breaking	broken

Here the infinitive is represented as being the unmarked form in the binary contrast 'container' vs. 'content', with a further binary contrast of 'incomplete' vs. 'complete', labelled as Content 1 (internal view) and Content 2 (exterior view). As corroborating data, we may simply point out that

(42) I am speaking

represents the subject involved in the midst of the event, in immanence, whereas

(43) I have spoken

represents the subject in transcendent position, having passed beyond the completion of the event: the content of the event is necessarily seen as a whole.

This contrast between the internal and external representation of a content seems to be a cognitive universal. The internal view is by nature continuate, the same continuate representation that is found in the so-called mass noun. Indeed the *-ing* morphology has in fact been borrowed as a derivational marker for making mass nouns: *roofing, flooring, plumbing, etc.* The external view on the other hand is that of a unit, since from an external view one necessarily sees the whole.

2.3 *Aspect*

Guillaume makes a very simple and coherent distinction between tense and aspect: tense concerns *le temps expliqué*, the Universe Time that contains the event, and aspect concerns *le temps impliqué*, the Event Time contained in the event (1964:47–48). Different representation of the shape or structure of the event consequently result in different aspectual forms. This way of describing aspect correlates with the definitions of others: Comrie, for example, describes aspects (1976:3) as "...different ways of viewing the internal temporal constituency of a situation." But Guillaume's definition allows for the making of subtle distinctions, as we shall see (6.5.1): since Universe Time may be either ascending or descending, differences of tense may themselves automatically carry differences of aspect.

The three forms of the quasi-nominal mood, because they represent the event from three different points of view, are the basis of the three marked aspectual forms of the verb, each with a suitable auxiliary:

(44) Prospective Aspect: *I will sing*
(45) Progressive Aspect: *I am singing*
(46) Retrospective Aspect: *I have sung*

Each of these compound forms, with an auxiliary in the non-past tense, contrasts with the simple non-past *I sing*, which is unmarked for aspect. The Prospective represents the subject in a position before the beginning of the event, with the event itself as purely potential. The Progressive represents the subject as engaged internally in the event, with the event itself as incomplete. The Perfective represents the subject in a position after the end of the event, with the event as complete, accomplished. In these forms it is always the auxiliary that carries the mark of tense; in (44) – (46) above it may be observed that the tense of all three forms is non-past, and it is typical of aspectual forms that they can be used throughout the paradigms of tense and mood, so that the equivalent past forms would be:

(47) I would sing
(48) I was singing

(49)   I had sung.

One may also find infinitive and subjunctive forms:

(50)   to be singing, to have sung
(51)   that she be singing.

There are two sets of auxiliaries in use in aspectual forms in English: the modal auxiliaries, as in (44) and (47), and the so-called grammatical auxiliaries, as in (45), (46), (48), and (49), (50), and (51). The grammatical auxiliaries *do, be, have*, which share certain common traits, will be dealt with in 2.3.2 below.

2.3.1 *The modal auxiliaries*
The modal auxiliaries are distinguished by the fact that they have no -*s* in the third person singular (sharing this morphology with the subjunctive) and have no infinitive or participial forms. Most, but not all of the modals have a simple past form as well as a non-past:

Non-past	Past
will	would
shall	should
can	could
may	might
ought	—
must	—
(dare)	—
(need)	—

Ought and *must* were originally past forms (as is shown by their final -*t*) but today have only present reference, and have no past forms:

(52)   You ought to go
(53)   I must go.

One can, however, use a transcendent infinitive with *ought* and obtain a past reference:

(54)   You ought to have gone

The only way to obtain a past with the idea of *must* is to change verbs however:

(55)   She had to go

since when one uses a transcendent infinitive with *must*

(56)   He must have gone

the reference is still present, since this is the so-called epistemic meaning of the modal; the meaning is

(57)   It is now obvious that he went.

The epistemic meaning of a modal auxiliary points to a conclusion to be drawn, rather than to a condition that will have consequences.

All these auxiliaries combine with the infinitive to form variations of the modal aspect, and only *ought* requires the infinitive with *to*. *Dare* and *need* have been added in brackets because their usage as modals is optional:

(58)   He dare not do it (modal)
(59)   He does not dare to do it
(60)   He need not do it (modal)
(61)   He does not need to do it.

It is notable that when *need* and *dare* are used as modals, the following infinitive normally loses its *to*.

The remaining auxiliaries form two related sets, since *will* and *shall* present the internal and external views of determination and *can* and *may* represent the internal and external views of potentiality.

The purpose of these brief comments on the modal auxiliaries is to present an outline of them as a subsystem of the English verb. There has been much written on the modals in recent years, and this extensive literature may be accessed in several full-scale monographs, such as Coates 1983, Perkins 1983, Woisetschlaeger 1985, Palmer 1990.

2.3.2 The grammatical auxiliaries

We have seen that English has only two tense forms, in that only two time zones (past and non-past) are expressed through the medium of morphological predication. But the language makes up for the paucity of tense forms by considerable development of the system of aspect, expressed through the medium of syntactic predication, and especially by the strategy of syntactic collusion, exemplified above, using an auxiliary for the verb form and a verbal (infinitive or participle) for the lexical content.

As mentioned in 2.3.1, the modals (*shall, can*, etc,) have a morphology that is similar to the subjunctive in that they never have -*s* in the third person singular (*he shall, he can*, etc.), have no infinitive or participial forms, and are never found in the imperative (*he shalls, *to shall, *shalling, *shalled and *shall! are all impossible).

The grammatical auxiliaries on the other hand are three in number (*do, be, have*) and may be found in the full morphological range of the ordinary verb, except that *do* may not be used in infinitive or participial form:

(62)   be talking, have talked, do talk (subjunctive)
(63)   was talking, had talked, did talk (past)
(64)   is talking, has talked, does talk (non-past)
(65)   be talking, have talked, *do talk (infinitive)
(66)   *being talking, having talked, *doing talk (present participle)
(67)   been talking, *had talked, *done talk (past participle)

The resistances, or forms that are not used, are marked with an asterisk. There is a regular resistance to having both auxiliary and verbal in the same form, a fact which makes the following forms redundant:

*being talking   (two participles)
*had talked   (two participles)
*(to) do talk   (two infinitives)

That the auxiliary *do* may not be used in either infinitive or participial forms may be due to the fact that this auxiliary takes the infinitive without *to* as its verbal content. Since the content of the two participles is formed from the content of the infinitive (and not vice versa) we may expect a resistance not only between the dependent content infinitive (i.e. *talk*) and a governing grammatical infinitive (i.e. *(to)* do), but also between the content infinitive (*talk*) and any other governing grammatical content derived from the infinitive, which includes both participles (*doing* and *done*).

Of these three auxiliaries *do* is mostly used for forming the negative and interrogative forms of the simple tenses:

(68)   I talk: do I talk? I do not talk (non-past)
(69)   I talked: did I talk? I did not talk (past)

In Shakespeare's day, one could say *I talk not* but this is no longer normal in Modern English except with the verbs *to be* and (for some regional variants) *to have*:

(70)   Tell him I'm not here
(71)   I haven't a clue.

It is sometimes claimed that this use of *do* in interrogatives and negatives is a meaningless manipulation so that the usual order of subject - verb can be maintained. But this claim is clearly untenable, since the choice of the *do* auxiliary occasionally produces meaningful contrasts with minimal pairs:

(72)   Why aren't you more specific?
(73)   Why don't you be more specific?
(74)   Why aren't you at the door?
(75)   Why don't you be at the door?

Sentences (72) and (74) have present reference, whereas (73) and (75) are suggestions, and one would expect (75) to run on

(76)   ... when he arrives.

All the auxiliaries are dematerialized in sense — their role is to bring grammatical form, rather than lexical content, to the arrangement. If this lexical dematerialization becomes complete, the auxiliary will lose its autonomy as a word and become a mere inflection as happened when Latin *amare habeo* evolved to become French *aimerai* (see, for example, Guillaume 1964:80–81).

Consequently, independent auxiliaries maintain some quantum of lexical content, sufficient to define their role as auxiliaries. The lexical meaning of *do* is very broadly generalised, since the verb stands as a 'pro-verb' for other verbs:

(77)   I asked him to look and he did
(78)   He went and so did I

Its basic sense is performative, since *to do something* means to carry it out. But even this element is lost in the pro-verb and the auxiliary since both of which may be used with stative verbs:

(79)   We have more children than they do; they don't have any..

The auxiliary *do*, therefore, simply represents the mechanical (i.e. grammatical) carrying out in time of the content of the replaced verb or of the dependent infinitive (Hewson 1990a).

The auxiliary *do*, by carrying the necessary grammatical representation for its accompanying infinitive represents the conditions for the occurrence of the whole event whereas the infinitive represents the lexical content of the event. If one denies the existence of the necessary conditions, the whole event is negated:

(80)   I do not talk (non-past)
(81)   I did not talk (past)

To put it another way: the 'grammatical' representation of the occurrence of the event is the 'necessary condition' for representing the whole as an experiential event. If this condition is denied, the event cannot be represented as experiential.

Since all auxiliaries express the grammatical conditions for the representation of the event, both negation and interrogation (which calls into question the occurrence of the event) are expressed in English through the medium of auxiliaries. Since the only finite verbal forms that lack auxiliaries are the simple past and non-past, the auxiliary *do* is utilized to remedy the lack in these two cases. Using *do* as a buffer in this way prevents the event which is doubtful (or denied) from being predicated directly of the subject: one avoids the contradiction of denying an event that one has represented as performed.

Whereas *do* as an auxiliary, however, does not occur in its infinitive and participial forms and is almost entirely restricted to the interrogative and negative of the simple forms of the verb, both *be* and *have* are utilized in a full range of verb forms and aspectual usage. It is not surprising, therefore, that the lexical relationship between these two verbs may be expressed in binary terms:

be	have
-------------------------->	-------------------------->
immanent view of	transcendent view of
existence (= existence)	existence (= essence)
(intransitive)	(transitive)

The related verbals may also be placed in binary contrast

talking	talked
-------------------------->	-------------------------->
interior view of	exterior view of
the materiality	the materiality
of the event	of the event

Consequently, we may delineate the two verbal aspects in question as follows

```
            talking
| ----------be---------->|

            talked
|<----------------------| have
```

The auxiliary *be*, as well as supplying the grammatical conditions for the representation of an experiential event, also expresses, by its dematerialized lexical content, the notion of immanence to the materiality of an event; *have* likewise expresses the notion of transcendence to the materiality to an event.

2.4 *Voice*

It is of particular interest in this regard to examine a minimal contrast that arises in English:

(82) He has struck
(83) He was struck.

In these cases, we are again presented with the problem of the limit. The auxiliary *be* in (85) locates the grammatical subject within the limit, but in (84) the auxiliary *have* locates the subject outside the limit:

```
            struck
    <------------------------- x | x
                                be | have
```

By means of this simple mechanism, English expresses a difference of voice. The verb *be*, in locating the subject as bound by the interiority of the event, is suitable for representing the subject as a 'patient', and therefore the construction serves as the normal representation of passive voice. The auxiliary *have* on the other hand, by representing the subject as not bound by the event is suitable for representing the subject as an agent, and therefore the construction naturally expresses the active voice, transcendent aspect.

Just as for the aspectual forms, we find that for every simple active form of the verb there is a compound form representing the passive, and likewise for every compound form there is a secondary compounding to form the equivalent passive:

ACTIVE	PASSIVE
(to) strike	(to) be struck
striking	being struck
struck	been struck
(that) he strike	(that) he be struck
he strikes	he is struck
he struck	he was struck
he is striking	he is being struck
he was striking	he was being struck
he will strike	he will be struck
he would strike	he would be struck
he has struck	he has been struck
he had struck	he had been struck

2.5 *The verbal paradigms of French*

By way of contrast with the verbal paradigms of English that we have been examining, the verbal paradigms of French are substantially different, especially in the indicative. We have seen that there are five different tense forms where English has only two: *je parle, je parlerai, je parlerais, je parlai, je parlais*.

In the case of French, we notice that the future belongs to the tense system rather than the aspect system, and that there are two futures and two past tenses, although one of these (the *passé simple*) is now only written and is not used in conversation. There are also no modal auxiliaries in French, and nothing to compare to the English auxiliary *do*. It will come as no surprise, therefore, that in the next five chapters, we shall propose a verbal content system for French that is very different from the English verbal system.

CHAPTER THREE
CHRONOGENESIS

3. *Introduction*

It was in 1929 with the publication of *Temps et Verbe* that Guillaume first put forward the idea that the content system of the verb is composed of three successive stages (1929:8–9). In his subsequent teaching, he was forever repeating that one has to find out about the content system through the medium of the expression system:

> La tâche du linguiste-grammairien est, toujours et partout, de découvrir le psychique sous le sémiologique et, là où il s'agit de structure ou de système, de se représenter la structure ou le système psychique auquels renvoient la structure ou le système sémiologique apparents.
>
> Le donné, en l'espèce, c'est la sémiologie de la langue, les signes dont elle se sert pour rendre son état psychique de définition. Et l'inconnue à découvrir, c'est le psychisme rendu sous signes, autrement dit signifié. (1971:77).
>
> (The task of the linguist-grammarian is, always and everywhere, to discover what is mental beneath what is morphosyntactic (physical) and, wherever there is structure or system, to figure out the mental structure or system to which the observable morphosyntactic structure or system pertains... The data, in this instance, is the morphosyntax of the language, the signs which it uses to indicate the parameters of the mental systems. And the unknown to be discovered is the mental machinery marked by these signs, i.e. the grammatical meanings).

In other words, the meaningful system of grammatical contrasts can only be discovered through the medium of the morphology that marks the grammatical contrasts of the system. Or, in Guillaume's own terms, the mental (i.e. cognitive) structure of a language can only be discovered through the examination of its semiological (i.e. morphosyntactic) structure.

3.1 *Three morphosyntactic types*

If we subject the simple verb forms of French to a cursory examination, we shall find the following data: (1) three forms that are not inflected for person: *parler, parlant, parlé*; (2) two so-called subjunctives, the second of which is seldom, if ever, heard in colloquial speech today: *que je parle, que je parlasse*;

(3) five forms that regularly occur in main clauses and that can be classified as indicative: *je parle, je parlerai, je parlerais, je parlai, je parlais*.

These ten forms constitute the basic morphology of mood and tense in French: these are the simple forms of the verb (in that they consist only of single words) and there are no other moods or tenses of the verb that are not represented by these ten forms. There are, of course, a multitude of aspectual forms, made up out of more than one word by the strategy of syntactic collusion, *but it is important not to confuse the aspectual relationships introduced by these compound forms with the systemic relationships that the simple forms have between themselves.* (The interplay of tense and aspect is treated in detail in 6.5.1 above). The delimitation of the basic system of the verb, in short, can best be done by concentrating on the simple forms, and later examining the relationship between the simple forms and the compound forms.

3.1.1 *Three chronogenetic stages*

The first three forms, *parler, parlant, parlé*, represent what Guillaume calls the quasi-nominal mood (1964:186; 1989:21). As the name indicates, these forms can readily be used as nouns, and the two participles can also be used as adjectives. These three forms can thereby represent events, but such events are not allocated to any time spheres and may not be predicated directly of the subject of a sentence. They may be considered, therefore, as verb forms in which the time image is but little developed, and Guillaume consequently classifies the quasi-nominal mood as Stage I in what he calls the chronogenesis (1929:8; 1945:23; 1964:186,fn 4), which is the cognitive development of the time image in the content system of the verb. At this level, Event Time (capitals indicate the linguistic representation, not the event itself) is represented as fundamentally static: a container and its contents.

Stage II in the chronogenesis produces the subjunctive, distinctive verb forms that must be predicated directly of a subject, and which are no longer suitable for use as a noun or adjective. In the subjunctive forms the event is no longer represented as static, but as a movement that takes place between an initial moment and a final moment. This dynamic representation requires the support of a subject, noun or pronoun; consequently, in constrast to the quasi-nominal forms, the subjunctive is no longer syntactically independent. (In French the subject is a separate word, whereas in Latin and in other Romance languages the subject is an internal pronominal support). At this second level there are no time spheres; the whole of time is represented as a vast present.

At the third stage of the chronogenesis, we see the introduction of contrastive time-spheres which will complete the development of the representation of the time image for the French verb. The experiential time of the speaker, the present, is seen as dividing the whole of Universe Time by forming a threshold which separates time which is not yet (the future) from time that has already been (the past). The subjunctive, in other words, represents an event that is unrelated to the speaker's immediate experience of time; the indicative, on the other hand, represents an event that is placed in relationship to the speaker's immediate experience of time: either the event is represented as being contemporaneous with the speaker's mental operations (the present) or it is represented as being anterior (the past) or posterior (future) to the speaker's immediate experience. In passing, we may note that French has a single present tense (*je parle*) but two past tenses (*je parlai, je parlais*) the former of which is seldom, if ever, heard today in colloquial usage. Likewise, there are two future tenses (*je parlerai, je parlerais*) the second of which is called the conditional in the traditional grammars but which shows by its morphology its close relationship to the simple future.

3.2 *Stage I: the quasi-nominal mood*

The notion of chronogenesis is essentially that of a three stage building up of the time-image that is specific to the French language. Guillaume proposes that at each of the three levels Universe Time is seen as an horizon running from an infinity in the past to an infinity in the future (1964:195). Also at each stage, he chooses to represent the view of time above the horizon as that of incidence, which becomes Ascending Time at Stage II, and the view of time below the horizon as that of decadence, which becomes Descending Time at Stage II. (We shall endeavour to clarify the ambiguity of these terms in 3.2.1 below).

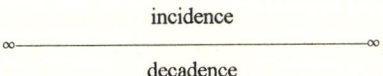

Consequently, the quasi-nominal mood has three possibilities: the infinitive, which is totally in incidence, the present participle which is partly in decadence and partly in incidence, and the past participle which is totally in decadence. These three possibilities of representing Event Time are presented in Diagram 1. The arrows at Stage I in Guillaume's diagrams are always vertical, to indicate static representations (1989:45), as opposed to Stages II and III, where horizontal arrows indicate the movements of Ascending and Descending Time. At this level of representation, therefore, the representation of time is but crude: Guillaume depicts it as an immense present (i.e. Universe Time) which has neither time-sphere nor movement, and in which events may be conceived of as nominal elements, that is, as having dimension in space or time.

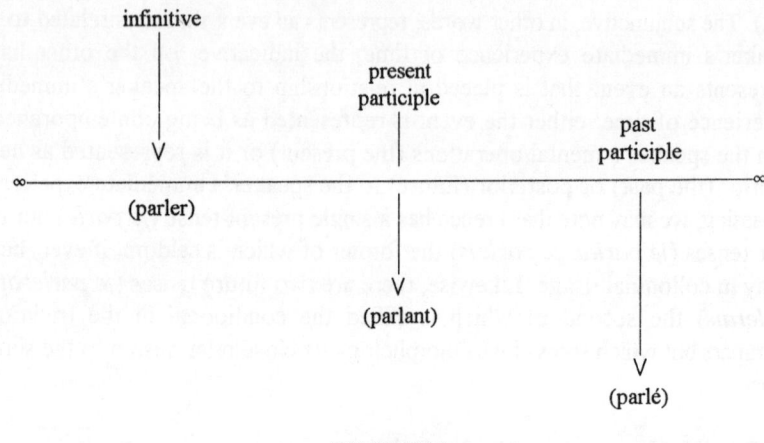

DIAGRAM 1

3.2.1 *A simpler view of the quasi-nominal forms*
Guillaume makes it quite clear that the three forms at this stage cannot be differences of tense (*1989*:44):

> Dès l'instant qu'on interdit, au sein de la représentation de l'infinitude du temps, la discrimination horizontale, on dissipe du même coup complètement la distinction d'époque, pour lui substituer, abstraction faite de l'époque, une distinction verticale, qui n'est plus alors, en toute époque — l'époque devenue indifférente — que celle de l'inaccompli, de l'accomplissement et de l'accompli.
>
> (As soon as one eliminates from the heart of the representation of the infinitude of time all horizontal discrimination, one immediately does away with tense distinctions, replacing them, regardless of tense, with vertical distinctions which are nothing other, in any time zone — time zones being irrelevant — than unaccomplished, accomplishment, and accomplished).

These latter distinctions are fundamentally aspectual. The forms *parlant* and *parlé* are clearly imperfective (accomplishment) and perfective (accomplished), respectively; and the infinitive, which represents the possibility of the whole event from beginning to end, indicates an event that is to be accomplished.

Guillaume was one of the pioneers of the introduction of the notion of aspect into Western European linguistics, using this originally Slavic concept in *Temps et Verbe* to describe the distinctions in French between *formes simples* and *formes composées* (1929:20), and comparing aspect in Russian and in French (1933/1964:46ff), an article that was subtitled *Esquisse d'une théorie psychologique de l'aspect*. But he did not so readily attribute the category of aspect to other forms; even in his 1945 book he still treats the Latin perfect forms as separate tenses, and it was left to Valin (1965/1994:44–45) to point out that the *perfectum vs. imperfectum* distinction of Latin (represented vertically by Guillaume) is an aspectual distinction.

If we treat the three quasi-nominal forms of French as simply aspectual distinctions, we do not need to represent Universe Time at this level, these forms being self contained (having only Event Time), which is why they can be used as nominals. In this case we can do away with the use of vertical arrows as symbols of static representations, and with a static representation of the incidence vs. decadence distinction, terms which otherwise represent movement. This move would seem to be all the more appropriate since Guillaume himself, in the passage above, indicates the irrelevance of Universe Time to the representations of this stage.

3.2.2 *Functions of the quasi-nominal forms*

The morphology at this level indicates that some kind of internal or morphological predication is functioning, since in each of the three forms a further morpheme is added to the simple stem of the verb. In the common spellings for an ordinary verb, these morphemes are *-er* for the infinitive, *-ant* for the present participle, and *-é* for the past participle. As aspectual forms they may be categorized as follows:

```
parler      performative aspect
parlant     imperfective aspect
parlé       perfective aspect
```

The three corresponding Event Times may be diagrammed as follows, with Guillaume's French terms (*1989*:44):

```
inaccompli        |x---------------->|     performative
accomplissement   |<-------x - - - - -|    imperfective
accompli          |<----------------x|     perfective
```

If these three meanings are then realized as nouns, *parler* would represent the event as an abstraction (external view of a complete event), *parlant* would represent the event as materially in progress (internal view), and *parlé* would represent the event as materially complete (final limit of interior view). The infinitive, in fact, is used nominally to represent the event as an idea, a potential act, rather than as a real occurrence: *Tout savoir, c'est tout pardonner* "To know all is to forgive all". In other words, the infinitive simply gives a name to the event as something realizable. In the case of the infinitive, one can only tell from the context whether the event is in fact realized or not:

(1) Je lui ai demandé de chanter
    "I asked him to sing (unrealized)"
(2) Je l'ai entendu chanter.
    "I heard him sing (realized)"

In the case of the past participle, on the other hand, which represents the total materiality of the event, the event is necessarily represented as complete. Such a representation will more readily be used as an adjective than a noun, and, if used as a noun, may in fact hypostatically be used to represent the person or thing bound by the result of the event: *un fiancé, les morts*. It is of interest to note that one such past participle, when used as a noun, represents the simple materiality of what is complete: *le passé*.

The present participle, since it, like the past participle, contains an element of Descending Time within its representation, is more commonly used as an adjective than as a noun. If used as a noun, it too is more likely to hypostatically represent the person carrying out the event than the simple process of the event itself: *un passant, un étudiant*. Like the past participle, it takes on the gender of the person so represented: *une fiancée, une étudiante*.

For all the similarity between English and French at this particular level (three forms, an infinitive and two participles), there are nevertheless, in spite of these similarities, significant differences: (1) the French infinitive is a morphologically marked form, just as are the present and past participles in French, whereas the English simple infinitive is an unmarked form in contrast to the marked forms of present and past participles; (2) usage of the infinitives and participles sometimes differs significantly between the two languages:

(3)   J'ai entendu chanter les enfants   (8)   Chanter c'est un plaisir
(4)   I heard the children sing   (9)   Singing is a pleasure
(5)   I heard the children singing   (10)   To sing is a pleasure
(6)   J'ai entendu chanter la chanson   (11)   C'est un plaisir de chanter
(7)   I heard the song sung   (12)   It is a pleasure to sing.

In (2) and (3) the French infinitive in (1), which has an active sense, may be translated by either an infinitive or a present participle. In (7) the French infinitive in (6), which has a passive sense, is translated by a past participle. The French infinitive used as a subject in (8) may be translated by either a present participle (9) or an infinitive (10), whereas only an infinitive may be used in English (12) if an impersonal subject is used (12).

3.3 *Stage II: the subjunctive mood*

Guillaume considers the subjunctive mood as the second stage of development in the chronogenesis (1929:29ff; 1964:193ff; 1971:82). At the first stage (the quasi-nominal mood) the representation of the event is essentially spatial and the three basic forms represent the three possible relationships of a semantic content to its grammatical container: the simple container (infinitive), partly full (present participle), and full (past participle). At the second stage, however, the event thus far represented spatially is now represented temporally, that is as a progression between a beginning and a conclusion. Time is a transcendence of space, and in Stage II the form of the spatial container of Stage I is transcended and the cognitive processing leads to a new representation: that of the form of the so far amorphous content: Stage I, in other words, establishes the form of the container, and its relation to the content; Stage II establishes the form of the content.

We have seen that in the verbal system of standard French the choice of morphological forms at Stage II is binary, at least in literary usage. This eventuality is made possible by the fact that the event in progress may be seen either from the point of view of Ascending Time (present subjunctive) or from the point of view of Descending Time (imperfect subjunctive). The viewpoint of Descending Time will lead to the representation of an event being carried along by the flow of time as it appears to come from the future, pass through the present and flow off into the past: the orientation is towards the past; the view is also, as always in Descending Time, the interior view of the materiality of the event. The viewpoint of Ascending Time on the other hand, will represent the event as coming to be, the addition of its consecutive moments, which may be projected towards a completion in the open prospective of the future: the orientation is towards the non-past, and as always in Ascending Time, the event is represented from the exterior, as a complete whole. We may represent this simple binary contrast of Ascending and Descending Time as follows.

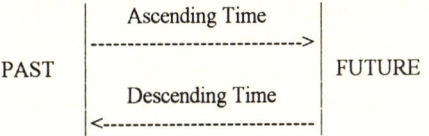

This state of affairs allows the so-called present subjunctive (in Ascending Time) to be used to represent non-past events, and the so-called imperfect subjunctive (in Descending Time) to be used for the representation of past events as in (13) – (14).

(13) Je ne crois pas qu'il le sache
      "I don't think he knows"
(14) Je ne crois pas qu'il le sût
      "I don't think he knew"
(15) Je ne crois pas qu'il ait su

In conversation (15) replaces (14) in the same way that the passé composé replaces the passé simple in indicative usage.

In literary usage the two subjunctives are also used for establishing sequence of tenses, so that only the imperfect subjunctive is considered appropriate after the indicative tenses in Descending Time, namely the imperfect and the conditional (see Chapter Six).

It is interesting to note that at Stage II, the event represented in the form of its temporal content rather than that of its spatial container is no longer syntactically independent: it must always be predicated of something that is itself represented spatially, namely, a noun or a pronoun that may stand as its syntactic support. From the point of view of discourse, therefore, the only role open to a subjunctive is that of predicate to a subject.

The forms of Stage II, however, still do not represent the event as an experiential reality, for the simple reason that they are not allocated to any experiential time-sphere: they are not represented as standing in any relationship whatever to the speaker's own experiential existence in time. Subjunctive events in French are, therefore, represented as belonging to the totality of time, which is an abstraction, and represent time as thought of by the speaker rather than as experienced by the speaker. The representations of Event Time at Stage I have become the model, by extrapolation, for the representation of Universe Time as a purely imaginary construct at Stage II. Consequently, as we shall see, the subjunctive represents the idea of the event, the potentiality of the event, rather than the empirical occurrence of the event. As a result the normal subjunctive occurs in subordinate clauses: in Guillaume's terminology it is typically an *idée regardée*, a notion that is viewed or judged through the 'lens' of other notions, through the filter of an *idée regardante* (1989:9, 12–13). Because of this subordinate role, it is normal, in grammatical discussions, to quote subjunctive forms with the subordinating conjunction *que*: *que je sois, que je fusse*.

3.4 Stage III: the indicative mood

The indicative is, in Guillaume's terms, the third and final stage in the development of the time image of the chronogenesis (1929:9, 1964:186, 1971:80–82, 1989:25). The nominal type of representation is introduced in Stage I. At Stage II, the verbal event is no longer represented as self contained, but as part of the contents of Universe Time, a so-called finite verb, a secondary stage of representation. The abstract event of Stage II is further defined at Stage III by being allocated to a time-sphere of Universe Time. The total view of the chronogenesis as proposed by Guillaume (without the adjustments suggested in 3.2.1 and 3.2.2) is presented in Diagram 2.

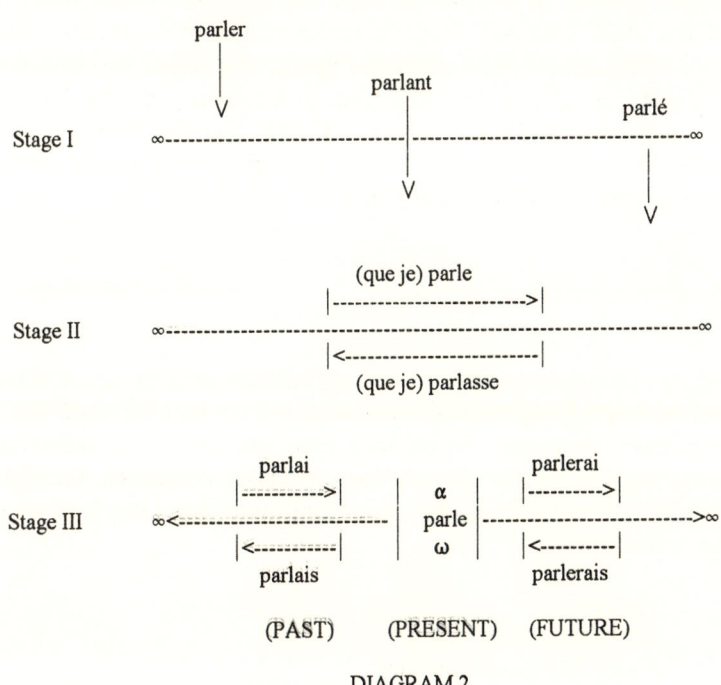

DIAGRAM 2

An event that is represented by an indicative form, therefore, is one that is predicated of a subject and viewed as a movement that takes place within Experiential Time, Universe Time as experienced by the speaker or hearer. Such a view represents the event as an occurrence, rather than as the mere idea or possibility of occurrence represented by the subjunctive. This difference between indicative and subjunctive will be analysed in detail in Chapter 7.

This is achieved, as in English, by introducing into the construction of the indicative the representation of the speaker's own consciousness of experi-ential time. In English the present is not itself represented as a time sphere sphere, but as a limit or pole of contrast to make possible the binary relationship of past and non-past. In French, by contrast, the present is itself represented as a time sphere of the indicative. The simple present form, *je parle*, therefore represents the narrow threshold between time that is not yet and time that has been.

As with all thresholds, this representation is necessarily built up of the omega moment (the last quantum of time that has been) and the alpha moment (the first quantum of time which is not yet). Since the representation of the present tense, in dividing the infinity of time into a past and a future, cuts across the horizon of time, and thereby penetrates from the level of incidence into the level of decadence, Guillaume proposes (1964:61, 1971:93) that the French present represents the alpha moment in incidence (i.e. Ascending Time) and the omega moment in decadence (i.e. Descending Time):

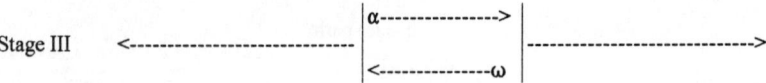

Stage III

This kind of a representation of the present would show the time within which one is free (incidence) being endlessly converted into the time by which one is bound (decadence). And since, as we have seen, any part of an underlying representation may be used for the purposes of surface expression, the alpha quantum (or alpha chronotype) may be used to express an event that is about to occur in the immediate future:

(16)   J'arrive!
       "I'll be right there!"
(17)   Je pars dans quelques instants.
       "I'll be leaving in a few minutes"

The French present in (13) would normally be translated "I'm coming right away, I'll be right there" in English. In similar fashion the omega quantum (or omega chronotype) may be used to represent an event that has gone on in the past and is still continuing in the omega moment:

(18)   Je parle depuis dix minutes
        "I've been speaking for ten minutes"
(19)   Il pleut depuis lundi
        "It has been raining since Monday"
(20)   Depuis combien de temps habitez-vous cette maison?
        "How long have you lived in this house?"

Any native speaker of English will immediately recognize that to translate these last three examples into English, the present perfect is required. The systemic differences seen here are analysed in detail in Chapter Eight. Other distinctive usage of the French present is discussed in full in Chapter Six.

Once one recognizes that the representation of the present separates the infinity of time not only horizontally but also vertically, the four indicative tenses that remain are easily assigned to their respective positions (1964:198ff, 1971:94–95). The future and conditional, for example, are morphologically marked as belonging to the time-sphere of the future by the distinctive mark of the -r- which is found, without exception, in every verb in the language. The two past tenses, the imperfect and the preterit (we are considering here the literary form of the language which is more conservative than the colloquial form) are unmarked in this contrast. The marker /-r-/ thereby distinguishes the past from the future, marking the horizontal contrast. But the vertical contrast is also to be found in both time-spheres, and the verb endings of the imperfect, which represent the decadent view of the past, are found again in the conditional, and are instrumental in marking the decadent view of future time. The normal future is consequently the representation of future time in incidence and the preterit (the *passé simple* or *passé défini*) is the representation of past time in incidence. We have, therefore, a system of the indicative which may be diagrammed as follows:

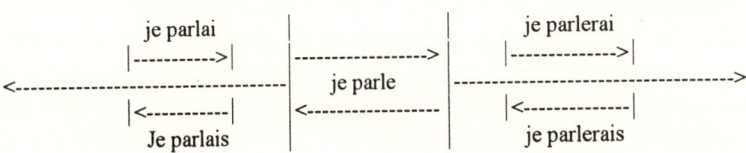

The relationship between the imperfect and the conditional that is marked in the morphology is discussed in detail in Chapter Six, and also the notional relationship of present and imperfect that appears in reported speech:

(21)   J'ai faim. Il a dit qu'il avait faim

In (19) it may be observed that the present of the speech act is replaced by the imperfect in reported speech.

Speakers of Indo-European languages tend to think of the division of the representation of time into time-spheres as being a basic requirement of any language. Certainly, such divisions are to be found throughout the spectrum of Indo-European languages, and speakers of such languages tend inevitably to look for such systems in languages belonging to other phyla and families, and sometimes to misinterpret the morphological categories they find in the verbal systems of other languages as being experiential time-sphere categories. But many languages have a fully coherent system of representation of time without analysis into time-spheres based upon the introduction or representation of the experiential present. The representation of tense in Indo-European languages, therefore, fulfills a need, but it is not the need to represent past, present or future, or indeed any other time-sphere.

It would appear, in fact, that the problem that is solved by the representation of time-spheres is the problem of representing an event as occurring within experiential time. If time is seen as a vast present, as in Stage II, (the subjunctive) in the representation of the French verb, any event that is represented as contained in this vast sea of time must necessarily remain vague and imprecise. But if the moment of the present can be represented as dividing future time from past time, then the representations of both the past and the future are bound by the intrusion of the present and by contrasting with each other, so that each may become a container within which an event occupying time may be placed, and thereby represented as an experiential occurrence. The Romance division of time into past, present and future stems at least in part, it appears, from the interplay of mechanical and representational requirements.

3.5 *Conclusion*

It was Jakobson who first pointed out that children's acquisition of their phonological systems shows staging: that later elements, such as front rounded vowels, cannot be acquired until other elements have first been acquired, namely back rounded and front unrounded vowels (1971/1990:298). Jakobson also noted that this staging was equally in evidence in aphasia: that what was acquired last was lost first. In fact Jakobson states quite categorically (1971, 1990:299): "Every phonological system is a STRATIFIED STRUCTURE, that is to say, is formed of superimposed layers" (emphasis in original).

The notion of chronogenesis as first presented by Guillaume in 1929 is a recognition of a similar kind of cognitive staging in a grammatical system, in this case the French verbal system. In the chronogenesis Guillaume perceives a three stage build-up of a time-image. The tense system of a language such as French, with its multifold contrasts, is a complex structure, and Guillaume insists that the analysis and reconstruction of its developmental stages is a fundamentally important task for linguists (1929:8).

At the same time he made an important statement of method, in a now famous footnote (1929:8):

> *La pensée en action de langage exige réellement du temps.* Il y a là un principe de grande portée en linguistique psychologique et en linguistique générale (emphasis in original).
> " (Thought operating in language requires time. This is a principle of major importance for both mentalist (today we would say *cognitive*) linguistics and general linguistics)."

In other words the choice of a given verb form in a sentence means that there was a mental operation, requiring real time, to find that place in the content system where such a representation could be created. In short, just as there is necessarily scanning of stored vocabulary (as in Penfield's experiments during brain surgery: 1959:227–228) to find *le mot juste*, there is also scanning of grammatical content systems in order to create the appropriate grammatical form for a given context. Given the necessary staging involved, any such scanning would necessarily proceed from Stage I through Stage II to Stage III.

In the above quote, from the 1920's, therefore, any proponent of cognitive linguistics from later in the century would necessarily recognise the mark of a distinguished predecessor.

CHAPTER FOUR
ASPECT

4. *Introduction*

In attempting to determine aspectual forms in the French verbs, we shall start from the point of view of the morphosyntax, and note that all compound forms are marked for transcendent (i.e. perfect or retrospective) aspect, whereas the simple forms are unmarked in this contrast. The compound forms, in short, show the same tenses as the simple forms: as well as the simple present tense, *je parle*, there is an aspectual compound form which corresponds by having the auxiliary in the same tense: *j'ai parlé*. For every simple form in the language, in fact, we shall find a corresponding compound form, so that the future and conditional, *je parlerai, je parlerais*, have the corresponding compound forms, *j'aurai parlé, j'aurais parlé*. Likewise, the two past forms, *je parlais, je parlai*, have their corresponding compound forms: *j'avais parlé, j'eus parlé*.

What is even more striking in the French verb, in fact, is that as well as a whole array of simple forms and compound forms, there is an array of forms showing two stages of compounding. For example, as well as a simple future *je parlerai*, and a compound future *j'aurai parlé*, there is also what is called by the French grammarians a *surcomposé*, or double compound: *j'aurai eu parlé*.

	Immanent	*Transcendent*	*Bi-transcendent*
Infinitive	parler	avoir parlé	avoir eu parlé
Pres. Part.	parlant	ayant parlé	ayant eu parlé
Past Part.	parlé	(eu parlé)	
Subjunctive 1	parle	aie parlé	aie eu parlé
Subjunctive 2	parlasse	eusse parlé	eusse eu parlé
Present	parle	ai parlé	ai eu parlé
Imperfect	parlais	avais parlé	avais eu parlé
Passé Simple	parlai	eus parlé	—
Future	parlerai	aurai parlé	aurai eu parlé
Conditional	parlerais	aurais parlé	aurais eu parlé

Table 1

For each of the compound forms, in short, a double compound form is possible, although some of these — such as the imperfect subjunctive *que j'eusse eu parlé* are seldom if ever used. Although these forms have been used in literary works since at least the sixteenth century, some have considered them to be marginally acceptable, and recent surveys in Europe (see Walter 1988:172) have shown that consistent use of them is not universal among French speakers.

Nevertheless, the grammars all report these forms and some, such as Damourette & Pichon, give a wide range of examples. There have also been several extensive studies (Foulet 1925, Cornu 1953, Stefanini 1954, Haltus 1986, Ayres-Bennett & Carruthers 1992) giving detailed information on their history and usage. Consequently any study of aspect in the French verb must take into account the full array of forms shown in tabulated form in Table 1, where the tenses have been listed vertically, and the aspects listed horizontally, to show clearly the interrelationship of tense and aspect in the paradigm. In the indicative, for example, there are five tenses, and three aspects: Immanent, Transcendent, and Bi-transcendent are the terms used by Guillaume (e.g. 1964:190).

4.1 *Distinguishing tense from aspect*

One point of this analysis that causes much confusion must be dealt with first. Many of the grammars of French, especially those used as teaching texts in the schools, will refer to the passé composé *j'ai parlé* as a past tense. The same confusion is to be found even in the writings of distinguished French linguists, such as Benveniste (1966b:69ff), for example. This confusion stems from a failure to perceive that the verb forms themselves, as may be seen from the coherence of their paradigms, are clearly markers of a cognitive system. Indeed, as Annette Vassant has pointed out (1988), Benveniste, although he talks of 'system', does not conceive of the forms of the French verb as representing any kind of underlying system.

Admittedly, from the point of view of usage, the passé composé is normally used to refer to events that occurred in the past. But, from the point of view of what is directly observable linguistically, namely the data of the morphosyntax, there is no doubt that the only marking of tense in the passé composé is to be found in the marked present tense of the auxiliary. It is the juxtaposition of this present tense with a past participle that enables the whole compound form to represent a past event. That does not make the whole form into a past tense any more than the use of a present to indicate future time will make such a present into a future tense. In such a sentence as

(1)   He is leaving for Montreal next weekend

the tense is incontrovertibly present, but the reference is to future time. Linguists, who insist that their methodology must always be rooted in the directly observable in order to make it coherent, to give it rigour, must call such a verb form *non-past tense*, and must steadfastly refuse to call it a future. (It goes without saying that they should also be able to give some account of such a phenomenon, and ultimately be able to explain how and why a non-past tense may be used in future reference).

It must be admitted, furthermore, that once one has agreed to call such forms as *j'ai parlé* instances of the present tense in transcendent aspect, then the total array of verb forms in French becomes much more manageable and understandable, and the usage and interrelationship of the various verb forms begins to take on a patterning that is much simpler to grasp.

4.1.1 *The surcomposé in student grammars*

Many students of French are unaware of the existence of the *formes surcomposées*, in spite of the fact that they have become very frequent in colloquial usage, and in spite of the fact that many of the student grammars give extensive examples of these forms. Grevisse, for example, in *Le bon usage* (1959:578–582) gives examples from classical French authors going back to the seventeenth century, and from such acknowledged prose masters as Bishop Bossuet (1627–1704). Damourette et Pichon (V:292–302) give several pages of forms collected from literary and other sources, including the following from the great French comparativist Antoine Meillet (p.295): "Quand l'abrègement de ces voyelles *a eu déterminé* l'amuissement, la voyelle inaccentuée de la syllabe précédente, se trouvant en syllabe finale, A SUBI à les mêmes mutilations" (*Caractères généraux des langues germaniqes*:89). The grammar of Wagner and Pinchon (1962) gives a selection of examples (pp. 342–343), and the brief and succinct *Grammar of Present Day French* of J.E. Mansion (1959) deals with these forms briefly in section 82, giving a full array of the indicative forms in section 395.

4.1.2 *The mechanism underlying the French aspectual contrast*

Gustave Guillaume, as early as *Temps et Verbe* (1929) and subsequently in important articles in the following decades (collected in Guillaume 1964), and also in the volumes on the French verb in the posthumous *Leçons de linguistique* (especially 1971, 1974, 1986) labels the three different aspectual sets shown in Table I as follows (a) Immanent Aspect: *Formes simples* — those forms of the verb expressed in a single word (b) Transcendent Aspect: *Formes composées* — those verb forms expressed in a compound consisting of auxiliary plus past

ASPECT 51

participle of the main verb (c) Bi-transcendent Aspect: *Formes surcomposeés* — those forms expressed in three words, consisting of auxiliary plus past participle of the auxiliary plus past participle of the main verb (1964:73–86, 1971: 177ff, 1986:150). He explains the functioning of the content system enshrined in these forms in terms of *temps impliqué*, or time enfolded, the time within the event, later renamed Event Time (temps d'événement) by Roch Valin (1965, 1994:40), the time represented as lying between the initial and final moments of the event that is represented:

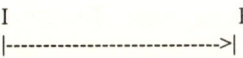

(1) I = initial moment of the event
(2) F = final moment of the event
(3) The arrow represents the unfolding of the event as each successive moment follows, from the initial moment until the end of the event.
(4) Every event (in order to be represented as an event) requires its own interior time.

This interior time may be represented as a static space (Infinitive Mood) or as movement between two poles: the initial and final moments of the event (Indicative and Subjunctive). Event Time is a representational mechanism that relates to the event only, and does not concern time exterior to the event. Or, to put it another way, it represents only the time 'contained' within the event, whether this interior time be represented statically (quasi-nominal mood), or in motion (subjunctive and indicative). Event Time is the basis of aspectual distinctions. The time exterior to the event, that contains the event, called *le temps expliqué* by Guillaume (1964:73–86) and renamed Universe Time by Valin (1965, 1994:40), is, by contrast, the basis of tense distinctions.

In Chapter Six we shall examine the contrasts of Universe Time that lead to tense distinctions. In this chapter we shall show that contrastive ways of representing Event Time are the basis of aspectual distinctions. In short, tenses are formed by the representations of Universe Time, whereas aspects are formed by different representations of Event Time.

4.1.3 *Simple forms*

In all the simple forms of the verb only the time interior to the single event represented is in question. In a form such as *parlant*, for example, the container of the event is represented as only partly full, whereas with *parlé* the container of the event is represented as full. In such a form as *il parlait*, where the verb is predicated of a subject, the subject is represented as engaged in the activity of a past event; in *il parle* he is represented as engaged in a present event; and in *il parlera*, he is represented as engaged in a future event.

In the simple forms of the subjunctive and indicative moods, consequently, the subject is represented as being 'interior' to the event, i.e. as occupying a position within the event, and somewhere between its initial and final moments. Hence, the term 'immanent aspect'.

4.1.4 *Compound forms*

With the compound forms the subject is represented as occupying a new space posterior to the completion of the original event. This new space is defined by the Event Time of the auxiliary, while the Event Time of the original event is represented by the past participle. We may compare the two types of representation as follows:

	il parle <----------X---------->
parlé <-------------------------	il a <----------X---------->

(1) The tense of the auxiliary in *il a parlé* is the same as that of *il parle*.
(2) The subject of *il parle* and *il a parlé* is marked in each case by X in the diagram.
(3) Whereas the subject is represented as being interior to the main event in *il parle*, it is represented as interior to the auxiliary in *il a parlé*, and the main event is now represented by the past participle *parlé*.
(4) Analytically *il a parlé* indicates present 'possession' of a previous event that is itself represented as complete.

In all the compound forms (*formes composées*) in French the subject is represented as directly involved with the event of the auxiliary, and no longer actively involved with the event represented by the past participle. The subject, in short, has now been 'removed' from the event represented by *parlé* and has been placed outside it in the time of another, subsequent event (*a*). Hence, the term transcendent aspect.

4.1.5 *Double compound forms*

The *formes surcomposées* (or super-compounded, double compound forms) are simply an extrapolation of the compound forms. Just as the latter, by relocating the subject in the time of the auxiliary, allow the original event to be represented as transcended, as an event prior to the auxiliary, so too the bitranscendent aspect shows a second stage of transcendence.

What was the auxiliary in the compound forms is itself transformed into a past participle, and a new auxiliary created that opens up a further space of event time and that is posterior both to the event time of the original auxiliary and to the event time of the original past participle:

		il parle <--------x----->	(A)
	parlé <-----------------	il a <--------x----->	(B)
parlé <-----------------	eu <-----------------	il a <--------x----->	(C)

The effect of such a mechanism is to represent the event of (B) as occurring before (A), and that of (C) as occurring before (B). If (A) is present tense, (B) is represented as occurring before the present, as anterior to the present. This is achieved by blocking off the space of the present with the event time of the auxiliary, so that the event represented by the past participle is necessarily thrust into the period prior to the present (i.e. the past). If there is a necessity for expressing the priority or anteriority of one past event over another, the form in (C) provides the means. It does this by representing the event time of the original auxiliary (*avoir*) by the past participle and by creating a new auxiliary with an event time which will occupy the space of the present.

As we shall see, form (B) is commonly used to represent a simple past event and is one of the most common forms of the language. Form (C), however, is normally only used to represent what necessarily occurs before an event of type (B). The common auxiliary used in these forms is *avoir*, although a lexically determined set of verbs is commonly found with the auxiliary *être*. Typical of this set, for example, is *partir*.

    (A) Quand il part   "When he leaves"
    (B) Quand il est parti   "When he left"
    (C) Quand il a été parti   "When he had left"

The occurrence of form (C) with verbs of this set is rare, and its occurrence with the pronominal verbs is even rarer. The formation of the *surcomposé* with pronominal verbs uses the auxiliary *être*: *il s'est eu réveillé, elles se sont eu levées*.

4.1.6 *Usage of French aspectual forms*

In a very high percentage of dependent clauses of time in French, the verb of the subordinate clause is found to be in the same tense as the main clause. This situation is therefore the norm, which should be taught to those who study French as a second language. Mansion gives the following examples (1959:213):

(2) Il sort quand il fait beau
     "He goes out when it is fine"
(3) Il sortit quand il fit beau
     "He went out when it was fine"
(4) Il sortait quand il faisait beau
     "He went out whenever it was fine"
(5) Il sortira quand il fera beau
     "He will go out when it is fine"
(6) Il sortirait quand il ferait beau
     "He would go out when it was fine (if it was)"

A context is required to make proper sense of (6). If someone says "Je sortirai quand il fera beau", this may later be reported under the form *Il a dit qu'il sortirait quand il ferait beau*. In both (5) and (6), the agreement of tense is essential to French, whereas English does not have a future in the subordinate clause and

(7) He will go out when it will be fine

would be classified by a native speaker of English as 'stylistically foreign'. We should note, however, that English has the non-past tense in both clauses, given that the auxiliary of *he will go out* is in the non-past tense, and that there is no future tense in English, the future being represented aspectually. If one tries to transpose the English pattern into French, however, where future aspect (English) would become future tense (French), the result is a gross clash of tenses, which is contrary to the norm of French as established above:

(8) *Il sortira quand il fait beau

If a future *tense* occurs in the French main clause, a future *tense* is also required in the subordinate clause of time. If a present *tense* occurs in the main clause, a present *tense* will also be required in the subordinate clause. This parallelism of tenses is also the norm of English usage as in the English translation of (5) above, once one perceives that *He will go* shows the regular non-past tense of English and represents the future aspectually with a periphrastic form. As we shall see below, it is quite normal for aspects to differ in the two clauses.

4.1.7 *Modern use of the composé as a preterit*

We note in passing that sentence (3) would only be used in narrative or literary style and would not be used in conversation. The passé simple has disappeared from use in conversation over the past two hundred years, and may be heard today only on the lips of the very old, and then only in remote settlements far from the contacts of urban life. In ordinary standard, it has been replaced in spoken French by the compound passé composé:

(9)   J'ai vu ce film hier
        "I saw that film yesterday"

The English present perfect could not be used in such a sentence:

(10)   *I have seen that film yesterday

The translation in (10) is ungrammatical, since the English present perfect may only be used with adverbials indicating present time.

The same restriction applied to the French passé composé in the seventeenth century, but no longer applies today, since the compound form has taken over the uses of the now obsolescent passé simple. Sentence (3) would be heard in normal conversation as:

(11)   Il est sorti quand il a fait beau.

The strict parallelism observed in (2) – (6) is again noticeable in (11) and is also to be found whenever the verb in the main clause is found in other of the compound forms. Mansion gives the following (1959:213):

(12)   J'étais sorti quand il avait fait beau
        "I had gone out when it was fine"
(13)   Il sera sorti quand il aura fait beau
        "He will be out when it is fine"
(14)   Il serait sorti quand il aurait fait beau
        "He would be out when it was fine"

A context is also required to give the right interpretation to (14): He said he would be out when it got fine.

4.1.8 Expressing anteriority

In sentences (3) – (6) and (11) – (14), the two different verbs represent events that are roughly contemporaneous; neither takes temporal priority over the other. In many cases, however, it is important to indicate that the action in one clause is over before the action in the other begins:

(15)   When he had eaten he went out.

Otherwise, we are confronted with ambiguous statements:

(16)   When he ate he went out.

The most natural sense of this sentence would be that he went out to eat, that the eating was contemporaneous with his absence from the house, since both verb forms are identical in both tense and aspect.

When this necessity of indicating the priority of one event over the other arises, French (as English) makes use of the compound aspectual forms to represent the prior event:

(17)   Il sortit quand il eut dîné.

Again we observe that there is a parallelism of tenses, and that the compound is used to indicate the priority or anteriority of the act of eating:

dîné	il eut
<-----------------------	----------------------->
	il sortit
	----------------------->

By showing the two representations in diagram form, we indicate the parallelism of *eut* and *sortit* (= simultaneity) and the priority of *dîné*.

Again Mansion notes the strict parallelism of forms in this type of sentence and also gives the following, where complete identity of tenses is maintained while exploiting aspectual forms to represent the anteriority of the event in the subordinate clause (1959:214):

(18)   Il sort quand il a dîné
       "He goes out when he has eaten"
(19)   Il sortait quand il avait dîné
       "He always went out when he had eaten"
(20)   Il sortira quand il aura dîné
       "He will go out when he has eaten"
(21)   Il sortirait quand il aurait dîné
       "He would go out when he had eaten"

And again we need to give a context for (21): *Il a promis qu'il sortirait quand il aurait dîné* (He promised that he would go out when he had eaten).

Sentences (18) – (21) are appropriate for either colloquial or literary style, but (17) is appropriate only for literary or narrative style since it uses the passé simple which would be replaced in colloquial style by the passé composé. There then emerges the possibility for a *surcomposé* in the subordinate clause in order to express anteriority to the event represented by a *composé* in the main clause

(22)   Il est sorti quand il a eu dîné.

In this way, the parallelism of tenses and forms is observed,

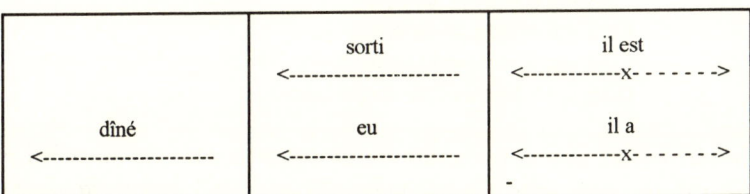

It is not surprising that the *formes surcomposées* have come into ever increasing use with the loss of the passé simple in conversational French and the growing use of the passé composé to replace it.

The same pattern is followed with the other tenses, and Mansion gives the following:

(23)   Il était sorti quand il avait eu dîné
       "He had always gone out when he had eaten"
(24)   Il sera sorti quand il aura eu dîné
       "He'll be out when he has eaten"
(25)   Il serait sorti quand il aurait eu dîné
       "He would be out when he had eaten"

The last sentence, of course, requires the context *Il a dit qu'il...*.
There are consequently three different ways of translating English *When he has eaten*... (Quand il a dîné, aura dîné, aura eu dîné) and six ways of translating *When he had eaten* ... (Quand il eut dîné, a eu dîné, avait dîné, avait eu dîné, aurait dîné, aurait eu dîné). The differences at first sight appear to be very complex, but once one understands that each language is coherently exploiting its own quite different resources in the representation of the same or similar experiences, the complexity evaporates. It is only when we allow the systems of one language to interfere with those of the other that we get complexity, error and confusion.

Mansion also points out that the same sequences occur with a dependent relative (i.e. adjectival) clause, and with a basic sentence type of *Those who lose pay* will yield the following comprehensive array of sentences (1959:214):

(26)   Ceux qui perdent paient
         Ceux qui perdaient payaient
         Ceux qui perdirent payèrent
         Ceux qui perdront payeront
         Ceux qui perdraient payeraient

         Ceux qui ont perdu ont payé
         Ceux qui avaient perdu avaient payé
         Ceux qui auront perdu auront payé
         Ceux qui auraient perdu auraient payé

In the second set, where the forms are all compounded, the so-called passé antérieur is not used, since it is rare in main clauses, and *formes surcomposées* are not found.

Then using the sentence type *Those who had finished first left*, he shows that another set of sentences will indicate the the anteriority of the event represented in the subordinate clause. The parallelism between the sentences in (26) and (27) is striking.

(27)   Ceux qui ont fini les premiers partent
         Ceux qui avaient fini les premiers partaient
         Ceux qui eurent fini les premiers partirent
         Ceux qui auront fini les premiers seront partis
         Ceux qui auraient fini les premiers seraient partis

         Ceux qui ont eu fini les premiers sont partis
         Ceux qui avaient eu fini les premiers étaient partis

Ceux qui auront eu fini les premiers seront partis
Ceux qui auraient eu fini les premiers seraient partis

Again we notice that the passé antérieur is not used in the second set, and the last sentence, with the conditional forms, would require a context to make good sense: *Normally, those who had finished first would have left.*

There are of course sentences where, for special expressive reasons, this parallelism of tenses will not hold. But unless such reasons exist the native speaker will commonly align the tenses according to the patterns we have seen. Those who do not use the *surcomposé*, will normally use the Pluperfect instead:

(28)   Il est sorti quand il avait dîné
       "He went out when he had eaten"

This is of course a perfectly acceptable alternative usage since the imperfect tense of the Pluperfect (as marked on the auxiliary) forms an *assiette* or background for the event presented by the passé composé.

When we come to look at sequences of tenses in other languages, however, we shall find that the modern French tendency to use a *surcomposé* instead of the so-called Pluperfect in (28) is part of a more or less universal pattern to parallel the tenses in subordinate clauses of time with those in the main clause. A brief examination of the data of English will show the same parallelism.

4.2 *Sequence of tenses in English*

If we translate the sentences in (26) and (27) above into English, we find that English, having only two tenses, cannot reproduce the array of forms that are found in the French sentences, but nevertheless demonstrates, just as does French, a completely coherent sequence of tenses. One has to realize of course that English expresses the future and conditional by means of aspect, and normally requires an adverb to get the equivalent translation of the imperfect. The tense of the auxiliary, however, will always be the same as the tense of the simple forms of the verb.

(29)   Those who lose pay
       Those who lost always paid
       Those who lost paid
       Those who lose will pay
       Those who lost would pay

Those who have lost have paid
Those who had lost had always paid
Those who have lost will have paid
Those who had lost would have paid

As in French, the last sentence requires an adverbial *Normally* to give a suitable context. It is very informative to note the switching of the verb *lose* in the first set of sentences, and of the auxiliary *have* in the second set. The identical phenomenon will be found in the sentences that express anteriority.

(30)   He goes out when he has eaten
       He always went out when he had eaten
       He went out when he had eaten
       He will go out when he has eaten
       He would go out when he had eaten

       He has gone out when he has eaten
       He had gone out when he had eaten
       He will have gone out when he has eaten
       He would have gone out when he had eaten

Again we should add an initial *Normally* to the two sentences that contain *would*. It should also be noted that the English sentences are by no means an exact parallel to the French set, because of the differences between the two systems. The present perfect of English is quite different from the passé composé, and as a result the sentence *He has gone out when he has eaten* would become in French *Il lui est arrivé de sortir quand il a eu dîné*. The English sentence would in fact be more natural with an added *sometimes*.

4.3 *Use of the surcomposé in main clauses*

Henriette Walter reports (1988:170–172) that the *surcomposé* is used in both main and subordinate clauses throughout the whole of southern France, but used only in subordinate clauses in the Centre East and Centre West, and not used at all in the most northern regions. This means that the majority of French citizens use these forms in subordinate clauses, while a large minority also use them in main clauses.

One usage of the *surcomposé* in main clauses parallels the rare use of the *passé antérieur* in main clauses:

(31) Il eut vite mangé
(32) Il a eu vite mangé

Just as the passé composé replaces the passé simple in normal conversational usage, the sentence in (32) may be used to replace the literary norm in (31). In both cases we are confronted with an event that is over so quickly that we are looking at the *fait accompli* in the past. This is of course a stylistic trick which suggests that when we go back to the time in the past when the event should be taking place, we are already too late, because things have happened so quickly. The English translation *He quickly finished eating* uses two verbs (finish, eat) to indicate that we are confronted by the end of the eating rather than by the eating itself; the French sentence achieves the same result simply by using the aspectual forms illustrated in (31) and (32).

Another usage is the one that was used in the survey mentioned by Henriette Walter (1988:170):

(33) Il a eu coupé, ce couteau

which in English would be *It has cut a few times, has this knife*. Here again we are dealing with a stylistic exploitation of the *forme surcomposée*: when we go back in the past, this knife already has a history of cutting: the use of the *surcomposé* extends the historical reference deeper into the past. The English translation adds the understatement *a few times* to underscore the extended usage of the knife. We could also say in English *It has done some cutting, has this knife*, where *cutting* is explicitly quantified.

4.4 Conclusion

It may be observed, from the regularity and coherence of the above examples, and the simplicity of the mechanism that determines the tense and aspect forms that are found in them, that the use of transcendent compound forms to express anteriority is a simple cognitive mechanism. It is in fact a mechanism that is exploited by a wide variety of languages.

It may also be observed that the *surcomposé* is a coherent and elegant solution to some of the problems of expressing anteriority in a language that uses transcendent compound forms to represent simple past events. Table I, at the beginning of this chapter, gave the actual forms utilized in the aspect system of French. The following table summarizes the simple cognitive mechanisms exploited in the content system.

A	B	C
Moment A, definition of a space occupied by the unfolding of the event	Moment B, definition of a space which is beyond the space in A, and from which A is seen as a complete event	Moment C, definition of a space which is beyond space B, and from which B's view of A is itself seen as a complete event
immanent aspect = simple forms	transcendent aspect = compound forms	bi-transcendent aspect = double compound forms

Put into purely cognitive terms, we may see Moment A as the locating in perception, memory, or imagination of the record of an actual or potential event. Moment B is then a later position (a platform) from which the memory of A is recalled or renewed, as when a speaker says *I have read that book*. Moment C, finally, is a later or further platform in the memory, from which memory B is itself surveyed, as if one were to say *I told you yesterday that I had read that book*. In such a case the memory of the speaker returns to the moment yesterday when the memory of a prior memory was recalled. It would appear that these two stages would be the normal practical limit for such recall.

CHAPTER FIVE
VOICE

5. *Introduction*

A universal trait of language is the representation of transitivity, which in Indo-European languages concerns the interrelationship of subject, verb and object. All languages have noun-like entities and verb-like entities, and all languages show some kind of arrangement of predication between these noun-like and verb-like entities. In both French and English finite verbs must always be predicated of a grammatical subject, and this grammatical subject must be a nominal: i.e. a noun or its representative (e.g. pronoun, noun clause, etc.). It is this relationship between the verb and its grammatical subject that gives rise to the phenomena that we classify under the traditional category of voice.

Much has been written in recent years from a typological point of view concerning the universal nature of the grammatical relations of the verb and its arguments (e.g. Comrie 1981/1989, Foley and Van Valin 1984, Van Voorst 1988, Lazard 1994), but this work tends to deal more with the morphosyntax (what Hjelmslev (1935:XII) called the expression side of language), and has little to say concerning the grammatical meaning involved (the content side of language in Hjelmslev's terms). The analyses presented here will show that voice is more simply treated as a matter of content, being dependent on the meaningful role to be attributed to the subject. With intransitive verbs, there is no limit to the role of subject; it may be agent with active voice, patient with passive voice, mixed with middle voice. With transitive verbs, on the other hand, because the prototypical object in Indo-European languages is patientive, the prototypical role left to the subject, by default, is that of agent. In fact we cannot talk intelligently about voice unless we can distinguish the grammatical elements 'subject' and 'object' from semantic roles such as 'agent' and 'patient', a contrast which will be examined in 5.1.

Much has also been written, from a variety of theoretical points of view, on pronominal verbs (which we have designated (5.3) as representing middle voice), and on the contrast between pronominal verbs (*le verre s'est cassé*) and intransitive active verbs (e.g. *le verre a cassé*) with an inanimate subject (e.g. Ruwet 1972, Rothemberg 1974, Burston 1979, Hirschbühler 1986, Zribi-Herz 1987, Labelle 1992).

The role of agent normally requires an animate, and the role of patient is most easily filled by an inanimate: *I kicked the table* is a normal sentence, whereas *The table kicked me* is not. The use of an inanimate subject for an active verb (*The glass broke* vs. *I broke the glass*) consequently presents a problem for an analysis that relies entirely on *form*: how can *glass* be both subject and object of the verb *to break*? How is one to explain that the intransitive sentence (*The glass broke*) is active not passive?

From a cognitive point of view the answer is not far to seek: *The glass broke* means that the glass gave way, was unable to resist the force to which it was subjected. The sentence is genuinely active: it does not mean that the glass was deliberately broken. The formalist account, by contrast, treats the subject as un underlying accusative (i.e. direct object) that has been 'promoted' to subject position (the 'unaccusative hypothesis'). In the account presented here we avoid such unnecessary manipulations and the jargon that accompanies them. It is important at all times to keep in mind that linguistic systems are necessarily simple: they are learned and mastered by very small children. In 5.6 we return to this issue to see what conclusions may be drawn from our own proposals, concerning such minimal pairs as *il a rougi* vs. *il s'est rougi*, and *il a cassé* vs. *il s'est cassé*.

5.1 The grammatical representation of agent and patient

There are two conflicting views of the relationship between subject and verb in an Indo-European language such as French. One is the 2000 year old tradition of European grammar, reaffirmed in Jespersen (1924, 1965:100) and Guillaume (1982:129) that the verb is dependent on its subject. The other, stemming from Tesnière 1959, is that the subject is dependent on the valency of the verb.

This is not the proper occasion to argue this issue at length. Let us simply say that verbs in Indo-European languages such as French and English agree with their subjects, not their objects[1], and that Tesnière, in englobing both subject and object in the valency of the verb, confused two issues that should have been kept separate. The valency of the verb, a function of its lexical meaning, is certainly relevant to the establishing of direct and indirect objects, but the status of the subject in no way depends on the valency of the verb: *every* finite verb *requires* a subject - a sure indication that the finite verb is dependent on, is predicated of, its subject. Even the imperative, which has no formal subject, is predicated, like the vocative, of the person addressed, which is why, in the normal usage of both these forms, the person addressed is present.

We tend to think of the grammatical subject in a language such as French as being the agent, i.e. the individual from whom the action of the verb stems:

---

[1] The agreement of the past participle with the direct object is such sentences as *Je les ai vus* is a participal agreement; the verbal agreement is to be found in the auxiliary *ai*.

(1) Richard parle vite
     "Richard talks quickly"

In (1), Richard is admittedly the point of departure of the action of the verb. But if the verb is intransitive the grammatical subject can also be the patient, i.e. the individual to whom the action of the verb is done:

(2) On a battu Richard
     "They beat Richard"
(3) Richard a été battu
     "Richard was beaten"

Sentence (2) shows *Richard* as the direct object to an active voice verb, whereas (3) shows *Richard* as grammatical subject of the same verb in the passive voice.
The prototypical roles exemplified in these simple examples may be questioned when we turn to transitive subjects that are not prototypical, not clearly agents. We may paraphrase (3) as follows, using a transitive verb, for example:

(4) Richard a subi une défaite
     "Richard suffered a defeat"

Here we have a representation of the same situation, but the subject *Richard* plays the role of agent: how can an individual play both roles in the same situation?
First it must be said that (3) and (4) are two quite different representations of a single situation, and that such pairs are quite common

(5) a. He was subjected to an intolerable burden
    b. He bore an intolerable burden

In (5a), the passive sentence, the subject is portrayed as victim, in (5b) he is represented as actively carrying on under an intolerable strain: two different views of the same situation. Similar elements may be found in (3) and (4). The active sentence, for example, may be used when the subject is the instigator of the fight and consequently gets what he deserves.
Within the role of agent, therefore, it is common to find all kinds of peripheral usages as well as the prototypical usages. An extensive discussion of the thematic roles of agent and patient may be found in Dowty (1991). As Dowty notes (1991:571): "...role types are simply not discrete categories at all, but rather are cluster concepts, like the prototypes of Rosch and her followers (Rosch & Mervis 1975)."

5.2 *Passive voice in French*

Passive voice in French is distinctive: it requires the use of the verb *être* in the appropriate tense, to which is joined the past participle of the verb in question. For every simple active form, therefore, there is a corresponding compound passive form:

QUASI-NOMINAL	battre battant battu	être battu étant battu été battu
SUBJUNCTIVE	que je batte que je battisse	que je sois battu que je fusse battu
INDICATIVE	je bats je battis je battais je battrai je battrais	je suis battu je fus battu j'étais battu je serai battu je serai battu

Likewise, for most compound forms of the verb, there is a corresponding passive, composed of three words:

QUASI-NOMINAL	avoir battu ayant battu eu battu	avoir été battu ayant été battu eu été battu
SUBJUNCTIVE	que j'aie battu que j'eusse battu	que j'aie été battu que j'eusse été battu
INDICATIVE	j'ai battu j'eus battu j'avais battu j'aurai battu j'aurais battu	j'ai été battu j'eus été battu j'avais été battu j'aurai été battu j'aurais été battu

Passive forms of the *surcomposé* may also be found composed of four words: (See Grevisse, *Le bon usage*, para. 661, remarque 2a):

(6) que j'aie eu battu   que j'aie eu été battu
(7) j'ai eu battu   j'ai eu été battu

These forms, however, with their string of past participles tend to be cumbersome and are very rare in formal style.

5.2.1 The role of the subject

As we have seen above, the different voices of the verb present the subject in different roles; as we investigate these roles, certain very clear patterns emerge.

First, although the grammatical subject can play a variety of roles, the grammatical object prototypically plays the role of patient. If the verb is transitive (i.e. has a direct object), therefore, the only role the subject can play is that of agent: the role of patient has been subsumed by the object.

subject	verb	object
agent	---------->	patient

If, on the other hand the verb is intransitive, the subject is free to play either role, according to the voice of the verb, or even to play a role that is part agent and part patient (middle voice).

voice	subject	verb
ACTIVE	agent	x---------------------->
MIDDLE	agent/patient	x--------><----------
PASSIVE	patient	x<---------------------

In the shift from active voice to passive voice, we see a complete reversal of roles: the patient is the grammatical object in the active voice and the grammatical subject in the passive voice:

(8) Jean a battu Richard
(9) Richard a été battu par Jean

It is also possible to allow the grammatical subject to play any role between the two poles of agent and patient, so that distinctions of active and passive voice become confused:

(10) Jean se bat
(11) Jean se lave les mains

Such verb forms have traditionally been called *reflexives*, which is obviously a misnomer, since many of these verbs are not at all reflexive: the reflexive is simply the prototypical middle voice, where the subject is equally agent and patient. The example in (10) would be translated *John is fighting*[2], and that in (11) *John is washing his hands*. There is an element of reflexivity in (11), since John is washing his *own* hands, but a reflexive verb could not be used here in English, and in (10) the *se* form of the verb is used because a fight necessarily involves reciprocity, not reflexivity: one needs an opponent who will fight back. The more appropriate term *pronominal verbs* is used today in most modern grammars for these middle voice verbs. The genuine reflexives are consequently only a sub-category of the pronominal verbs, where the agent does an action to himself and is, therefore, also the *patient*:

(12)   Je me vois dans le miroir
       "I see myself in the miror"

A very great number of pronominal verbs, in fact, are not at all reflexive:

(13)   Ce livre se vend très bien
       "This book is selling well"
(14)   Cet hôtel se cache derrière une grande usine
       "This hotel is hidden behind a large factory"

In the active voice in French, the subject is represented as free, as being in control of the event: the prototypical agent. In the passive voice, the subject is represented as bound, as being controlled by the event: the prototypical patient. In the middle voice, as represented by the pronominal verbs, the subject is at one and the same time both bound and free, or alternatively, neither one thing nor the other. The pronominal verbs are, therefore, clear-cut examples of middle voice, the *via media* between active and passive, and French is a language that has a distinctive morphosyntax of middle voice, as was pointed out by Guillaume as long ago as 1943 in a strikingly original article in *Le français moderne* (1943, 1964:127-142). It is not unusual for Indo-European languages to show distinctive markings for middle voice. The Ancient Greek aorist and future, for example, had contrastive active, middle, and passive paradigms. Latin had its deponent verbs: passive forms with active meanings: *nascor* "I am born"; *morior* "I die". Even English, which does not normally distinguish active from middle:

(15)   I grow flowers. Flowers grow.
(16)   I sell books. Books sell.

---

[2] If he is fighting, he is being hit as well as hitting. English, which has no equivalent morphosyntax of middle voice, tends to represent such events as active. Active voice in English, in comparative terms, is medio-active: Latin deponents are typically translated as English actives.

(17)   I'm cooking the turkey. The turkey is cooking.

nevertheless has such oddities as

(18)   He was born a pauper.

which, while passive in form, does not have an active correlate:

(19)   *His mother bore him a pauper

Middle voice values are, in fact, very common, and every language, under close scrutiny, will reveal elements, within its representations of transitivity, that may be considered instances of middle voice - verbal elements that are neither truly active nor truly passive, but occupying the middle ground between these two polarized voices: a recent book by Kemmer (1991) has in fact presented an extensive survey of the range of middle voice forms. It is obviously unthinkable that the variety of activities that must be represented at some time by speakers will all unambiguously be either active or passive; middle voice allows for an alternate representation of the middle ground between the two polar positions.

Damourette & Pichon, in their massive seven volume grammar of French (1911-1936) have collected what must be the most perfect illustration of the semantic contrast of all three grammatical voices in French (Vol 5:662):

Si c'est Villeroi qui commande dit le Prince Eugène, je le battrai. Si c'est Vendôme nous nous battrons. Si c'est Catinat, je serai battu.

Here we have the three possible results of a battle: *win* (active), *draw* (middle), and *lose* (passive). Translating such contrasts into English is very difficult: se battre is normally translated "to fight", but the second sentence would make no sense if translated in this way. Possible translations are as follows: (1) "... I will give him a beating...we will give each other a beating...I will be given a beating", (2) "... I will batter him...we will batter one another...I will be battered."

5.3 *The pronominal verbs*

Much has been written in recent years on the pronominal verbs, from such early studies as Hatcher (1942) and the massive Guillaumean style study by Stefanini (1962), through later volumes such as Donaldson (1973), Rothemberg (1974), to the wide ranging study by Geniušiené (1987) on the typology of reflexives in IE languages. A recent study by Melis (1990) attempts to find a prototypical meaning for each of the traditional sub-categories: subjective, objective, dative, reflexive, reciprocal.

Instead of trying to find a variety of underlying meanings all marked by the same morphology, as Melis does, we shall attempt to show that this distinctive morphosyntax marks a single underlying meaning, that stems from a single, simple, cognitive strategy: the elimination of the two polarized voices, active and passive, to produce a third voice that is neither active nor passive. This is achieved by introducing a clitic pronoun that would normally be reflexive: the prototypical role of a reflexive is to deflect the operation of the verbal lexeme back toward the subject, so that the subject and object are one and the same.. Here it must be understood that for a verb to be transitive, the action must pass across (*trans*) from an agent to a patient, and that normal transitivity is aborted when the action is deflected back to the subject. If the reflexive pronoun plays the role of indirect object, this deflection may be only partial, as in *Il s'est lavé les mains*, where the result is a mixture of active and middle.

The middle voice created by this strategy of using a reflexive pronoun is capable of presenting a whole range of surface values which vary all the way from close to the active, through the median values of reflexive and reciprocal, to values that are close to the passive, as the following examples will show (see also 5.5).

(20) quasi active in sense
se souvenir "to remember"
s'en aller "to go away"
s'évader "to escape"
se lancer "to dart"
(21) reflexive and reciprocal
Il s'est regardé dans le miroir
"He looked at himself in the mirror"
Ils se sont regardés, l'un l'autre
"They looked at each other"
(22) quasi passive in sense
La clef s'est retrouvée
"The key has been found"
La maison s'est bâtie en trois jours
"The house was built in three days"

A notable feature of the pronominal verbs of French is that their compound tenses use the auxiliary *être* - the auxiliary of the passive:

(23) Je m'en suis souvenu
"I remembered it"
(24) Je me suis dit
"I said to myself"

Another feature of note is that many of them may be translated by the English auxiliary *get*, which often has a sense of *become*, a verb closely related to *be*: *to be* is the result of becoming:

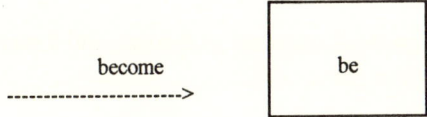

We may, therefore, make a long list of such verbs and their English equivalents:

se marier	to get married
se lever	to get up
se laver	to get washed
s'habiller	to get dressed
se déshabiller	to get undressed
s'évader	to get away
s'établir	to get established
se rétablir	to get well
se lasser	to get weary
se coucher	to get to bed
se fâcher	to get angry

Syntactically, it may be noted, French pronominal verbs function partly like active verbs and partly like passive verbs, since their compound forms are only distinguishable from passive forms by the use of the extra object pronoun:

(25) Il s'est décidé
"He made up his mind"
(26) Il est décidé
"It is decided"
(27) Elle est blessée
"She is injured"
(28) Elle s'est blessée
"She got hurt"

In (27) and (28), it may be noted that even the agreement of the past participle co-incides in both sentences.

5.4 *The verbs of resultant state*

There is, moreover, a group of verbs which, in their compound aspectual forms, are indistinguishable from the passive:

(29)   Elle est blessée   (passive)
(30)   Elle est partie   (non-passive)
(31)   Elle est née   (non-passive)
(32)   Elle est morte   (non-passive)

The most common of these verbs are as follows, and it may be noted that most of them fall readily into pairs:

aller	venir
sortir	entrer
partir	arriver
mourir	naître
retourner	revenir
monter	descendre
rentrer	
devenir	
tomber	
rester	

These verbs are commonly called the 'verbs of motion' in the traditional grammars, but the name is quite inadequate, since such verbs as *courir*, *marcher*, etc., are not in the set whereas such a verb as *rester* is. A more appropriate title for these verbs would be 'verbs of resultant state', a title which, when understood, explains why they belong to a special category. All these verbs represent actions which, when completed, result in a state of affairs where the subject is no longer free. The verb *mourir* "to die" is perhaps the most obvious example. With actions such as *running* (*courir*) or *walking* (*marcher*) the subject, upon completing the running or walking, is immediately free to resume running or walking. But once one is *dead* (*mourir*), one reaches a state from which it is no longer possible, in the normal human condition, to continue dying. It is this state, where the subject is no longer free to continue the event, that we call the resultant state.

An examination of the 'verbs of resultant state' reveals that they all represent events that, when complete, may no longer be simply resumed. If I enter a room, for example, I am then *in* the room, and from that position within can no longer continue entering. In order for the act to be done again, I am obliged to go outside again, to the original position: I am forced to leave the resultant state, since in the resultant state I am bound, no longer free to carry out the event. The inverse (*sortir*) is equally true, which is why these verbs tend to run in pairs. Likewise, once I reach the top of the stairs (*monter*), I am no longer in a position to keep going up; once I reach the bottom of the stairs (*descendre*), I am no longer in a position to keep going down.

There are, moreover, obvious good reasons why a verb such as *tomber* does not have a counterpart with which to form a pair. The person falling comes to rest on the ground or floor, which forms a limit to the fall, and establishes a resultant state. But one does not normally move in the opposite direction, nor is there any common limit for such upward movement.

Of the other verbs which do not form obvious pairs, *rentrer* is a simple compound of *entrer*, and *devenir*, as well as being a compound of *venir*, has, as we have seen, its own resultant state:

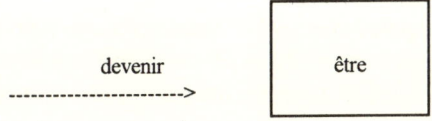

Becoming results in being: once one has become a doctor, for example, one then *is* a doctor, and is no longer free to continue *becoming* one.

The only remaining important verb in this category is rester *to remain*. It is not immediately obvious why this verb, which appears to lack the notion of dynamism, of reaching a goal, should also fit this pattern. There are, in fact, usages of this verb to be found with the auxiliary *avoir*, especially where the sense of the verb is equivalent to *demeurer* "to stay", "to dwell":

(33)   Il a resté deux jours à Lyon (Littré)

Nevertheless, the auxiliary *être* is the common one:

(34)   Je suis resté pour m'informer là-dessus
        "I stayed behind to find out about it"

Sentence (34) reveals the verb as intentional: I decided to stay behind, remained therefore when the others left, and as a result here I am (or there I was): the act of remaining can only take place when one is expected to leave; the state of remaining results. Being in the state of remaining, the subject is no longer free to exercise the act of remaining: he is quite simply there. He can only exercise the act of remaining if he is again expected to leave; then, and only then, can he choose the option of staying or leaving.

It is of interest that *rester* can represent the *act*, as in (34), or the state:

(35)   Il est resté deux ans.

In both cases, the auxiliary is the same. The same feature is commonly found with the other verbs of resultant state:

(36)   Papa est sorti
         "Dad is out (state)"
         Papa est sorti à deux heures
         "Dad went out at two o'clock (act)"
(37)   Richard est mort
         "Richard is dead (state)"
         Richard est mort en 1988
         "Richard died in 1988 (act)"

In other words, the *passé composé* of these verbs can represent either the event itself or the resultant state of the event. And finally, it should be observed that there is a close resemblance between the passive and the expression of resultant state, since the passive itself often represents a resultant state:

(38)   Richard est blessé (passive)
         "Richard is wounded"
         Richard est mort (active, resultant state)
         "Richard has died, is dead"

5.4.1 *Resultative verbs as a morphosyntactic category*

This group of 16 verbs that we have described above is a somewhat arbitrary one, for two reasons: (a) in other languages, it may be a slightly different selection of verbs that shows these features, and (b) even in French, there are verbs, other than those cited, that occasionally follow the same pattern. Grevisse, for example, (*Le bon usage* §658) lists some 50 verbs that may on occasion take *être* as the auxiliary of the passé composé. The verbs in this list by Grevisse are not as common as the 16 given above, but there are no surprises among them: it is quite conceivable that *croître* "increase" and *diminuer* "decrease", for example, which form a neat pair and suggest resultant state should also occasionally follow the same usage as the verbs of resultant state. And it is quite natural that verbs like *atterrir* "land, as a plane" and *aborder* "land from a ship" should follow the same pattern as *descendre*.

If we compare the selection of verbs that follow this pattern in Italian and German, we may observe a certain arbitrariness in the selection, since these two languages also include their verb *to be* in this category, while French does not. Compare the items in (39).

(39)   je suis tombé   sono caduto   ich bin gefallen
         j'ai été   sono stato   ich bin gewesen
         j'ai dormi   ho dormito   ich habe geschlafen
         je suis resté   sono restato   ich bin geblieben

As Vincent has pointed out, Italian is more conservative than French in this regard, and "the situation in Old French seems to have been more like that found in Modern Italian" (1982:91), where the *be* auxiliary is more frequent with intransitive verbs than in Modern French.

We may also note that English in an earlier period had forms such as *I am come, he is gone, he is fallen,* etc.

(40)   I am come that ye might have life
         (King James Bible, 1611)

The usage is not unknown in Modern English either, since we often hear

(41)   Is he gone yet?

The construction is also to be found in the literary forms of Modern English

(42)   The nymphs are departed
         (Eliot: *The Waste Land*)

The common usage with these verbs in Modern English, however, is unquestionably with *have* as an auxiliary.

Another curiosity of Modern English, however, is the following usage:

(43)   I'll be finished my exams by Tuesday

which is felt by many speakers to be 'more natural' than

(44)   I'll have finished my exams by Tuesday.

What is truly remarkable about (43) is the use of the auxiliary *be* with a full transitive verb = one that has an explicit direct object: *exams*. This may never be done in French, where a primary requirement for the auxiliary *être* is that the verb should be intransitive.

5.4.2 *Change of auxiliary with transitive verbs*

In fact, we may observe an immediate shift of auxiliary if a verb is made transitive:

(45)   Je suis monté
         "I went upstairs"
(46)   J'ai monté mes bagages
         "I carried up my luggage"

(47)   Elle est sortie
       "She went out"
(48)   Elle a sorti un mouchoir
       "She took out a handkerchief"

Grevisse also gives the following (§656, n.2):

(49)   Il a entré du tabac en fraude
       "He smuggled in some tobacco"
(50)   Il a tombé son adversaire
       "He toppled his opponent"

This distinction is important, since it indicates quite clearly that the choice between the auxiliaries *avoir* and *être* with these verbs is a function of voice. When these verbs are intransitive, their lexical sense, or Aktionsart, produces the effect of a resultant state in the *passé composé*, and consequently triggers the use of the middle and passive auxiliary.

It is obvious that in French *avoir* is the unambiguous auxiliary of the active voice. Any verb that becomes transitive by adding a direct object must be active, since only the 'patient' can play the role of direct object, and if the patient occupies that category, the only role available to the subject is that of agent. In such circumstances, when the subject is unambiguously agentive, the auxiliary *avoir*, auxiliary of the active voice, *must* be used. It is only when the verbs in (45) to (50) are intransitive (where the subject may consequently be less than fully agentive) that the auxiliary *être* becomes possible.

5.5 Middle voice

If Richard is the patient and John the agent of a fully transitive verb, we have a SVO structure, and the auxiliary must be *avoir*:

(51)   Jean a vaincu Richard

With a verb that shows only SV structure, other options are open. Since there is no object, the patient may also become the subject and we may have either of the following:

(52)   Jean a vaincu
(53)   Richard est vaincu.

In the case of SV structures, therefore, the verb may be either active with auxiliary *avoir* or passive with auxiliary *être*.

We suggested above (5.3) that a middle voice is created in French (and the same is true of Romance languages in general) by eliminating the two polarized voices, active and passive, by using a reflexive-type subject to reflect the action of the verb back to the subject, so that the subject cannot be categorically agent or categorically patient. In short the subject of a pronominal verb is necessarily part agent, part patient. This was put into a simple formula by Guillaume (1971a:202):

sujet = agent + patient = 1

In short the subject of a pronominal verb contains both agentive and patientive elements, either of which can be reduced to a mere quantum, but neither of which can be reduced to zero. The result is the range of surface values noted above (5.3), which varies all the way from borderline active to borderline passive, with the reflexives and reciprocals squarely in the middle of this range.

5.5.1 *Morphosyntax of middle voice*

Middle voice, which represents an indeterminate state of affairs between active voice and passive voice, in many languages utilizes some part of the morphosyntax of the passive forms. The formation of the morphology of the middle voice in Greek, for example, is the same as that of the passive, except in the future and the aorist, which have distinctive middle voice forms. Latin, like Greek, also uses passive voice morphology for middle voice, which results in the so-called deponent verbs: verbs that have a passive morphology but are all translated by active verbs in English: *proficiscor* "I set out" (= *partir*), *morior* "I die"(= *mourir*), *obliviscor* "I forget", *loquor* "I speak". This is another example of a set of middle voice verbs sharing the same morphology as the passive. (For discussion, see Guillaume 1943, 1964:127–129).

Middle voice verbs may be identified in French, therefore, not only by the use of so-called reflexive pronouns, but also by the use of the auxiliary *être* with intransitive verbs that are not passive. With the pronominal verbs, the reflexive type pronouns are also used, even when the sense of the verb is not truly reflexive, and may appear to be fully active:

(54) se laver to wash oneself
(55) se souvenir (de) to remember
(56) se lamenter to lament
(57) s'abstenir (de) to abstain
(58) se débattre to struggle

As Grevisse observes (*Le bon usage* §797, translation mine) "It is sometimes difficult to observe the value of the reflexive-type pronoun in the pronominal verbs". The value of the pronoun is reasonably obvious in (54) above, but not in (55) - (58). This has led some analysts to propose that *se* in pronominal verbs in Romance languages is two, or even three different pronouns, each with a different value. Other writers (e.g. Garcia 1975) quite properly insist that such a conclusion is methodologically unsound and stems from a failure to find the underlying value or invariant that underlies the variant usage. Once one allows two identical elements, which show neither morphological or syntactic contrasts to each other, to be analysed as two different elements, all coherence of methodological procedure has been sacrificed, and the door is open to ad hoc solutions of all kinds.

The use of a reflexive type pronoun with a transitive is a clear indication that the basic transitivity of a verb has been blocked by not allowing the event to be represented as passing across (*trans* = "across") from an agentive subject to a patient, but has been turned back upon the subject. A verb marked in such a way is neither fully active (because of the aborted transitivity), nor fully passive (because the subject cannot be fully patientive when there is an object pronoun). Such reflexive verbs are prototypical exemplars of middle voice: *je me lave* "I wash myself". From this prototype the usage may spread to intransitive verbs such as *se fâcher* "to get angry", *se lamenter* "to lament" where the subject does not act freely, but in response to some external causation. As a result, in all the Romance languages, we see the pronominal verbs used in a full range of middle voice values that vary all the way from the quasi active to the quasi passive.

5.5.2 *Agentive and patientive senses of middle voice*

Because it covers a range, a gradient, between the poles of agent and patient, the subject of a middle voice verb may consequently cover a wide variety of senses.

There are many verbs, for example, that are marked in French as middle voice where the subject is largely agentive, but some small patientive element is inherent in the notion of the verb. We have already noted *se fâcher* (note English *to get angry*, and Latin deponent *irascor*) where the subject does not carry out the act entirely of his own volition, but is the victim (i.e. patient) of circumstances: something makes him angry, and in respect to this something he is patientive - he undergoes anger because of an external stimulus or cause. (Anger is a passion; the word *passion* itself is derived, as is the word *passive* from the Latin deponent verb *patior* "I suffer"). *Se réveiller* "to wake up" (Latin deponent *expergiscor*), *s'endormir* "go to sleep", *s'ennuyer* "get bored", *se lamenter* "lament", *se tromper* "make a mistake", *se noyer* "drown" likewise are not normally based upon conscious volition, and the subject of such verbs is necessarily partly patientive, in similar fashion.

When one comes, however, to such examples as

(59)   Le poulet se mange froid

we see a subject that is *predominantly* patientive, that would be translated by an English passive:

(60)   Chicken is eaten cold/ can be eaten cold
        *(The) chicken eats itself cold
        *?Chicken eats cold

The use of middle voice here indicates that *chicken* is in some small way agentive in this sentence, sufficiently to prevent the use of the more obvious passive; it means that chicken is good to eat when cold, that the eater does not have to make an effort of will to eat cold chicken, that the tastiness of the chicken helps the eater (the agent) in his act, may even cause him to carry out the act, in which case the chicken, being in a small way a causative element, is not fully patientive; in such cases middle voice is a more suitable representation than passive voice. The same is true for

(61)   Ce livre se vend très bien
        "This book sells very well"

where the attractions of the book are partly cause of its excellent sales record.

Consequently, there is a very large number of verbs whose lexical sense is neither clearly active or clearly passive, and these are categorized or marked in French by the typical use of reflexive-type pronouns. Other languages also have such distinctive lexical sets, and indeed it is remarkable that a high percentage of Latin deponents would be translated into French as pronominal verbs, even though there is no etymological relationship between the two types, one (Latin) being marked in the morphology and the other (French) being marked in the syntax.

5.5.3 *Reflexive and reciprocal senses of middle voice*

As well as the middle voice verbs that have a clearly agentive or clearly patientive sense, there is a set of verbs that do not belong to either one wing or the other of middle voice, but solidly occupy the exact middle ground half way between the two poles: such are the reflexives and reciprocals.

In the case of the true reflexives, which may now be seen as a sub category of middle voice, the subject is equally agentive and patientive, in a true 50-50 balance. We have suggested above that this may be seen as the prototypical usage of middle voice, from which the usage has evolved to the more peripheral agentive and patientive types:

(62) Il s'est coupé avec le rasoir
      "He cut himself with the razor"
(63) Elle s'est regardée dans le miroir
      "She looked at herself in the mirror"

In sentences such as (62) and (63) it can be seen that the subjects, in doing the action to themselves are equally and identically agent and patient.

The same is true of reciprocal verbs, which share the same morphosyntax, and require further syntactic material to eliminate the consequent ambiguity:

(64) Elles se sont regardées dans le miroir
(65) Elles se sont regardées dans le miroir l'une l'autre
(66) Elles se sont regardées dans le miroir les unes les autres

Sentence (64) is ambiguous, since it could be either reflexive or reciprocal, whereas the ambiguity is resolved in (65) to indicate that two people looked at each other, and in (66) to indicate that more than two people looked at one another in the mirror.

We also find hidden reciprocals among the pronominal verbs. We may wonder why a verb such as *to assemble* should be pronominal: *s'assembler*, but a moment's reflexion reveals that it is impossible to assemble on one's own, and that such an activity requires reciprocity. The same is to be seen in

(67) se battre   "to fight"
      se fiancer   "to get engaged"
      se marier   "to get married"
      se débattre avec "to wrestle with (e.g. problem)"
      se ressembler   "to look alike"
      se mêler à   "to get involved"

Similar sets can be found in other language families, such as Bantu or Algonkian: the phenomenon of middle voice appears to be a linguistic universal.

Just as it is possible to have ambiguous sentences that may be interpreted as either reflexive or reciprocal, it is possible to have middle voice verbs that can be interpreted in various ways:

(68)   Les nageurs se jettent à l'eau
         "The swimmers dive into the water (active)"
         "The swimmers throw themselves into the water (reflexive?)"
         "The swimmers throw each other into the water (reciprocal)"
         "?The swimmers are thrown into the water (passive)"

The passive alternative is hardly possible with this particular sentence, except in extraordinary circumstances, because of the animate gender of the subject. But if the subject is made inanimate, the passive interpretation becomes the only alternative:

(69)   Les rebuts se jettent à l'eau
         "The garbage is thrown into the water"

It can be seen from these examples that the whole range of middle voice values is open to any verb whose lexical meaning can tolerate such variation. Given that questions of voice call into play the relationship of the verb to its subject, and given the wide range of middle voice values, it is not surprising that the nature of the subject will have an important role to play in the interpretation of middle voice forms.

5.5.4 Middle voice with pure intransitives

One is entitled to wonder why such a verb as *s'en aller*, with its Spanish (*irse*, i.e. *ir-se*) and Italian (*andarsene*, i.e. *andar-se-ne*) correlates, is allocated to middle voice. The answer lies in the goal-oriented nature of the lexeme *aller* in French (Hewson 1976), whence the impossiblility of saying

(70)   *Nous allons de cette maison
         "We're going from this house"

while it is perfectly proper to say

(71)   Nous allons à cette maison
         "We're going to this house"

Consequently, if one wishes to use *aller* to indicate a departure, adjustments are necessary. First of all the pronoun *en* is required to add the notion *from* to give the lexeme a biderectional sense (*aller* = à, *en* = *de*). When this is done, we can imagine a subject going from A to B:

         A -----------------> B

In such a case it is clear that any subject who goes freely to B (=*aller*) is bound by the necessity of leaving A (=*en*), a situation that he cannot avoid. Given the strict lexical sense of *aller*, therefore, ("movement towards"), we need a middle voice verb to represent the consequences of this action, the departure ("movement away") that is a necessary entailment, by which the subject is bound, being no longer fully agentive in this extended sense of the verb.

As well as the pronominal verbs that use *être* as an auxiliary, there are also those non-passive intransitive constructions which we have called verbs of resultant state: *je suis allé, je suis rentré*. These are really active verbs, and the use of *être* in their compound forms is an element of *turbulence*, i.e. an irruption of unusual formations that disturbs otherwise regular paradigms. Guillaume (1964:141) even goes as far as to suggest that these verbs form a *fourth* voice in French, distinct from the other three. A pronominal verb can be recognized empirically in all its forms, but a verb of resultant state appears as an ordinary active verb until one gets to its compound forms, and even in these, as we have seen, the auxiliary *avoir* is not unknown. In conclusion, we may observe that middle voice elements, whether regular formations (e.g. reflexives) or elements of turbulence (e.g. verbs of motion), are universal features of language. It is enough to point at the peculiar syntactic behaviour of *finish* and *be born* in English to realize that English as well contains such elements.

5.6 *The contrast of active and middle with inanimate subjects*

A number of intransitive verbs can be found in both the active and middle forms, with a subtle contrast of meaning; Rothemberg (1974) notes for example that the subject in (72a) has a nature capable of producing the effect represented by the verb, whereas *mouchoir* in (72b) does not.

(72) a.   Jeanne rougit
          "Jean blushes"
     b.   Il vit le mouchoir se rougir soudain
          "He saw the handkerchief suddenly redden"

In short, the animate in (72a) where the active form is required is by nature more agentive than the inanimate *mouchoir* in (72b), where the middle voice form is requisite, the animate being more capable of carrying out the activity of the verb.

That is not simply a matter of animate vs. inanimate subject is shown by Labelle (1992) who takes the discussion a further stage with a detailed semantic analysis of *casser* and *briser*, the contrastive verbs "to break". Refining suggestions of Burston (1979) and Rothemberg (1974) she proposes the following contrast:

(73)   casser: x come to be apart (as its capacity of resistance is exceeded).
briser: x (forcefully) interrupt the continuity/integrity of y

She then gives examples (1992:405) showing the relevance of the lexical meaning of these verbs to the possible voice formations. The more active lexeme *briser* is found with middle but not active intransitive forms, whereas *casser* may be found with both active and middle:

(74)   *La branche a brisé
La branche s'est brisée
"The branch broke off"
(75) a. La coquille a cassé durant le transport
The (egg) shell broke during transportation
  b. L'oeuf s'est cassé durant le transport
"The egg broke during transportation"

The interesting contrast in (75) is explained by Labelle as stemming from the fact that subjects that represent 'rigid or taut materials (or entities) may be conceived as coming apart under stress.' The validity of this analysis is shown by the following paraphrases.

(76) a. The eggshell gave way during transportation
  b. *The egg gave way during transportation

In short, subjects that represent items that by their very nature are capable of 'giving way under stress' may be found with the active form of *casser*, otherwise middle voice will be used. With the more active verb *briser* the active voice will normally result in a transitive verb.

(77)   Elle a brisé le silence
"She broke the silence"

The examples illustrate the subtle interplay of lexical and grammatical meaning.

5.7 *Conclusion*

The phenomenon of voice appears to be a true linguistic universal, since all languages need ways of representing transitivity, and Klaiman (1991) has traced the varying strategies used by the world's languages to represent voice distinctions. Likewise all languages must find ways of representing the varying relationships of intransitive verbs to their subjects, since the subject of an intransitive verb can be agentive, patientive, or to some degree both agentive and patientive.

In Indo-European languages we see the problem of middle voice dealt with in various ways. There are indications that the earliest forms of Indo-European had only two voices: Active and Medio-Passive, where the middle voice was subsumed into the passive. This is the situation in Latin, Ancient Greek, and Sanskrit, where middle voice mostly shares a morphology with the passive.

In English, by contrast, we have a Medio-Active and a Passive, where verbs that clearly have a middle voice sense are in no way different from normal active forms. Other languages, however, have developed a full morphosyntax for the middle voice, distinct from both active and passive, as may be seen in French and the other Romance languages, where the pronominal verbs present a distinctive morphosyntax of middle voice.

In all these cases, however, the different voices mark the differing semantic relationships of subject and verb. If the subject plays a prototypically agentive role in the verb, the verb will be active. If the subject plays the role of patient, the verb will be passive. If the role of the subject is mixed, there may be a coherent morphosyntax of middle voice, as in French and the other Romance languages. Otherwise middle voice meanings may be subsumed into the passive to form a medio-passive as in Ancient Greek, or subsumed into the active to form a medio-active as in Modern English.

CHAPTER SIX
TENSE

6. *Introduction: tense and aspect*

Before examining the category of tense, it is important to get a clear picture of the difference, in representational terms, between tense and aspect as linguistic categories.

It is important that the distinction be made in representational terms and not in terms of what is represented. We need in short to distinguish between Past Tenses (the linguistic representation) and past time, the experiential, (non-linguistic) past. All of the following sentences, for example, represent an event in past time:

(1) I saw it.   Je le vis.
(2) I have seen it. Je l'ai vu.

The sentences in (1), however, achieve the representation of past time through the medium of tense, whereas those of (2) achieve it through the medium of aspect. The only tenses in (2) are to be found in the auxiliaries, and both are present (or non-past in English), whereas the tenses in (1) are both past tenses. The aspectual forms in (2) both represent the present possession of a complete event: any event that is complete in the present must necessarily have taken place in the past. The present perfect, by representing a position in the present that is necessarily *after* the event, is able to represent the event as past. In like fashion a prospective aspect, that represents a position in the present that is before the event, is able to represent a future as in English *I will see*. Here the auxiliary is again the non-past, but this time it is the future that is represented.

This caution is important because it is so often taken for granted that because a form represents the past it is necessarily a Past Tense. It has been argued, for example, that since the *passé composé* replaces the *passé simple* in French conversation, it therefore *functions* as a past tense, and from a functional point of view must be described as a past tense.

Il suit de ce qui précède que le passé composé, tout en contenant un morphème du présent, ne contient pas l'élément sémantique 'présent'. (Schogt 1968:39). (It follows that the *passé composé*, while containing a morpheme of the present, does not contain the semantic element "present").

This argument is a refusal to face fact; a refusal to admit the reality of the evidence that confronts the observer. The problem with such arguments is that they ignore completely the nature of the element that is being used, and look only at the way it is used; if I use a table knife to tighten a screw in a door hinge, the table knife functions as a screw driver, but we are not required to deny that it is a table knife. To allow function to determine form is to put the cart before the horse; it is form that determines function: a table knife is an object of suitable shape and strength to serve as a screwdriver.

The status of these compound forms, however, because of the cart-before-the-horse methods of mid-20th century linguistics, has been a matter of considerable dispute: Comrie, for example, has long discussions on the perfect (1985:32–35) and future (1985:43–48) as tenses in English, and equivalent discussions can be found in French on the status of the *passé composé*. Golian, in a survey of the question, notes that

> Christmann cite des linguistes et grammairiens qui pensent, comme lui, que le passé composé fait partie, dans le cas où il distingue un procès passé, des "temps" passés: A Meillet, F. Brunot — Ch. Bruneau, A. Dauzat, M. Grevisse, F. Kahn, E. Lerch, A. Sauvageot, H. Sten (1979:166–167).

Our principal point here, however, is that just as we no longer accept the Bloomfieldian phoneme, which was determined entirely by what is heard, we should also no longer accept the view that a tense is decided entirely by what it represents, without any examination of the other elements of the system, and of the contrasts and relationships to be found in the system. The set of forms given in Table 1 (§ 4.0) shows quite clearly that from the point of view of the paradigm of the French verb the *passé composé* is NOT a Past Tense, but a perfect or retrospective aspect representing past time.

6.1 *Defining tense and aspect in cognitive terms*

For Guillaume, as we have seen (4.1.2), the difference between tense and aspect rests upon a very simple cognitive distinction: aspectual contrasts are all based upon the representation of the event itself, are based upon 'Event Time', whereas tense contrasts are based upon the representation of 'Universe Time', the infinity of time that contains the event.

The difference is categorical. Event Time is that time which lies between the initial and final moments of an event. Such an event can be viewed from a variety of different positions by representing the subject as occupying such positions as in the following diagram.

TENSE

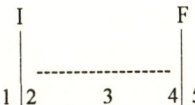

(I = initial; F = final); 1 = prospective, 2 = inceptive, 3 = progressive, 4 = perfective, 5 = transcendent or retrospective: traditional perfect

The event so represented does not, in and by itself, necessarily belong to any particular location in Universe Time: what is at issue in Event Time is the representation of an event as a temporal entity with a beginning, a middle, and an end, the traditional Aristotelian categories.

Aspect, as we have seen, deals only with the representation of Event Time, the time that it takes for an event to unfold from its initial moment to its final moment. Consequently aspect features positions from which the event is viewed ('aspect' being an excellent term for the category), common positions being the following, with numbers correlating to those in the diagram above.

1. before the initial moment: prospective (e.g. *will speak*)
2. at the initial moment: inceptive (e.g. Fr. *Soudain, il eut peur*)
3. between the initial and final moments: progressive (e.g. *is speaking*)
4. at the final moment: perfective (e.g. Slavic perfectives, Greek aorist)
5. after the final moment: retrospective (e.g. *j'ai parlé*)

Universe Time on the other hand is the time that contains events, rather than the events themselves; it is the background against which events are represented, and at the indicative level is divided into time spheres. All experience involves a *here and now*, and temporal contrasts that stand in relationship to the *here and now* of the speaker and hearer are the elements from which indicative tense systems are forged.

We have seen, for example, that the English indicative system is binary: any event that takes place in memorial time may be allocated to the past; anything that takes place in non-memorial time may be represented as non-past:

memorial time   non-memorial time
------------------------> ------------------------>

The French system is different because where English has only two simple forms of the indicative, French (and the same is largely true of other Romance languages such as Italian, Spanish, and Portuguese) has five simple forms of the indicative: a present that represents the *here and now*, two forms that allocate events to time that has been, and two that allocate events to time that is not yet.

6.2 *Tense in cognitive terms*

Penfield, when commenting on the "experiential responses of the flash-back variety" that were prompted by the application of an electrode to the cortex of a conscious patient during brain surgery, causing replays of earlier memories, comments (1959:53):

> When, by chance, the neurosurgeon's electrode activates past experience, that experience unfolds progressively, moment by moment. This is a little like the performance of a tape recorder or a strip of cinematographic film on which are registered all those things of which the individual was once aware.

We shall use this image of the moving film to develop an analogy of the cognitive processes underlying linguistic representations of tense, beginning with the notion of 'present', and showing how the bodily experience of the active memory, recording the stream of consciousness as indicated by Penfield (1959:59, 229), lies behind the linguistic representation of the present, this representation of the present being then the basis of tense systems in IndoEuropean languages such as French and English.

Film moves through a cinema camera at a speed of 24 frames a second. Each frame, as it passes through the 'chamber' (camera), is exposed to light and to the image transmitted by the light. In the diagram below, as the film moves from right to left, the unrecorded frames on the right pass through the camera and are exposed, thereby changing in status, and from this point on carrying an imprinted image (= X).

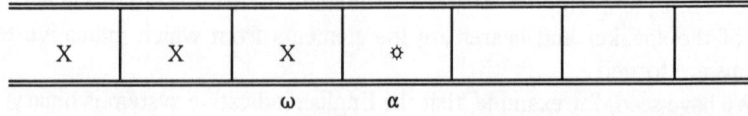

The frame that is most recently recorded represents the omega moment of consciousness, the most recent element to be recorded in the memory. The frame that is in the process of being recorded represents the alpha moment of consciousness, the earliest moment of the unfolding future that is to be recorded by the memory.

Because of the existence of this kind of memory operation, there exist two different kinds of memory cells in the brain: those that carry a memory trace and those that do not. Thus we have a physical reality, a mental reality that is somatic, that lies behind the linguistic category of tense, that determines the distinction in the English verbal system between 'memorial time' (i.e. past) and 'non-memorial time' (i.e. non-past). The prevalence of this kind of bodily distinction that underlies cognitive distinctions, and the linguistic distinctions that depend upon them, has been discussed at length by Johnson (1987). Having used the metaphor of light and sight to gain an appreciation of the nature of cognitive awareness of the present, it is necessary to warn against thinking of present awareness as simply visual. There is obviously interplay with a variety of different sensorial and mental inputs, and indeed there is interesting linguistic evidence that indicates awareness in the alpha moment of immediate experience that is already recorded in the omega moment. The following two sentences are revealing:

(3) Aie! Je me brûle le doigt!
     "Ow! I burnt my finger!"
(4) Il me vient une ideé.
     "I just had an idea."

The experience of burning the finger or having a bright idea, once it is realised, is already in the omega moment, so that the awareness of it, and the commentary on the fact, takes place in the alpha moment. Because the French present includes both alpha and omega moments, the commentary falls rightly within the scope of the French present tense. In English, where the omega moment belongs to the past tense, the only way to record awareness of the immediate burning of the finger or the sudden surge of the idea is by means of the preterit or present perfect, both of which have access to memorial time. There are many more parallels between the French present and the English present perfect, all of which are based on the requirement of a cognitive threshold between experience, on the one hand, and awareness of the experience on the other hand. The subject will be dealt with in detail in Chapter Eight.

6.3 *Tense and the experience of time*

What is the present in experiential terms? The work of Einstein teaches us that the experiential present is the individual's personal time, the time occupied by the functioning of the mind, in the same way that personal space is that occupied by the mass of the body.

We become aware of the relativity of time through the realization that the light that comes from some distant star reaches our eyes only years later. In other words, as we look out across space, we are also looking across time. If we had a supremely powerful telescope and could observe astronauts when they are walking around on the moon, we would only see what they do a second and a half after they do it since it would take that amount of time for the light to travel from the moon to the earth. Consequently, in Einstein's terms, there are no contemporaneous events — all events have their own particular time.

Even people sitting together in the same room occupy different positions in time as they do in space. The light reflected from various items in the room will reach the eyes of individual A in different sequences and at infinitesimally different times from those of individual B. That individuals A and B are spatially distinct is naively observable, although the space that separates them is infinitesimal, negligeable, in a universe where the *nearest* galaxy is 750,000 light years away. That the two individuals are equally distinct in temporal terms is not naively observable, but is nevertheless equally true. Such distinctions are irrelevant, however, for the normal purposes of human language. Individuals A and B are both *here* if I am in the same room, both *there* if they are in a different room. And both may be described as acting in the time that is *now* (i.e. present), which relates to my consciousness in the same way that *here* relates to my spatial presence. Or, if they are acting elsewhere, in another time, they are acting *then*, be it in the future or in the past. Some verbal systems distinguish between *then* and *now* and mark such distinctions morphologically. Latin, for example, has

stat	"he stands"
stabat	"he was standing"
stabit	"he will stand"

where *time now* is unmarked and *time then* is marked with -*b*-. The geometrical relationship of such forms, showing the present as a threshold between past and future, would be as follows:

PAST	PRESENT	FUTURE
<----------------------- ω	α ----------------------->	
stabat	stat	stabit

In French, where the present tense is also a representation of the threshold between past and future, the systemic contrasts are nevertheless quite different, since both present and past share a common unmarked stem, representing experiential time (memorial time plus the alpha moment), in distinction to the future, marked with a stem final /-r/, indicating non-experiential time.

PAST	PRESENT	FUTURE
<----------------------- ω	α ----------------------->	
aimai, aimais	aime	aimerai, aimerais

The English tense system, as we have seen, is completely different from either the Latin or the French system, being of the simple binary sort. In the English system the cognitive contrast is between memorial time (marked with /-d/) and non-memorial time (unmarked). In English, as a result, the omega moment is represented as the last moment of the past tense, the alpha moment as the first moment of the non-past tense: the experiential cognitive threshold divides the two tenses:

```
         PAST                NON-PAST
    ---------------->   ---------------->
        walked        ω   α      walks
```

As a result of this distinction between French and English, we see notable differences of tense usage when there is contrastive usage of alpha and omega chronotypes.

French, for example, can use the present tense to stress activity that belongs to the alpha moment of experience:

(5)   J'arrive!   ("I'll be right there!")
       Je pars à l'instant.   ("I'm leaving right away").

English in these cases tends to use either a future or a progressive, and the use of the simple non-past in such cases now has a slightly archaic or literary impression. Puck, for example, when sent on his errand around the world in Shakespeare's *Midsummer Night's Dream* says:

(6)   I go, I go, see how I go
       Swifter than the arrow from the Tartar's bow.

Today this would be "I'm going, I'm going, just watch me go".

When it comes to emphasis upon the omega moment, however, we see French using the present tense, and English shifting into the past:

(7)   Je viens acheter du lait
       "I came to buy some milk"
(8)   Elle sort à l'instant
       "She just left a moment ago"

English may also use the present perfect in these cases, and again we note the correlation of English present perfect and French simple present.

6.4 The parameters of tense in French

The chronogenesis of the French verb, as outlined in Chapter Three, is a content system, a structured system of related grammatical meanings. It is also a process, the generative development of a time image through three successive stages. It is at the third stage that the time image developed through the movement of chronogenesis becomes fully realized through the medium of a tense system.

Guillaume proposes that the basic time image of French is moulded by the representation of the present as a threshold between the past and the future. Like all thresholds, the French present is made up of a quantum or particle from each side: an α 'chronotype' from the future, and an ω 'chronotype' from the past. But according to Guillaume, these two particles are vertically organized in the content system of the verb in French and result in a vertical organization of incidence and decadence in past and future:

```
        PAST              PRESENT           FUTURE

      incidence      |      α       |     incidence
<--------------------|--------------|-------------------->
      decadence      |      ω       |     decadence
```

The present is, in this scheme, represented somewhat as the egg timer or hour glass, with the sand constantly dripping from the upper chamber (α) to the lower (ω). Or, to put it in Guillaume's terms, chronotype α is being continually converted into chronotype ω, and this mechanism of conversion is an integral part of the representation of the present in French. The French present as a result not only separates the past from the future; it also establishes a vertical hierarchy that results in two past tenses, one in incidence (*je parlai*) and one in decadence (*je parlais*), and two future tenses, one in incidence (*je parlerai*) and one in decadence (*je parlerais*).

6.4.1 The verticality of the present in French

When Guillaume proposes the verticality of the representation of the present in French what is at issue, therefore, is the distinction between incidence and decadence. This distinction being introduced into the indicative at the level of the present, from there affects representations in both the past and the future.

Such a notion has, of course, not been without its critics (e.g. LeFlem 1984:137a, Curat 1991:252–3), but methodologically it is a sound proposal because it is argued from the system, in a way that Jakobson, who understood the importance of arguing from the system, would certainly have approved. The morphology, for example shows a clear cut parallel between the imperfect and the conditional, which share common, identical inflections. Their morphology, in short, marks a systemic parallel. Guillaume also tried to trace a parallel between the morphology of the future and the preterit, but one can not take the comparisons very far: they are limited to the singular forms of first conjugation verbs:

FUTURE	PRETERIT
aimer-ai	aim-ai
aimer-as	aim-as
aimer-a	aim-a

Nevertheless, when we come to an appreciation of the terms 'incidence' and 'decadence' in cognitive terms, it will be seen that both the future and the preterit are typical representations of incidence.

For Guillaume, decadence represents the materiality of time flowing away into the past, so that the most recent (and therefore nearest) moment is the ω moment of the present. Incidence represents time as the sum of moments from the beginning of an event until the end, so that the initial (and therefore nearest) is the α moment of the present.

From a cognitive point of view we may view the alpha and omega moments either as simply sequential, as two different sequential frames upon the strip of film, or we may see them as qualitatively different: one (α) that is a bare frame that does not yet have a material recording, but is the potential container for a recording; the other (ω) that now carries a memory trace, a material record of a quantum of memorial experience, a content.

From a cognitive point of view, therefore, the verticality in Guillaume's representation of the present is an attempt to indicate that instead of treating the alpha and omega moments as simple sequential moments of experience, the French system involves a qualitative evaluation of these two moments whereby the alpha moment is represented as a container, and the omega moment as a material content. When we return to our analogy of the strip of film it can be seen that all the frames can be treated as containers, but that the future frames are qualitatively different from those that carry a recorded imprint.

X	X	X	✿			
		ω	α			

All the frames may be treated either as a container or as a content, but it is obvious that the future frames have a content that is zero, whereas the past frames have a material content. This distinction between the container and its content is a linguistic universal that we have already seen: it is the same distinction that is found in the count vs. mass noun distinction: *chicken, a chicken, oak, an oak, hair, a hair, newspaper, a newspaper.*

Consequently when Guillaume writes of the horizontal distinction between alpha and omega, as in the Latin system, we may understand a mere quantitative distinction between two sequential moments. When he introduces the vertical distinction, as in the French verbal system, we have to understand a qualititative distinction between a container and its content. In short these two moments may be represented as either quantitatively different, as in the Latin system, or qualitatively different, as in the French system. The qualitative distinction, as Guillaume saw very clearly, has important repercussions on the whole tense system, resulting in qualitative tense distinctions in both past and future.

In Guillaume's terms (1964:210–211) the present is a separating element between past and future by 'position' (the quantitative distinction) and also by 'composition' (the qualitative distinction).

6.4.2 *The breadth of the French present*

The French present, as well as representing both alpha and omega moments may also be used to express both past and future in particular contextual circumstances. The use of the present to represent the past is known as the Historic Present, and may be recognized as a stylistic trick to make the narration more vivid, since the writer thereby simulates the events as being simultaneous with the reader's consciousness — it is as if he were taking the reader back to the moment when the events were actually occurring. In imaginative and creative writing and speaking, this kind of utilization of the representational systems of language is extremely common, and is one of the distinguishing features of such discourse, whether the narrator be a distinguished novelist or a simple teller of folktales. The imaginative and creative use of the systems of tense and aspect is especially noticeable.

The use of the present to represent the future, on the other hand, is much more mundane:

(9) Il part demain
(10) Je vais à Montréal samedi

In cases such as these what is really being declared is a present intention or expectation of a future event, otherwise the future itself will be used:

(11) Il partira demain
(12) J'irai à Montréal samedi.

English likewise uses sentences such as (9) and (10) to emphasize that the event, since it has already been decided upon, is in a sense already in progress.

There are also sentences which indicate what are called 'eternal truths': those facts that do not change with the passage of time:

(13) La terre est ronde
(14) L'eau bout à 100 degrés Centigrade

All of these different usages indicate quite clearly that the French present, as a representational tense, is not limited to the here and now. The present limits the past and the future, both of which are defined in reference to the present, the past being the whole of memorial time that is beyond the omega moment, and the future being the whole of non-memorial time which is beyond the alpha moment. The present, however, may also be vast, as noted by Curat (1991:143). The only limitation to the range of the present is that the representation must incorporate some element of the here and now. Many presents clearly incorporate both alpha and omega chronotypes, but, as may be expected, there are variants where only one or the other is in fact involved, just as a plosive consonant may have allophones that show only a phase of the total plosive gesture. We may consider these variants as 'grammatical allosemes' of the total invariant meaning represented by the position in the system.

The items in (5) are repeated in (15) to show forms where only the alpha chronotype is involved:

(15) J'arrive!
Je pars à l'instant.

Other usages, by the fact that the English present perfect is used in translation, show that only the omega moment is involved.

(16) J'attends depuis dix minutes, et je n'attends plus
"I have waited for ten minutes, and I'm not waiting any longer"

Waugh (1975:449) quotes an exchange between two francophones where the ambiguity of the French present is played upon:

> Enfin, qu'est-ce que je fais?
> - Des sottises!
> - Je te demande ce que je dois faire.
> ("OK, what do I do?
> - Foolishness!
> - I'm asking you what I'm supposed to do").

The initial question, intending the alpha moment, has been deliberately understood as *What am I doing*, which of course stresses the omega moment. The first speaker comes back to insist on the alpha moment, by an auxiliary that resembles English *shall* in its semantic content. Like most plays on words, this exchange is next to impossible to translate.

When we come to examine the uses of the imperfect, we shall again find variants that represent or emphasize different elements of the invariant meaning, the *Gesamtbedeutung* (Jakobson 1936/1991), the *signifié de puissance* (Guillaume 1964:246–248), the 'grammatical sememe' that stems from the position in the system and the positional contrasts that result. All these variants are different possible actualizations of the grammatical sememe.

6.5 *Past tenses*

If we continue the analogy of the hour glass, used in 6.4 above to illustrate the distinction between incidence and decadence, we may distinguish the two past tenses as follows:

a) *Passé simple*. This tense represents in the system the incidence of a past event. It is the view of the sand in the upper chamber at the moment that it starts to run. The representation is therefore of a complete, integral, undivided event. (Exterior, unit view)

(b) *Imperfect*. This tense represents in the system the decadence of a past event. The sand from the upper chamber is continually accumulating in the lower, and the representation is therefore of an event that is materially in progress. (Interior, qualitative view).

We may alternatively present this contrast by means of vectors:

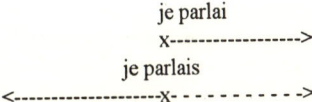

Immediately we notice that the subject has been placed at the beginning of the movement in incidence, but in the middle of the movement in decadence. Nor is this allocation accidental, since the integrality of the event represented by the Passé simple must be respected, and therefore the materiality of the event (the interior, continuate view), which is the focus of the Imperfect, cannot be addressed in the representation presented by the Passé simple (the exterior, unit view).

It would seem that memories of events, as total entities, are accessible from their initial moments: as Penfield comments (1959:53):

> Time's strip of film runs forward, never backward, even when resurrected from the past ... A particular strip can sometimes be repeated by interrupting the stimulation and then shortly reapplying it at the same or a nearby point. In that case it begins at the same moment of time on each occasion. The threshold of evocation of that particular response has apparently been lowered for a time by the first stimulus.

Consequently access to a memory, according to evidence provided by Penfield (1959:53), appears to be by the way of an initial moment: "It begins at the same moment of time on each occasion." It would appear that a speaker is able to identify what in computer terms is called an 'address', a location where the recall of a particular event begins. If the speaker can identify and locate memories or complete past events in this way, such memories become the prototype for a linguistic preterit. In short a preterit represents a complete event unfolding from a moment α, belonging to memorial time. Hence, in French the necessity of using either Passé simple or Passé composé when the duration of a past event is known: *Il travailla pendant trois ans; il habita Rouen de 1978 à 1985.* Although both of the events are of long duration, the imperfect may not be used because the adverbial modifiers indicate the events are complete.

In other words the representation of the event conveyed by the Passé simple is that of *a complete event beginning at a point R in the past*, where R represents the temporal point of reference for the past event.

It is not surprising, therefore, that the sense of the *passé simple* is often inceptive, i.e. it indicates the beginning or initiation of the event only, especially with verbs indicating actions that are durative: *Soudain, il eut peur / Soudain il fit noir*. Grevisse (p. 636) quotes Boileau:

(17) Qui ne sait se borner ne sut jamais écrire
"He who cannot set limits for himself never learned to write"

The verb *savoir* is not used here in its common sense of *knowing*, but in its inceptive sense of *coming to know, learning*. Likewise in a pair of sentences such as

(18) Il était bien triste quand il reçut ma lettre
(19) Il fut bien triste quand il reçut ma lettre

we know that in (18) he was already sad when he received my letter (i.e. the imperfect, representing decadence, presents part of the event as *accompli*, accomplished) whereas in (19) he became (inceptive) sad upon reading my letter (no part of the event is present as *accompli*; what is represented is the initial moment of the prospective *accomplissement* or accomplishment):

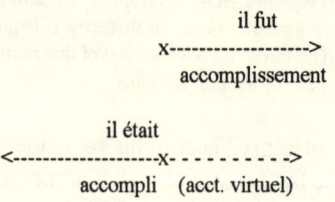

We shall continue to use Guillaume's terms *accompli* and *accomplissement*, and we shall use a broken line in the schema of the imperfect to designate the *accomplissement virtuel*, the completion of the event that is in progress, and that necessarily remains 'unseen' in any interior view of the event in progress.

6.5.1 *Imperfect and passé simple: tenses or aspects?*

It is clear from the above commentary that we could describe the Imperfect and Passé simple in aspectual terms, as completive vs. incompletive, simple vs. progressive, perfective vs. imperfective, and so on, terminology that would seem to fit at least partially. It is also obvious that what is at issue is, in a certain sense, the representation of Event Time, since both share the same Universe Time: it is not at all obvious that this is a contrast of one facet of Universe Time against another. Scholars such as Imbs (1960) and Martin (1971), who have in fact read and appreciated Guillaume, have opted to treat the distinction as one of aspect rather than tense, as noted above (1.8). Any study that treats the distinction as tense rather than aspect must therefore present cogent arguments to justify such a position.

There is in fact evidence from the system, both from the paradigm and from the content system, that indicates quite clearly that Imperfect and Passé simple are both elements of the tense system. Both the paradigm of aspectual contrasts (see 4.0) and the paradigm of active and passive voice contrasts (see 5.1) show that Imperfect and Passé simple belong to the same paradigmatic category, and demonstrate the same range of aspectual and voice contrasts as the other tenses. Such patterns in the data should play a determining role in establishing the linguistic category and the nomenclature used.

It is also notable that both voice and aspect systems normally have a full paradigmatic array; an aspectual contrast found at one point in the paradigm will also be found throughout the paradigm. But the contrast between Passé simple and Imperfect, found also in the contrast between future and conditional, is crucially not found in the present: French does not have two different paradigmatic forms of the present. Instead it is the dual nature of the French present, as outlined in 6.4 above, that forges the possibility of two different past tenses, and two different future tenses. It is this view of the coherence of the whole array of morphological forms and their meanings that leads in turn to the conclusion of the 'vertical' nature of the present in French.

Finally if the Passé simple and the Imperfect do not represent two contrastive time spheres within Universe Time, they very definitely illustrate two different ways of representing Universe Time. There are necessarily two contrastive ways of representing Universe Time, since time is movement, which cognitively is perceived as either figure against background or background against figure.

Clark (1973:35), for example, contrasts MOVING-EGO vs. MOVING-WORLD; these are changed to MOVING-EGO vs. MOVING-TIME by Fleischmann (1982:324). Guillaume (1964:195) uses the term Ascending Time for the former, Descending Time for the latter, and relates Incidence to Ascending Time, Decadence to Descending Time.

Cognitively, Descending Time is time that works in the mind, the time that records memory, whether we like it or not: it is the film running in the cine camera, from the spool that represents the future to the spool that represents the past. Ascending Time, by contrast, is the time of the linearity of thought, of the mind that works in time; it is the action recorded on the film, which runs in the opposite direction to the film's progress through the camera.

```
                Ascending Time
Incidence    ----------------------->    Movement of action

                Descending Time
Decadence    <-----------------------    Movement of film
```

In Guillaume's terms (1964:210) the present not only separates past from future, a horizontal separation, but also separates movement towards the future (Ascending Time) from movement towards the past (Descending Time), which he sees as a vertical separation.

Consequently, there are universally two different kinds of tenses: (1) tenses in Descending Time, as in Slavic languages, where the Immanent aspect of simple tenses is imperfective, and (2) tenses in Ascending Time as in Germanic languages, where the Immanent aspect of simple tenses is Performative (i.e. represents the complete performance of an event). There are some language families, such as Romance and Celtic, that have both types of tenses, hence the contrast in French, of Passé simple and Imperfect, which are primarily tenses, and only secondarily aspects, taking their aspectual contrast from the different Immanent aspect of the tenses in question.

As a footnote to this whole discussion we must point out that it is quite normal for grammatical labels to be only an approximation. The linguistic reality so labelled may often have overtones of another category, or even overlap with another category. We have already seen the overlap of aspect and voice in French, for example (e.g. *il est parti, il est blessé*), and in English there is some overlap of aspect and voice in the progressive (e.g. *I'm telling you it's true*, where the subject uses the progressive to indicate that he is not 'getting through', is not a full transitive agent). A similar phenomenon in reverse may be seen in French where a middle voice form (e.g. *il se meurt* "he is dying") because of the continual return of the action to the subject, gives the equivalent of a progressive aspect. Similar imprecision is also true, of course, of the labelling of natural categories in biology: there are occasional items that overlap with two different categories.

6.5.2 *The imperfect*

We have seen (6.5) that the subject of the *passé simple* remains 'trapped' in the initial moment of the event by the very nature of the representation, by the fact that the event is represented as an indivisible whole (external view) the content of which is not open to analysis: it is simply a complete event which begins at point R in the past.

The subject of the imperfect, by contrast, being involved with the internal content of the event, may occupy any position internal to the event, and the fascinating usage of the imperfect indicates that this fluidity is exploited to the full by speakers of the language. There are, of course, three basically contrastive positions for the object to occupy: the beginning, the middle and the end of the event:

```
              acct. virtuel
Type 1   x--------------------->
         accompli        acct. virtuel
Type 2   <-------------x---------->
                     accompli
Type 3   <---------------------------------x
```

The remarkably complex usage of the imperfect can be broken down and classified into instances of one of these three main types. In Type 1, the event is represented as purely virtual, and the representation is used to indicate potential, possible events. In Type 2, the event is represented as partially completed: this is the ordinary banal imperfect of everyday usage. In Type 3, the event is represented as all *accompli*; this type is used for stylistic effect, and has become notably frequent in the past quarter of a century.

In cognitive terms Type 2 may be considered as the prototype of the French imperfect, with types 1 and 3 being peripheral, and limiting cases. If we return to our analogy of the strip of film it can be seen that Type 2 is really an internal view of the event at any point between its initial and final moment. Type 1 may also be seen as the initial moment of the event, with the subject in position to act, but before the event has got under way. Type 3 likewise represents the final moment of the event, as in the following diagram of the strip of film:

X	Y	Y	Y	Y	Y	Y	X
1	2	2	2	2	3		

(X = time outside the event; Y = moments of the event; 1 = initial moment of the event, 2 = internal moments of the event; 3 = final moment of the event).

6.5.2.1 *Imperfects of Type 1*

The most noteworthy instances of usage of this type indicate a notion of 'brinkmanship': the event is represented as just on the point of occurring. Mansion, for example, quotes the following (1959:63):

(20)   Un pas de plus et je tombais dans l'abîme
       "One step more and I would have fallen into the abyss"

(21)   Si l'on ne m'eut prévenu à temps, je commettais une faute irréparable
"Had I not been warned in time I would have committed an irretrievable error"

The normal usage would be with the compound conditional: je *serais tombé* in (20) and *j'aurais commis* in (21). The effect of the imperfect, however, is to suggest the subject on the very brink of the event poised over the abyss in (20) and just saved in the nick of time in (21). An examination of our schema reveals the subject as being in position to carry out the event, occupying the initial moment of *accompli*, but with the whole of the event still to come; it is not surprizing that this potentiality offered by the system is utilized by native speakers to represent the brink of the event.

Such verbs may, of course, be ambiguous and Guillaume himself pointed out long ago (1929:68–69) that one can only know from the context whether, in the sentence

(22)   Un instant plus tard, le train déraillait

the train really did come off the rails or not. In other cases the context makes it quite clear that the event did not take place. The following, for example, is from a waiter responding to a complaint about a dirty glass.

(23)   Il n'avait qu'à me demander, et je lui changeais son verre
"He only had to ask me and I would have changed his glass"

Here we see the real sense of the subject in the initial position of the event, ready to carry out the rest of the event, which is never completed because the necessary prior conditions are not fulfilled.

There are also such usages with modal-type verbs, which Martin calls the *imparfait modal* (1971:99–103), where the context again indicates that there was a latent possibility or obligation which was never realized.

(24)   L'entreprise a réussi, mais votre incurie pouvait tout gâter
"The enterprise succeeded, but your carelessness could have spoiled everything."
Il fallait me prévenir
"You really should have let me know"
Ah! Je devais le savoir!
"Oh! I should have known!"

Other imperfects of type 1 are those used in subordinate conditional clauses to indicate a condition either contrary to fact or unlikely to be realized:

(25) S'il me voyait ici il serait bien heureux
 Si j'étais riche, je prendrais ma retraite.

These sentences also appear with equivalent compound forms:

(26) S'il m'avait vu ici, il aurait été bien heureux.

6.5.2.2 *Imperfects of Type 2*

Incompleted actions and states are the normal representations of Type 2 imperfects:

(27) Il parlait quand je suis entré
 Le ciel était bleu
 Elle portait une robe noire

It is also used to indicate habitual and repeated action, the continuation of the habit being represented by the *accomplissement virtuel*:

(28) Chaque fois que la porte s'ouvrait il levait la tête

Type 2 imperfects are also used for past reporting of utterances originally expressed in the present, and for other presents reported in the past; what is called in the traditional grammars the 'sequence of tenses'.

(29) Elle a répondu qu'il était malade
(30) Elle savait qu'il était malade
(31) Il demanda ce qui se passait

Since the ordinary present has a similar element of *accompli* (the ω moment), it is always the imperfect that is used to report it in the past.

Likewise, just as the French present may be used in a retrospective sense because of the element of *accompli* it contains, so may the imperfect of Type 2 be used to represent an event begun at a remoter period and still continuing. The conjunctions *depuis*, etc., which cause the use of the perfective forms when translating into English, again underscore a direct comparison with the present:

(32) Nous sommes ici depuis un an
"We have been here for a year"
(33) Nous étions ici depuis un an
"We had been here for a year"
(34) C'est la première fois que je mange du caviar
"It's the first time I've eaten caviar"
(35) C'était la première fois que je mangeais du caviar
"It was the first time I had eaten caviar"

The items in (34) and (35) are dealt with in detail below (8.2; 8.3.3).

6.5.2.3 *Imperfects of Type 3*

Just as we observed the utilization of Type 1 to represent the initial brink of an event, likewise Type 3 can be found, in stylistic usage, representing the very moment of completion of the event. Mansion (1959:63) quotes the following

(36) Je rencontrai un journaliste qui arrivait de Paris
"I met a journalist who had just come from Paris"
(37) Elle sortait à peine du couvent lorsqu'il la demanda en mariage
"She was hardly out of school when he proposed to her"
(38) Il rentrait du régiment lorsque je fis sa connaissance
"He was just out of the army when I met him"

In all cases, the event is so recent that the writer uses the imperfect to suggest that the subject was still actually involved in the final moment of the event. The result of this stylistic play is the suggestion of the immediate recency of the preceding event.

This type of imperfect is also used with dramatic stylistic intent to make a complete event more vivid and affective. Guillaume quotes a long passage (1929:68) that is narrated almost entirely in the imperfect, and the following is typical of this type of imperfect used for dramatic effect in a mystery novel:

(39) On découvrait Aerts pendu ... on découvrait sa femme, Emma, pendue, elle, à l'aide d'un drap (Simenon, *La péniche des deux pendus*)

Nothing could be more complete, instantaneous (or even inceptive) than the act of discovery. Teachers of French as a second language would cross out the imperfects in (39) as gross errors. Yet here is a famous mystery writer manipulating the mechanisms of his mother tongue for a maximum of effect:

the effect is to take the readers right back to the material moment (*accompli*) of the discovery and leave them there still thunderstruck at the horror of the discovery. The event is necessarily a complete one, but it is represented from the interior, qualitative point of view and not from the exterior, quantitative point of view which would be presented by the preterit.

Sometimes a whole passage may be presented in this manner, as the remarkable passage quoted by Mansion (1959:63) where there is a blurred flurry of movement:

> (40) Joe, immédiatement relevé après sa chute, à l'instant où l'un des cavaliers se précipitait sur lui, bondissait comme une panthére, l'évitait par un écart, se jetait en croupe, saisissait l'Arabe à la gorge ... l'étranglait, le renversait sur la sable, et continuait sa course effrayante.
> "Joe, getting up instantly after his fall, at the very moment when one of the horsemen charged upon him, leapt in the air like a panther, darted to one side, threw himself upon the hindquarters, seized the Arab by the throat, strangled him, threw him off in the sand, and continued his terrifying flight."

Because no event is represented as a complete whole, but all the events are seen from the inside, the resulting impression is an overlap of all the activity: no event is fully complete before the next one has already begun. The resulting impression is that of a wild, confused flurry of activity.

6.6 *Future and conditional*

Guillaume's proposal that the same incidence/decadence contrast found in the past is also found in the contrast of future and conditional is supported by the fact that the morphology of the conditional is an exact reflection of that of the imperfect, the only difference between the two sets of forms being the distinctive /-r-/ marker that the conditional shares with the future:

IMPERFECT	CONDITIONAL
je parl-ais	je parl-er-ais
tu parl-ais	tu parl-er-ais
il parl-ait	il parl-er-ait
nous parl-ions	nous parl-er-ions
vous parl-iez	vous parl-er-iez
ils parl-aient	ils parl-er-aient

We have also observed the use of the imperfect to suggest the brink of an event, with the subject represented as being *in position* to carry out the event:

(41)   Un pas de plus et elle était dans la rue

Here the imperfect replaces a more ordinary and uneventful use of the compound conditional

(42)   Un pas de plus et elle aurait été dans la rue

The compound conditional is required because the overall time zone is the past, whereas the simple conditional refers to future time. Compare

(43)   Un pas de plus et elle sera dans la rue
(44)   Un pas de plus et elle serait dans la rue

When said in the context of present time (43) indicates that her present movement will automatically take her into the street in the next moment: the event is represented as a prospective realization. In (44) on the other hand, the subject is simply represented as being *in the same position* as the subject of (43) but the rest of the event is represented as awaiting some further motivation. We may diagram these two different verbs as follows:

```
                          sera
                    x---------------------->
FUTURE TIME
                         serait
                    x- - - - - - - - - - - ->
```

The future *sera* is the representation of an event seen as a complete whole beginning at point R(F), a possible point of reference in future time. The conditional *serait* is the representation of the same event in the mode of decadence, an incomplete event ready to begin at the same point R(F), but having no material content, remaining only the possibility of an event.

We are immediately confronted by an obvious question: why is the future event represented by the conditional always a non-event? Why is it always 'awaiting some further motivation'? This question is all the more important because of the contrast with the imperfect, which can and does represent a real experiential event, so that even sentences such as (41), as we have already pointed out, are ambiguous, and the ambiguity can only be resolved by the context.

The answer to the question, however, is quite simple: there can be no *accompli* in future time, since *accompli* is the representation of the 'materiality' of the event, which is not possible for an event that has not yet occurred. On the strip of film, all these frames would be blank. The materiality of the event remains a perpetual possibility.

The future is therefore seen as an event to be realized since it has the necessary memory cells to record it already allocated as a total group with the materiality of the event not in question. Its representation therefore resembles that of the Passé simple, a complete event beginning at a point R, with the subject in position to carry the event to its conclusion.

The conditional, like the imperfect, represents, by contrast, the materiality of the event, the content of the memory cells which, in future time, is necessarily zero, no matter which of the memory cells is examined. In the circumstances, the subject would be unable to move out of initial position, and would remain, necessarily 'on the brink' of a future action.

The most common sense of the conditional, therefore, is that of the unrealized event, the event which could be realized because the subject is in the appropriate position to carry it out.

6.6.1 *The future in the past*

In recording the stream of consciousness, the alpha moment is continuously being transformed into an omega moment. In verbal systems this may be represented as a simple temporal, quantitative change, another simple addition to the memory of consciousness. In the French system, however, we see this change also represented as a qualitative change from incidence (external view) to decadence (internal view). And since the omega moment is always a past in relation to the alpha moment, decadence, in the French system, always represents a past, an earlier stage of an equivalent incidence.

We have seen, for example, that in the sentence *Il était bien triste quand il reçut ma lettre* the imperfect represents an event already in progress before the event in the preterit occurs.

In similar fashion we find usages where the conditional is treated as a past form of the future, sometimes called the 'Future in the Past' in the grammars. Reported futures, with main clauses in the past, for example, become conditionals:

(45)   Ceux qui perdront payeront
         Il a dit que ceux qui perdraient payeraient

(46)   Ceux qui auront fini les premiers pourront partir
         Il a dit que ceux qui auraient fini les premiers pourraient partir

Consequently, whenever a future is to be expressed in the matrix of past time, it will be transformed into a conditional (giving rise to the term 'Future in the Past' that is found in some grammars):

(47) Il m'a dit qu'il serait prêt dans deux ou trois minutes
"He told me he would be ready in two or three minutes"

Mansion gives the following:

(48) Il refusa de me conseiller.   Je ferais comme je voudrais.
"He refused to advise me."   "I was to do as I thought fit."

In other words, it is understood that he either said or implied *Vous ferez* (or *Faites) comme vous voudrez* "(You will) do whatever you think fit (or even, in more brutal terms, Do as you please)". The future usage of the original is transformed into the conditional when the remark is reported as a past event.

6.6.2 *Conditional clauses*

There is a similar parallelism of tenses to be found in conditional clauses, where a difference of tenses is used, as in English, to mark the temporal difference between condition and consequence. Since conditions necessarily precede their consequences, a condition in the present tense will be followed by a consequence in the future:

(49) S'il perd il payera
"If he loses he will pay"

Since we conclude that the subject in (49) has not yet lost, the present tense in this case must be understood as an alpha present, the present in incidence, followed suitably by the future, also at the level of incidence. Removing the condition from the present into the past results in making the condition and its consequence more remote, and transferring them to the level of decadence:

(50) S'il perdait il payerait
"If he lost he would pay"
(51) S'il avait perdu il aurait payé
"If he had lost he would have paid"

In such cases the imperfect becomes the past of the present, and the conditional the past of the future; it may be seen that the forms in (51) are simply the compound forms of the tenses in (50). Since the two tenses in decadence are both capable of representing simply the possibility of an event, the condition and its consequence are both at a further remove.

There are also hidden conditions, where the condition is not made explicit, but the consequence is reported in the future tense because of the implicit condition.

(52) A cette heure il sera à Montréal
"He'll be in Montreal by now."

Here it is known that the subject has gone to Montreal, and if all has gone according to plan, will be at his destination. If however the speaker is not sure that the subject has indeed left for Montréal, but suspects that he has, the conditional is used.

(53) A cette heure il serait à Montréal
"He would be in Montreal by now"

Here it is understood that *if he had left* he would be in Montreal after such a lapse of time.

6.6.3 *The conditional of probability*
Another usage of the conditional is found in the suggestion of probabilities. Mansion gives the following (1959:70):

(54) Ce seraient les Chinois qui auraient inventé la poudre à canon.
"It would seem to be the Chinese who invented gunpowder."

(We note again the correspondence of tenses found in relative and temporal clauses, as described in the chapter on aspects). In this sentence, the Chinese are represented as *in position* to invent gunpowder, but the writer is loath to attribute the realization of the event, being unsure of the facts.

It is but a short step from the nuance in (54) to

(55) On a proposé de percer un tunnel qui relierait directement les deux vallées
"It was proposed to dig a tunnel which would connect the two valleys directly"

In (55), it is the tunnel that is represented as being in a position to connect the two valleys, but the realization of the event cannot be attributed simply because the tunnel is as yet only an imaginary one.

The carrying out of the event, therefore, in terms of incidence and decadence, is the transforming of each future moment of the event (incidence) into a past moment of the event (decadence). It is in this purely mechanical fashion that decadence, in representational terms, is the 'past of incidence'.

6.7 *Conclusion*

In all these varying usages and utilizations of the system of tense in French, it is remarkable that certain simple binary contrasts are being played upon. It is out of such simple contrasts that every representational system is forged, and different languages will make use of different elements of contrast to forge different representational systems. Every language, consequently, lends itself to different forms of exploitation, as its speakers struggle with the problems of representing and expressing the passing parade of everyday experience in all its multitudinous facets. And most remarkable is the intuitive way that speakers play, in opportunistic fashion, with the mechanical resources of content systems.

Guillaume frequently comments that once languages have found operative mechanisms that produce useful results they continue to find additional ways of exploiting these mechanisms. In indicative tense systems events are seen as unitary elements incorporated in Universe Time, whether that time be represented in binary (past vs. non-past) or tertiary form (past, present, future). Universe Time is therefore the time that incorporates, Event Time is the time that is incorporated. But Universe Time itself may be seen as descending (view of decadence) or ascending (view of incidence), the kind of binary contrast that seems to be a cognitive universal, since we find it used in so many linguistic systems. When we come to an examination of the indicative tenses of French we find that this contrastive view of Universe Time allows for two different tenses in both past and future, and for a representation of the present that is based not only a quantitative movement, whereby one moment of time (α) becomes another (ω), but also as a qualitative movement, whereby a moment of experience becomes reshaped as a moment of memory, a content that is open to examination.

CHAPTER SEVEN
MOOD

7. *Introduction*

Since we have already dealt with differences of mood in Chapter Three, and with the uses of the Indicative Mood in Chapter Six, the main thrust of this chapter will be a description of the Subjunctive Mood and its usage in French, especially contrastive usage with the Indicative which will demonstrate the fundamental cognitive contrast between subjunctive and indicative.

There is an extensive literature on the French subjunctive, much of it comprehensively surveyed in Marcel Cohen's *Le subjonctif en français contemporain* (1965:15–16), a work which also has over 200 pages of examples. As Schogt has pointed out (1968:53), there are three fundamental positions that one can take towards the subjunctive: (1) to see it as a *valeur* in the Saussurean sense, that is as a single position in a system, as exemplified in the work of Guillaume (1929, 1951, 1971), Imbs (1953) and Moignet (1981), (2) to present it as two or more subcategories, as do de Boer (1954) and von Wartburg & Zumthor (1958), or (3) to provide a simple listings of usages, with no attempt to provide any systemic view.

7.1 *A simple cognitive contrast*

The approach taken here is based on a conviction that the French subjunctive must be a unitary *valeur*. This conviction, in turn, is a consequence of the following fundamental observations.

1. Languages are learned by very small children; their fundamental contrasts (e.g. indicative/subjunctive) must be reasonably simple.
2. There are minimal pairs (*Je comprends qu'il a/ait acheté un auto*) which show regular meaningful contrasts between indicative and subjunctive in French: the contrast in these pairs is fundamentally the same in each case.
3. Where there are regular contrasts there is evidence of underlying systemic differences. The regularity of sound change in historical linguistics, for example, is based on systemic change (see 1.1 above). The exploitation of grammatical systems likewise produces regular contrasts in discourse.
4. Cognitive lexical contrasts, such as that between *connaître* and *savoir* in French, are necessarily subconscious (i.e. native speakers are unaware of

what the distinction is, and may have difficulty describing it), but nevertheless perfectly regular and coherent. Cognitive grammatical contrasts, equally subconscious, are also equally regular and coherent.

One might be led to expect, if the subjunctive is represented as an intermediate stage between quasi-nominal and indicative forms, that children would learn to use it before the indicative. Such is not the case, and we also note that in some dialects of English subjunctive forms are never heard at all. The reason for this state of affairs is that the subjunctive level has no representation of Mental Time, the here and now, or egocentric time that leads the speaker to divide Universe Time into time zones, whether binary, as in Germanic, or ternary as generally in Romance. Consequently the subjunctive is not 'entrenched' (Rosch et al. 1976): Deane claims (1992:194–199) that of the factors that lead to entrenchment, the most important is egocentricity, as in the notions of self, and of the here and now. As a result subjunctives are not normally as entrenched as indicatives.

What follows is an attempt to delineate a cognitive contrast between indicative and subjunctive, and to show how this simple contrast explains a vast range of complex usage.

7.2 *The subjunctive as a position in a system*

Morphologically and syntactically we have distinguished three moods in the French verb, traditionally called quasi-nominal (3.2), subjunctive (3.3) and indicative (3.4).

Each of these moods is a subsystem within the verbal system and the three of them relate together in a three stage cognitive progression, the chronogenesis. Guillaume sees the chronogenesis as a mechanical system of successive cognitive stages which must be involved in the development of every verbal form, so that every verbal form used in discourse is the product of one of these three stages, and therefore is morphologically marked as being of either quasi-nominal, subjunctive, or indicative mood. The infinitive from the quasi-nominal mood is the basic verbal representation of the lexical meaning, which is why it is the form used for representing the verb in the dictionary. The second level of representation is that of the subjunctive which represents the verb as operational, as a movement in time, and therefore requiring the grammatical support of a subject. At the third level of representation this image of the event made possible by the subjunctive is allocated to experiential time; it is represented as being past, present, or future, an event taking place in the world of experience. A brief examination of each of these levels will enable us to identify the place of the subjunctive in the cognitive system of the French verb.

7.2.1 *Quasi-nominal mood*

The mood contains the nominal forms of the verb: infinitive, present participle, and past participle, all of which may be found functioning as independent nouns: *Signifier, c'est employer un signifiant pour présenter un signifié*. The two participles may also function as adjectives. None of these forms, however, may be predicated, in a directly subordinative role, to a subject pronoun: their syntactic usage differs from that of subjunctive and indicative.

7.2.2 *Subjunctive mood*

Subjunctive and indicative are forms that require to be predicated of a grammatical subject in French. They represent the event as movement between two poles, the initial and final moments of the event, the beginning and the end. This movement may be represented in the regime of 'incidence', where the event is seen externally as a whole, or in that of 'decadence', where each moment of the event is represented as adding to what has already been achieved from the beginning (Guillaume 1971:94). In the case of the subjunctive, there is a representation of Event Time, of movement between an initial moment and a final moment, but the event so represented is never allocated to a contrastive position in Universe Time. Consequently, in modern French, with the disappearance of the imperfect subjunctive, the so-called present subjunctive may be found after past tenses, present tenses, or future tenses.

> Elle veut/voulait que je l'appelle tout simplement Pauline.
> *She wants/wanted me to simply call her Pauline.*
> Elle ne comprenais/comprends/comprendra pas que je sois marié.
> *She didn't/doesn't/won't understand that I was/am married.*

The subjunctive therefore represents an event that unfolds in time, and that consequently requires (being itself only an attribute) to be predicated of a grammatical subject. But the event so represented remains unrelated to experiential time (past, present, or future) and is used to represent potential events, possibilities of occurrence.

7.2.3 *Indicative mood*

The indicative too represents the event as a movement between two poles, the initial and final moments of the event. The indicative event, however, is not only represented as containing Event Time, but it is also allocated to a time sphere: past, present or future, the categories of experiential time.

The major distinction between indicative and subjunctive therefore is that the indicative event is represented as taking place within experiential time, past, present, or future, whereas the subjunctive is not. The subjunctive is represented as incorporated into Universe Time, the present subjunctive at the level of incidence, the imperfect subjunctive at the level of decadence, but since there is as yet no representation of the present, the experiential reality of the speaker, Universe Time at this level has no division into time spheres: the whole of Universe Time is represented as a vast present with no boundaries.

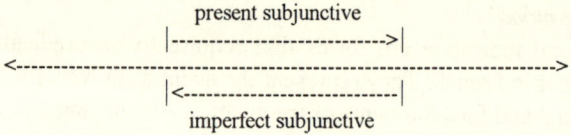

Only at the third level, the level of the indicative, where Universe Time is divided into specific time spheres by the intrusion of the present, does Universe Time become represented with precise distinctions.

7.3 *The indicative/subjunctive contrast*

This simple mechanical contrast, between events that are represented as occurring in definite times spheres (indicative) and those that are represented as abstracted from any such precise localization, may be used somewhat arbitrarily by different groups of speakers, both historically and geographically. We must carefully distinguish the mechanism itself from its function, the conventional 'utilization' or 'exploitation' of the mechanism, in much the same way that we would distinguish the category 'substantive' from the syntactic role 'subject', for which a substantive may be used.

All mechanical contrasts, in fact, lend themselves to arbitrary shifts of usage, as a specific group of speakers opts to develop or ignore a particular means of expression. Categories of subjunctive usage tend to vacillate with century and dialect: Latin for example frequently used the subjunctive after *si*, whereas modern French never does. To explain such vacillation it is not always necessary to presume that a shift takes place in the underlying system: the shift may simply be in the norm of usage. Whether one eats with knife in the right hand and fork in the left, as Europeans do, or with fork in the right hand, as Americans do, is a matter of usage. The reality of knife and fork is the same for both communities, for whom the reality of usage is nevertheless different.

The functional or pragmatic contrast that corresponds to the mechanical contrast between subjunctive and indicative in Modern French, is, as pointed out by Guillaume, the contrast of possible and probable (1929:32–33, 1971:188–202). The subjunctive is used for those instances that are assigned in discourse to the realm of the possible (*champ du possible*), the indicative being reserved for the expression of the realm of the probable (*champ du probable*). It should not be overlooked that what a group of speakers considers possible or probable may also be an arbitrary delineation: in 17th Century French one could find the subjunctive after *espérer* "to hope", whereas in 20th Century French one finds the indicative.

That which is possible must precede, in notional chronology, that which is probable: an event has to be possible before it can be probable. The inverse cannot be true. Guillaume expresses the relationship (1971:206) in the familiar binary unit:

```
     champ du possible              champ du probable
     --------------------->         -------------------->
     P₁              P₂   Q₁                        Q₂
```

$P_1 =$ position of impossibility, prior to the development of the field of possibility
$P_2 =$ position of fully developed possibility, possibility so great that it is ready to become probability
$Q_1 =$ initial position of probability, a simple transcendence of P_2
$Q_2 =$ final position of probability, the representation of certitude.

7.3.1 *Possible vs. probable*

The effects of this distinction are very easily demonstrable:

(1) Il est impossible qu'il vienne   (subjunctive)
(2) Il est possible qu'il vienne   (subjunctive)
(3) Il est probable qu'il viendra   (indicative)
(4) Il est certain qu'il viendra   (indicative)

In all these instances, we have a dependence of one idea or clause upon another. Guillaume calls the main clause in such cases the *idée regardante* (the viewing idea) and the subordinate clause the *idée regardée* (the viewed idea). It may be seen that in each of these cases the *idée regardante* sets up the matrix that determines the mood of the verb in the *idée regardée* (Guillaume 1971: 188–189).

It is also notable that the denial of probability in the *idée regardante* will also call into play the subjunctive:

(5)   Il est peu probable qu'il vienne

Denial of probability entails the refusal to enter the realm of the probable, and the matrix established is therefore that of the prior field of the possible.

7.3.2 *Affirmative vs. negative*

This same divergence of affirmative and negative is found in many instances where the verb of the main clause establishes the notion of belief or the affirmation of fact:

(6)   Je crois qu'il connaît votre père
(7)   Je ne crois pas qu'il connaisse votre père
(8)   Il est certain qu'il le sait
(9)   Il n'est pas certain qu'il le sache
(10)   Je vous dis que c'est vrai
(11)   Je ne vous dis pas que ce soit vrai
(12)   J'espère qu'il a raison
(13)   Je n'espère pas qu'il ait raison

All verbs of stating, hoping, declaring, believing, and all adjectival expressions indicating truth, certainty, etc., will be found to establish the kind of matrix exemplified here. A positive *idée regardante* will be followed by the indicative, and a negative *idée regardante*, which casts doubt on the reality of the *idée regardée*, will be followed by the subjunctive.

7.3.3 *Relative clauses*

The matrix of a relative clause is its preceding antecedent; if the existence of this antecedent is negated, we see the subjunctive used much as in the preceding section:

(14)   Voici un étudiant qui sait vous répondre
        "Here is a student who knows how to answer your question"
(15)   Il n'y a pas un étudiant qui sache vous répondre
        "There is no student who knows how to answer your question"

In (14) the existence of the student is affirmed; in (15) the existence of such a student is denied and the antecedent is a non-person. The verb of the clause relating to this antecedent is put into the subjunctive. The requirement of French is that if the antecedent is given positive chances of existing the verb in the subordinate clause is in the indicative, but if the antecedent is attributed negative chances of existing the verb will be put in the subjunctive:

(16)   Il y a beaucoup de gens qui le savent
(17)   Il y a peu de gens qui le sachent

In certain contexts and situations, this distinction may produce minimal pairs:

(18)   On cherche une secrétaire qui sait le russe
(19)   On cherche une secrétaire qui sache le russe

In (18), the speaker expresses confidence, in (19) doubts, about finding a Russian speaking secretary. Situation can easily determine the usage: one would expect to hear (18) in Eastern Europe, (19) in Canada, for example.

In similar fashion when the antecedent is an indefinite or interrogative expression, the dependent clause will be found in the subjunctive:

(20)   Qui que vous soyez ...   "Whoever you are"
(21)   Quoi que tu dises ...   "Whatever you say"
(22)   Quelques mots que tu dises ...   "Whatever words you say"
(23)   Quels que soient tes mots ...   "Whatever your words"
(24)   Quelque (Si) fort que tu sois ... "However strong you are"
(25)   Si longtemps que vous attendiez ... "However long you wait"

In all these instances, the subordinate clause (with conjunction *que*) relates to an indefinite antecedent, and since the antecedent is an unknown, the verb of the subordinate is subjunctive.

7.3.4 *Conjunctions*

Certain of the compound conjunctions can be broken down in similar fashion.

(26)   J'attendrai jusqu'à ce qu'il vienne
(27)   J'ai attendu jusqu'à ce qu'il est venu

In (26) and (27) we may consider that the conjunction *que* marks the beginning of the subordinate clause in each case, and that *jusqu'à ce* is a prepositional phase consisting of a compound preposition and its object *ce*, a demonstrative. When used with future reference, this *ce* refers to an unknown, undetermined moment, hence the use of the subjunctive in the subordinate clause, which, in (26) refers back to this indeterminate *ce* as an antecedent. In past time reference, on the other hand, the demonstrative *ce* will normally refer to a moment of memorial time, to a moment that is known, determined, hence the typical use of the indicative in (27), although the subjunctive can be used as well, which would indicate *until whatever time he came*. For further examples and a discussion of this very subtle contrast, see Matte (1989:208). Matte's Chapter 7 (175–242) on the subjunctive covers a wide range of usage and has many perceptive comments on subtle distinctions.

The conjunctions expressing negation are also followed by the subjunctive:

(28)   Il est sorti sans que vous le sachiez
        "He went out without your knowing"

Likewise events that are intended, or contingent on eventualities (and therefore indeterminate) are assigned to the subjunctive:

(29)   Je parle lentement pour que vous me compreniez
        "I'm speaking slowly so that you may understand me"
(30)   Parlez lentement de sorte que je comprenne
        "Speak slowly so that I can understand"
(31)   Mangez vite avant qu'il vienne
        "Eat up quickly before he gets here"

7.3.4.1 *The subjunctive with* après que

We expect the subjunctive with *avant que*, which represents an event that has not yet occurred, but not with *après que*, which has traditionally taken the indicative. More and more, however, the use of the subjunctive with *après que* has become very common, and in some instances this usage is clearly justifiable. Grevisse (1959:1015) gives a brief list of references to the discussions of this usage, and quotes the following from the French Constitution of 1946:

(32) a.   Le président du Conseil et les ministres ne peuvent être nommés qu'après que le Président du Conseil ait été investi de la confiance de l'Assemblée.
           "The Prime Minister and the Cabinet may only be named after the Prime Minister has received the Assembly's vote of confidence."

Here *après que* is the notional equivalent of *avant que*, as may be shown by changing *ne ... que* to *ne ... pas*:

(32) b.   ... ne peuvent pas être nommés avant que le Président ... ait été investi
           "cannot be named before ... has received ..."

The modal usage of clauses of time has fluctuated significantly over the centuries: it was normal for *when* clauses in Latin to be in the subjunctive, for example. The reason for this state of affairs is the dependent status of the subordinate clause of time, normally totally dependent upon the temporal reference of the main clause. Given this dependency, there may be a consequent tendency to leave the temporal reference of the subordinate clause open, by exploiting the temporal indefiniteness of the subjunctive. This tendency may be playing a part in the now frequent use of the subjunctive with *après que*.

There has been much lively and sometimes volatile commentary in both public forums and scholarly journals on the usage of the subjunctive with *après que*. Wunderli (1970) notes the absurdity of much of the criticism of the usage, pointing out that the subjunctive with *après que* has been around for centuries, although much more frequent today. Glättli (1970) takes him to task for this: quoting with approval a well-known French literary critic (Pierre-Henri Simon) who had declared in the 1962 number of *Esprit* that the use of the subjunctive after *après que* was a sign of a deranged mind, Glättli casts doubt on the reality of the evidence of earlier times. Wunderli replied (1970a), defending, for example, the reputation of the 17th century lexicographer Richelet, who had said that both indicative and subjunctive could be used with *après que*: a Frenchman who was extremely knowledgeable about his language, Richelet also had a reputation as a purist, so that he would be unlikely to make such a comment lightly. Glättli replied (1970a), but without adding any further substance.

At about the same time Marc Wilmet (1969, 1976) also discussed the issue, expressing the opinion that the subjunctive with *après que* would soon become a simple grammatical requirement. For this he was taken to task by Dolbec & LeFlem (1981), because such a view fails to take into account the meaning difference which exists between subjunctive and indicative. They reported on a small experimental study which they conducted with a hundred subjects, an attempt to establish the meaning variation of the different usages, indicative and subjunctive, with *après que*. They found that only 19% of their subjects used only one mood in such usage (14% subjunctive, 5% indicative) and that there were variations in the 18 test sentences between a low of 47% subjunctive (33a), and a high of of 88% subjunctive after *après que* (33b), with an overall average split of approximately one third indicative, two thirds subjunctive on a corpus of eighteen sentences.

(33) a. Un siècle après que ces paroles d'espoir (avoir) été prononcées, nous savons tous que la paix est une illusion. "A century after these words of hope were uttered, we all know that peace is an illusion".

b. Parce qu'elle a des ailes plus courtes que les autres rapaces, la petite buse peut atteindre ses proies même après qu'elles se (être) réfugiées sous le couvert. "Because it has shorter wings than other predators, the lesser buzzard can catch its prey even after it has fled under cover".

In these two polarized cases we can see a contrast between a simple temporal distance (a century later, after a recorded event) and a contingent possibility (even if the prey flees under cover). Dolbec and LeFlem noted, in fact, that with *même* (33b) and *ne...que* (32a) and other negative elements the percentages of subjunctive usage were consistently above 70%. The last word has not been said on this interesting alternation, but it is quite clear that a contrast of meaning, subtle but nevertheless real, is involved.

7.3.5 Value judgements

A very real difference between French and English occurs in clauses subjected to a personal value judgment. French regularly uses the subjunctive here, even though the event be experiential:

(34)   Je regrette qu'il soit venu
        "I'm sorry he came"

English regularly uses the indicative here, although in British English

(35)   I'm sorry he should have come

is a permissible alternative. Such sentences as (34) form a stumbling block to any naive explanation of the subjunctive as representing simply a potential event.

Speakers of a language, however, will play upon the means of expression in subtle and creative ways that are themselves clues to the informed and perceptive linguist of the nature of the underlying content mechanism.

In (34) the *idée regardée* is placed in the subjunctive because of the existence of an *idée regardante critique*. By using the subjunctive here, in fact, speakers of French bring the force of the critical evaluation to bear not upon the occurrence of the event (= indicative) but upon its very nature, upon the 'idea of the event'. In fact, it may be noted that outrage or scandal at an event may be expressed in English by the phrase

(36)   The very idea!

As a consequence, we may obtain minimal pairs in French with significant translations:

(37) Je comprends qu'il a acheté un auto
"I understand he bought a car"
(38) Je comprends qu'il ait acheté un auto
"I see why he bought a car"

In (37), the subject declares his understanding of the 'occurrence' of the event, in (38) of his understanding of the nature of the event, of the 'idea that lies behind the event' (in the chronogenesis the subjunctive 'lies behind' or underlies the indicative).

(39) Je suis d'avis qu'il l'a acheté
"I agree he bought it"
(40) Je suis d'avis qu'il l'ait acheté
"I agree with his buying it"

In (39) the subject agrees that the event has occurred. In (40) on the other hand, when he introduces an *idée critique*, a value judgment, he agrees with the principle of the event. The value judgment expressed in (40) is of the same type as that expressed in

(41) Il est bon qu'il l'ait acheté
(42) Il est dommage qu'il l'ait acheté
(43) J'approuve qu'il l'ait acheté
(44) Je regrette qu'il l'ait acheté
(45) Il est incroyable qu'il l'ait acheté

The use of the subjunctive in value judgments makes possible a much more generalized type of criticism: in explicitly criticizing the nature of the event rather than its occurrence one is implicitly criticizing all other possible occurrences of such an event by criticizing the underlying notion or principle of the event. This faculty is missing from the normal English usage; the following curiosity, however, was recorded in Canada from an English/French bilingual speaker:

(46) I approve that we have, and that we should have, such a system.

Although English was this individual's first language, he was struggling to express something that had become, for him, a naturally spontaneous idea: approval not only of the system in question, but of its underlying rationale. The sentence therefore is an instance of a subtle form of second language interference.

Value judgments may also occur with superlatives:

(47)   C'est le meilleur ami que nous avons
(48)   C'est le meilleur ami que nous ayons

Sentence (47) is a bland statement of fact; (48), on the other hand, introduces a value judgment whereby the speaker suggests an 'absolute superlative' — the best of all possible friends. The subordinate clause here is also a relative, and renews connection with the usage observed above: *best friend* is the antecedent of the dependent clause, and if such an antecedent is felt to be an empirical entity, the dependent verb will be indicative, if a potential entity (best 'possible' friend), the dependent verb will be subjunctive.

7.3.6 *Variable usage*

We said above that what a group of speakers considers to be possible or probable will be, to a certain extent, arbitrary and dependent upon historical, geographical or cultural conventions. Consequently, as well as minimal pairs, which yield different meanings and thereby give an insight into the functioning of the subjunctive/indicative distinction, there are instances of resistance to the regular and normal use of the subjunctive, with resulting historical changes in the usage. Historically, for example, instances may be found where a subjunctive would be required today (ex. from Guillaume 1971: 233):

(49)   C'est dommage, Garo, que tu n'es point entré
       Au conseil de Celui que prêche ton curé.

Modern usage would require us to correct this couplet from La Fontaine's *Fables* and to write *que tu ne sois point entré*, which would, of course, disturb the metre.

Elsewhere we find the indicative being used to record an indeniable, ineluctable fact:

(50)   Il serait stupide de nier que la terre est ronde
       "It would be stupid to deny that the earth is round"

Normally a subjunctive would be used after *nier*, but in this case, the fact itself resists the subjunctive usage. On the other hand, the subjunctive may also appear where we would normally expect an indicative

(51)   Le fait que Napoléon ait vaincu les Prusses à Iéna ...

The antecedent of the relative clause *que Napoléon ait vaincu* ... is the noun *fait*. Surely nothing could be more empirical, more determined, or have more positive chances of existence than 'a fact'. And yet it is, in some way, the nature of this antecedent that is a direct cause of the subjunctive in the dependent clause. Is a value judgment involved? It is conceivable but doubtful. We notice, however, curious possibilities in English:

(52)   The fact that Napoleon could conquer the Prussians at Jena....
(53)   The very fact that this should have happened ...

Not all speakers of English are able to accept (53) in this context (i.e. of an event that did happen), and the usage appears to be essentially British. Nevertheless, (51) – (53) point to another sense of 'fact': the notion of historical abstraction, fact as an abstract entity in an historical scheme, fact removed from the world of immediate experience, fact as 'idea'. In such a context, it is perfectly permissible for the noun 'fait', as an antecedent, to be considered not as an empirical event but as an abstraction, causing the use of the subjunctive in the subordinate relative clause.

7.4 *Facing the problems of subjunctive usage*

Such conflicting usage has often not been honestly faced by linguists. Consequently, two different, and equally indefensible attitudes are frequently sanctioned: (1) to ignore all such conflicting usage and to concentrate only on the generalities that may otherwise be drawn from the data, and (2) to conclude that there are no generalities: that all is accident and contingency. The former attitude is simply anti-scientific, since scientific procedure requires that the enquiry should cover all of the data (the scientific Canon of Exhaustiveness); the latter attitude fails to take into account that minimal pairs with subjunctive vs. indicative contrast regularly show quite basic differences of meaning which cannot be attributed to accident or contingency. There is a regularity of meaning but, as with all grammatical meanings, it is not always easy to delineate the underlying meaning in a coherent fashion.

The secret of Guillaume's success in this regard is his reconstruction of the underlying content system out of basic binary contrasts, contrasts whose 'operational results' may be viewed on the surface of language, at the level of discourse. But that is not sufficient, since the underlying and surface elements must be correlated: the apparent anomalies can only be 'coherently' explained (a requirement of the scientific Canon of Coherence) if a distinction is made between the mechanisms of the underlying content system and the notions that underlie the usage or manipulation of those mechanisms. Guillaume proposes that it is the binary opposition of 'possible/probable' that underlies the meaningful usage of the underlying system. The use of the subjunctive in (51) for example (*que Napoléon ait vaincu*) may be analysed in two stages. In the first stage, we analyse the *valeur* (to use a Saussurean term) of the antecedent *fait* in order to justify the use of the subjunctive in the relative clause. Since the indicative is commonly used in this particular context of (51), our explanation must be able to illuminate the native speaker's intuitive feeling that the subjunctive here has a special value, that it presents the fact as an idea, as an item in an argument.

Our suggestion that the noun *fait* in this sentence has a contextual meaning (alloseme, *signifié d'effet*) of 'abstracted experience' rather than the more common meaning 'empirical experience' may at once satisfy the native speaker and justify the use of the subjunctive, since the abstracted experience may appropriately be related to the realm of the possible or potential. But this still does not explain how the subjunctive provides this meaning, and we must therefore proceed to the second stage of the analysis, which will take us to the underlying linguistic mechanism.

Here we observe once more that a single simple binary contrast between abstract (or indeterminate) Universe Time and concrete (or determinate) Universe Time is utilized for a vast range of expression. The subordinate event in (51) is represented mechanically as an event in Universe Time, but abstracted from any precise localization.. Wherever a subjunctive is found, this same basic contrast is the underlying mechanism (at the level of representation) that is functioning to produce the total range of usage that is to be found in discourse (at the level of expression).

This element of meaning brought to the context and situation, in other words, is the stable element that is found in every subjunctive. What is not stable, on the other hand, is the complex web of meanings and overtones that any particular context and situation will bring to a particular subjunctive usage, and thereby mould and change every subjunctive usage into a different contextual meaning.

7.5 *Conclusion*

Mood as a linguistic category is dependent upon the stages of cognitive processing of the verbal time image.

In French, the quasi-nominal mood is a preliminary image of the event as an entity, represented simply as a static container (infinitive), as a content that is incomplete (present participle), or as a content that is complete (past participle). These three representations relate to three fundamental cognitive faculties:

memory, perception, and imagination. The past participle represents the event as if it were in the memory; the present participle as if it were being perceived; the infinitive as if it were in the imagination.

The second developmental stage of the time image results in the subjunctive, where the event in incidence (Ascending Time) forms the present subjunctive, and the event in decadence (Descending Time) forms the imperfect subjunctive. At this level the event is represented as taking place in Universe Time; the event so represented, however, is not allocated to experiential time, past, present, or future.

The third developmental stage adds to the delineation of Universe Time already established at the subjunctive level, the representation of the moment of the present, which in turn defines both past and future. The representation of the present introduces the element of personal experience (a 'shifter' in Jespersen's terminology), and identifies the events represented as experiential, as belonging to Universe Time divided into time spheres which can be identified with mental experience (recorded, being recorded, to be recorded).

We are now in a position to review Guillaume's chronogenesis in terms of different developmental aspects of the recording of experience in the memory.

At the quasi-nominal level we have three different forms which represent fundamental mental experience viewed statically. Guillaume expresses the view that at this initial stage time is not represented as either descending or ascending (1964:187), and consequently he represents the three forms at this level with vertical arrows, rather than horizontal arrows (which would indicate Ascending or Descending Time). This representation with vertical arrows is the one that we have reproduced above in Chapter Three (3.4).

Rather than annul or cancel the movement of Universe Time at this level as Guillaume does (1964:187, 1971:45), however, it would be more reasonable to conclude, as we have done above, that the full representation of Universe Time does not emerge until Level Two of the chronogenesis, and that Universe Time is in fact an extrapolation from the kind of time that is represented at Level One, which from a cognitive point of view is purely mental time, the time of consciousness, so that the three representations of Level One of the chronogenesis can be described as follows.

    past participle   linguistic representation of the event as the kind of experience that is already recorded in the immediate memory present participle   linguistic representation of the event as the kind of experience that is in process of being recorded by sensory perception, about to be recorded in the memory

infinitive   linguistic representation of the event as the kind of experience that is still in the imagination, before being recorded in sensory perception and memory

The recording of memory, as shows in the analogy of the movie camera, operates in Descending Time: recent memories become more distant memories with the passage of time. Descending Time is indeed, to use Guillaume's term, 'time which operates in the mind' (see for example 1964:60) since the memory records the passing parade of life, whether we like it or not: the recording of the stream of consciousness is fundamentally passive, and the past participle, which represents the event as if it were a memory trace, has a fundamentally passive meaning, which justifies its exploitation in the formation of passive voice forms. It is this aspect of mental time, time inside the mind, that also becomes the model for a representation of Universe Time, time outside the mind, as Descending Time.

The imagination, by contrast, operates in Ascending Time: it is an exploration from the present into the future. It is an illustration of 'the mind which operates in time' as opposed to 'time which operates in the mind'. If the infinitive is seen as the imaginary rehearsal of an event, the kind of rehearsal that takes place within mental time, it would provide a model for the representation of Universe Time, time outside the mind, as Ascending Time.

In this way Universe Time, ascending and descending, would be a novel creation of Level Two of the chronogenesis, an extrapolation from the limited representations of Level One, and would lead to the possibility, at Level Two, of representing events in Universe Time, time outside the mind. The recognition of time outside the mind, in contrast to Mental Time, is also a recognition of self consciousness, a contrast of the me and the non-me. Such representations are later productions in the development of child language, as are the use of first and second person pronouns. The representations at this level, and also at the later third level, are also predicated of the persons of self consciousness, the me, and the non-me, whether the non-me be second or third person, and if third, animate or inanimate — the persons of the universe. The representations of Level Two in the French verb are as follows.

present subjunctive	linguistic representation of an event as occupying an undefined segment of ascending Universe Time, predicated of a personal subject
imperfect subjunctive	linguistic representation of an event as occupying an undefined segment of descending Universe Time, predicated of a personal subject

Neither of these events, however, is represented as being in experiential time, since at this stage of the representation Universe Time is purely imaginary time, there being no *point de repère*, no bench mark to relate it to experience. This is provided at the third stage of the chronogenesis, where the kinetic view at Level Two is seen in relation to the fundamental representation of conscious experience at Level One. If Level One represents Mental Time, and Level Two represents Universe Time, time outside the mind, Level Three represents Mental Time in Universe Time, a combination of the two earlier levels. The whole of the indicative mood, in short, is dependent upon the introduction of the present of consciousness into Universe Time. It is this representation of the present which provides the bench mark missing at Level Two of the French verb.

present	representation of an event as occupying a segment of Universe Time coeval with consciousness, as partially in the memory (Descending Time) and partially in the imagination (Ascending Time)
preterit	representation of an event as occupying a segment of ascending Universe Time coeval with the memory
imperfect	representation of an event as occupying a segment of descending Universe Time coeval with the memory
future	representation of an event as occupying a segment of ascending Universe Time that is still in the imagination
conditional	representation of an event as occupying a segment of descending Universe Time that is still in the imagination

From this overview we can comment on several noteworthy features.

The representations in Descending Time depict the materiality of the event: they give an interior view of an event as if it were being recorded and passing segment by segment into the memory. This is the typical view of the French imperfect, and indeed the imperfect tenses of Indo-European languages as a whole are constructed on the representation of descending Universe Time.

The difference between a future and a conditional is that the future represents a segment of ascending Universe Time as a complete event, whereas the conditional represents the materiality of the same kind of segment, a materiality that is yet to be, a mere potentiality. Consequently the conditional, by its makeup, represents the mere possibility of an event: all the conditions for an event, without any part of it being realised.

The imperfect subjunctive, since it represents the event as a material entity in Universe Time, contains an unsatisfactory form of representation for a subjunctive, or at least for the kind of subjunctive used in Modern French.

The preterit, since it does not represent the materiality of the event, is a less than satisfactory representation of a real event in the past. It is not surprising that the passé composé, which is able to represent the materiality of a complete event in the past, has replaced the preterit in ordinary conversational usage, nor that the imperfect subjunctive has, for all practical purposes, disappeared from usage.

CHAPTER EIGHT
PRESENT AND PRESENT PERFECT

8. *Introduction*

When one defines the present in concrete cognitive terms, it is then possible to show how this mental experience of recording consciousness can be represented differently in different linguistic systems, and possible to explain differential usage between two different tense systems, such as those of English and French. There are certain differences of usage that are absolutely consistent between the two languages, showing quite clearly that what is in question is a difference in the underlying system, in this case the different cognitive representation of the present. A survey of all the different usage shows quite clearly that it can be explained as the result of a single fundamental systemic contrast.

At several points throughout this study we noted cases where the French present must be translated by a past in English, or by the English present perfect. There are also cases where the French Passé composé may be used with adverbs of past time, where the English present perfect may not, usage that has long puzzled the grammarians. A penetrating Guillaumian study by Korrel (1991) on this question, contrasting the usage in English and Dutch has broken new ground in proposing a fundamental systemic difference as the underlying cause of these distinctions, and we shall here take the analysis one stage further by treating this systemic difference in terms of alpha and omega moments. We shall also show that the two problem cases that Korrel lists in her study (1991:115–117) can also be satisfactorily explained by the notion of threshold.

8.1 *Concrete cognitive activity*

The experiential present, in cognitive terms, is the activity of recording the stream of consciousness, the moment of recording experience in the memory, when the memory acts in recording mode. It is that time when the areas of the cortex that are allocated to recording the short term memory are busy at work.

To understand what is entailed in such cognitive activity, we have used the analogy of the film in a movie camera passing through the chamber where it will be exposed to light. The fundamental physical difference between film that has been exposed and film that has not leads to a comparison with the cognitive functions of memory and imagination. The contrast between memory and imagination, in turn, underlies the linguistic binary distinction between memorial and non-memorial time, between a past and a non-past. In this way we relate a linguistic distinction to a cognitive activity, in the style of Johnson (1987, 1992), thereby dealing with linguistic distinctions in concrete rather than abstract terms:

> We are beings of the flesh. What we can experience, how it can be meaningful to us, how we can reason about it, and how we communicate this understanding to other people depends on the patterns of our bodily experience (Johnson 1987; Lakoff 1987). The form meaning can take for us is prefigured in the way we inhabit our world, through our spatial and temporal orientation, our manipulation of objects, our perceptual interactions, and our bodily movements (1992:347).

Inevitably a physical distinction between memorial and non-memorial time calls into play the necessity of a threshold, where a given cluster of brain cells, which previously has carried no memory trace, is used for recording a moment of experience. Thereafter each such brain cell carries a memory trace, just as each frame of the unexposed film, as it passes through the camera, is exposed to the light and thereafter joins the sequence of frames of exposed film that will then need to be developed. This threshold lies between those cells that carry a memory trace and those that do not; it is this threshold that is the universal experience we call the present.

8.2 *The nature of a threshold*

If we zero in on this moment of the threshold on the moving film, we may distinguish the two separate frames that form the core of this operation: one that has just been exposed, the last one in the sequence of exposed frames; and one that is in the chamber, with the shutter open, the first one in the sequence of not yet exposed frames. The last of the exposed frames we have called the omega moment, since it is the most recent moment of the past, the last moment of the past. The frame in the chamber we have called the alpha moment, since it is the first moment of the future. These terms are extrapolated from the original proposals by Guillaume (see, for example 1929:51, or 1964:60–61), merely giving Guillaume's original term 'chronotype' a concrete cognitive sense.

The present may thus be viewed as the threshold between past and future, formed, in the manner appropriate to every threshold, by a quantum of the past and a quantum of the future. Any threshold that separates one space from another is necessarily composed of a quantum from each of the two spaces: a threshold that did not itself have dimension would of course be inexistent. We have already used the analogy of the saw cut: when a sheet of plywood is sawn in two the cut of the saw has a certain dimension, so that the two resultant pieces of plywood are no longer as big as the original single sheet. If the cut is accurately made, it cuts a quantum from each of the two existing halves, each of which will be slightly less than half of the original sheet.

8.3 Cognitive contrasts, lexical and grammatical

All languages, as we know, analyse experience differently. French distinguishes *savoir* and *connaître*, where English has only *to know*. English, on the other hand distinguishes *say* and *tell*, where French has only *dire*, or *make* and *do*, where French has only *faire*. It is not surprising, therefore, that different languages should choose to represent the cognitive experience of the present in different systemic ways, and that grammatical subsystems should be just as language-specific as lexical subsystems.

English, as we have seen, is traditionally analysed by the grammarians as having only two tenses, and represents the future periphrastically, by means of aspect, not by tense. We have analysed the two tenses of English (2.1.3) as forming a simple binary contrast between memorial and non-memorial time, so that *I talk* in the English tense system represents not so much the moment of the present, of the here and now, but frequently represents an event that has a permanence, that occupies future time as well:

```
------------------------> ------------------------>
                         ω  α
```

Presumably it was to circumvent this representation of permanence that the so-called progressive *I am talking* was developed and came into full flower in the middle of the seventeenth century.

French, by contrast, has both past and future tenses, and the present in such a system necessarily represents the no-man's-land between past and future (see 6.4 above). The representation incorporates at least the alpha and omega moments, thus effectively representing the present of cognitive experience in the system of tenses.

```
                         ->
<------------------| ω  α |-------------------->
                         <-
```

(The small arrows indicate that in the French present there is a contrast between indidence (->) and decadence (<-) that is analysed in 6.4.1).

Because of this fundamentally different structure of the tense system, French represents the cognitive experience of the present, the alpha and omega moments, as a separate entity within the tense system, whereas English simply uses these two moments of experience as a threshold to make the break between past and non-past. In the English representation of tense, the present is seen as a watershed: one switches between past and non-past. In the French representation, on the other hand, the present is seen as a summit from which the rest of the landscape can be viewed.

8.3.1 *Contrastive usage: past versus present*

As a consequence of these diametrically different representations of the same cognitive experience, there are fundamentally different usages of tense in French and English that the translator, for example, has to be aware of. If for example we wish to represent an event as belonging to the most recent past, which includes the omega moment, we find the past tense used in English, but the present tense used in French. The person left waiting on a street corner rendezvous may comment to their late arriving friend

(1)   You finally arrived!

Or a colleague may enter an office and say

(2)   I came to get your signature

In both cases the event is so recent that it reaches into the cognitive present, and includes the omega moment, which is of course represented in the English system as the last moment of the past tense. In the French system, however, where the omega moment is represented as a segment of the present tense, the natural tense in both these cases is a present:

(3)   Enfin tu arrives!
(4)   Je viens chercher ta signature

The same phenomenon occurs with such sentences as

(5)   He just left
(6)   I just told you that

which pose a problem of representation in French that is solved by the use of the idiom *venir de*, which allows the speaker to use the present to represent this omega moment where the Anglophone speaker uses the past:

(7) Il vient de partir
(8) Mais je viens de te le dire

8.3.2 Contrastive usage: present perfect versus present

Much better known to the teachers of both languages are the differences of representation that occur with such words as *since* and *depuis*. Where an event continues over a period of time into the present, the present perfect must be used in English, whereas French uses the simple present tense, as in the following.

(9) J'habite ici depuis dix ans
     "I have lived here for ten years"

If one were to say in English

(10) I live here for ten years

the meaning would be that I have just arrived on a ten year stay, after which I am scheduled to go elsewhere, as in

(11) I live here for ten years, and then I go to France for ten years
(12) I work here for ten years, and then I retire.

In other words the use of the non-past tense in English necessarily carries with it the representation of the alpha moment and the time which follows it, that is from the present into the future, not into the past.

The use of the present perfect, on the other hand, indicates the present possession, in the alpha moment, of a past event which includes the omega moment:

```
<----------------------|---------------------->
       lived          ω α     have
```

Both of these moments, however, are already represented in the French present, which we may represent as follows:

```
                           habite
<- - - - - - - - - - - - -|<-- -->|
                           ω α
```

(The extended dotted line indicates that the event has been extended by the adverbial phrase *depuis dix ans*.) This extended dotted line is not an inherent part of the verbal representation, but an addition which is brought to the representation by the adverbial phrase.

When this usage with *since* and *depuis* is transferred from the present connection to a past connection, the parallel that we find between the French present and the English present perfect is repeated in a parallel between the English past perfect and the French imperfect:

(13) Il habite ici depuis dix ans
"He has lived here for ten years"
(14) Il habitait ici depuis dix ans
"He had lived here for ten years"

Just as the omega moment of the present, representing the point of view of decadence, leads from the present towards the past, the element of *accompli* in the imperfect, representing the point of view of decadence, leads from the past into time before the past reference point.

8.3.3 *Contrastive usage: the first time*

We may note that English also uses the present perfect with the phrase *It is the first time that* whereas French here uses the simple present tense.

(15) C'est la première fois que je mange du caviar
(16) This is the first time I have eaten caviar

The English usage may in fact be considered strange: why would I use a present perfect here when I have never before eaten caviar? The answer here lies once more in the problem of the threshold, this time the threshold between the actual eating and the claiming of a first. One must start (or at least intend) to eat *before* it can be a first time. One cannot claim a first time before one is actually involved with the activity. Once the involvement has started, then the claim can subsequently be established.

It is this priority that is shared between the omega and alpha moments. The eating occupies the omega moment, and the establishment of the dependent claim of a first time then appropriately belongs to the alpha moment. Hence the use of the present perfect in English, where this contrast is available, and the use of the simple present in French, which contains both moments in its representation.

Since we have argued that the regularities that appear in discourse are entirely the result of systemic differences at the level of tongue, it is no surprise to observe that when the reference is entirely in the past there is the same correspondence between the English past perfect and the French imperfect that we had already observed in section 8.3.2:

(17) C'est la permière fois que je mange du caviar
"It's the first time I have eaten caviar"
(18) C'était la première fois que je mangeais du caviar
"It was the first time I had eaten caviar"

Again the element of *accompli*, the element of decadence in the imperfect, provides the experience, and the subsequent element of *accomplissement*, the element of incidence, provides the appropriate place for making the subsequent claim of a first time.

Korrel (1991:117–119) interestingly picks up on this particular usage of *This is the first time*, and notes that it is equally valid for *second time, third time*, and so on. It is also of interest to note that *This is the last time*, which is a statement about the future rather than about the past, is normally not followed by the Present Perfect. If eating caviar leads to an allergy, we may expect *That's the last time I eat caviar.*

8.3.4 Contrastive usage: immediate physical realizations

Here it is important to realise that language usage is not conscious but subconscious, not logical but psychological. These subtle distinctions of the priorities of a threshold show up in more than one way. Verbs in French, for example, typically show either *à, de*, or zero before a dependent infinitive. But there are three verbs and only three, that show variation: an alternation between *à* and *de*.

(19) Il a commencé à/de manger (recommencé, continué)

What do *begin, begin again*, and *continue* have in common? The answer is the problem of the threshold. Does one begin to eat by sitting down at the table (= à) in preparation, or does one begin to eat only after taking the first bite (= de)?

```
              I                F
              |                |
      à -->   | --> de         |
              |                |
              |---------------->|
```

(I = initial moment of event; F = final moment of event; *à* = movement of approach to the initial moment; *de* = movement away from initial moment).

Note that *se mettre à*, with its notion of "getting down to" (=à) allows of no variation: only the preposition *à* is allowed. The verbs *recommencer* and *continuer* pose the same problem as *commencer* and for the very same reason: at what cognitive moment does the notion of continuing operate? Does one continue to eat before taking the next bite (intentional), or after taking it (resultative)? English recognizes the same problem by exploiting the contrast between infinitive and gerund.

(20)　He began to eat　　　= Il a commencé à manger
(21)　He began eating　　　= Il a commencé de manger
(22)　He continued to eat　= Il a continué à manger
(23)　He continued eating　= Il a continué de manger

The infinitive with *to* represents an event prospectively: the gerund represents an event that is already under way: (20) and (22) indicate that the act of beginning and the act of continuing precede the first bite; (21) and (23) indicate that both beginning and continuing here depend on the first bite.

We have already seen the exploitation of the two distinct moments of the threshold of the present in the usage with *C'est la première fois que*; we also see it where there is a mental happening followed by an immediate conscious awareness, as in

(24)　Je change d'avis
　　　"I've changed my mind"
(25)　Il me vient une idée
　　　"I've just had an idea"

In both (24) and (25) there is instantaneous recognition (moment α) of an immediate prior mental operation (moment ω). Korrel (1991:116) records the use of the non-past in Dutch for similar instantaneous recognition of physical sensations (breaking a tooth, burning one's fingers).

8.3.5 *Contrastive usage: passé composé versus preterit*

The fifth and final major difference between English and French that concerns the present is the use of the passé composé in French where English may not use the present perfect, but only the preterit. This occurs typically where the sentence contains an adverb of past time.

(26)　J'ai vu ce film hier
(27)　"I saw (*have seen) that film yesterday"

This usage presents a significant problem for francophones, who are used to translating the Passé composé with the English present perfect, as is perfectly appropriate when there is no explicit reference to a particular time in the past:

(28) J'ai vu ce film
(29) "I have seen that film"

If the translation is perfectly appropriate when there is no adverb of past time, why does it become impossible, as in (27) when an adverb of past time is introduced?
The problem here is that the auxiliary of the English present perfect, as we have seen, contains only the alpha moment in its representation. The omega moment, since it is not included as an element of the auxiliary, automatically becomes included in the representation of the past participle:

$$\underset{\omega \mid \alpha}{\overset{\text{seen} \quad \text{I have}}{\longleftarrow \mid \longrightarrow}}$$

The sense of this combination is to indicate present possession of a complete event which must necessarily have taken place in the time preceding the time of the auxiliary, namely the past *up to and including the omega moment*. It is this inclusion of the omega moment in the representation of the past participle that causes the phenomenon of 'present reference' (as the grammarians call it) that is a necessary and fundamental part of the representation of the English present perfect. And it is this inclusion of the omega moment in the representation of the past participle that results in a semantic clash with any adverb indicating past time divorced from the present.

The French passé composé, on the other hand, since its auxiliary contains both the alpha and omega moments in its representation, indicates possession of a past event that lies entirely in the past, since the past participle, in this combination does not include the omega moment, already included in the auxiliary. The French passé composé may represent a past event without encumbrance, and may therefore be used with explicit adverbs of past time.

8.4 *Conclusion*

The conflicting usage of present tense between French and English might lead one to the conclusion that all is inconsistency and conflict: present tense in French is translated not only by the English non-past, but sometimes by a future, sometimes by a past, sometimes by a present perfect. When one makes a careful examination of the usage, however, regular and consistent patterns emerge, and the systematic differences indicate clearly that they are based upon systemic differences, simple distinctions that belong to an underlying cognitive system.

PART TWO
THE EXPRESSION SYSTEM

CHAPTER NINE
SEMIOLOGY, THE SYSTEM OF SIGNS

9. *Introduction*
The principle focus of concentration of this book has been upon the mechanisms of content systems, an area of linguistics that, apart from the work of Jakobson on Russian (1932, 1936, 1957), and that of Guillaume on French (1929, 1945, 1964, 1971), has suffered almost total neglect.

Guillaume also wrote quite extensively about what he called semiological systems, the systems of signs that relate to the content systems we have been describing. The term 'expression systems', coined by Hjelmslev (1935:xii) is the one that has traditionally been used in English, and is the one that we have used and will continue to use. Guillaume's analyses of expression systems are not always as profoundly convincing and intuitively penetrating as his analyses of the content systems, but his views are nevertheless frequently perceptive, and a survey of some of them will form a fitting complement to the above survey of the content systems of the French verb.

9.1 *The arbitrary nature of the sign*
An important Saussurean doctrine is that of *l'arbitraire du signe*, the arbitrary nature of the linguistic sign (see 1.3 above). It is important, however, to understand exactly what Saussure meant by this doctrine, which has been much misunderstood. Saussure did not mean that a sign can not be motivated, and in fact many signs are motivated in some way, and Saussure himself discusses the obvious motivation of onomatopoeic signs (1916:101-102).

The proper sense of the Saussurean principle is that the link between signifier and significate, or in more modern terms between morpheme (form) and sememe (meaning), is arbitrary only in the sense that it is not requisite, and the morpheme or signifier could at any time be changed for something else: in the game of chess a lost rook can be replaced by a spice bottle (see 1.3). It is this arbitrary nature of the sign, of course that makes linguistic change possible.

At the same time we must take fully into consideration the importance of the element of motivation in the formation of the morpheme. We see, for example, the functioning of analogical levelling that is a constant force to reduce irregularities in the morphology, such as the change of Old French *amons, amez*, to Modern French *aimons, aimez*, the shift from *dive, dove*, to *dive, dived* in British English (although the older form has been maintained in American English), or Saussure's own example (1916:138) of the change from Old High German *was, waren* (equivalent of English *was, were*) to *war, waren* in Modern German.

There is, in short, a constant pressure to make the expression system a direct reflection of the content system. This is to be expected, since the role of the expression system is to mark the content system, to provide that which is only conceivable (content) with a mark that is perceivable (expression). Morphemes, which are perceivable, are markers of sememes, which are not perceivable in themselves, but only conceivable (Valin 1968, 1994). The role of the morpheme, in short, is to make the sememe perceivable, to give it a perceivability.

Guillaume, in his lectures, endlessly preached the importance of distinguishing *les faits psychiques* (meaning contrasts), which are not directly observable, from *les faits de sémiologie* (formal contrasts), which are. The former, in fact, can only be determined indirectly through the latter: if we conclude that standard French has five different indicative tenses, it is because we start from the five morphological sets in the indicative paradigm of every normal verb that give contrastively different effects in discourse.

In his earliest work (1919:11–13) Guillaume compared this procedure to that of the classical comparative method in Historical Linguistics. In historical comparative work, there is the reconstruction of a theoretical formal entity (e.g. an asterisked morpheme) from forms in the daughter languages *that share a common meaning*. In analysing underlying content, there is the reconstruction of a theoretical cognitive entity from a variety of surface meanings or functions *that share a common form*. Guillaume expressly states (1919:27) in the last sentence of his *Avant-propos*, that his main aim in the work is "the definition of a method for the semantic study of forms" (translation mine).

If we were to concentrate only on the evidence of morphemic differences, however, we would be obliged to consider the forms *finir, vendre* as not being the equivalent of *aimer, jouer, parler*. In English, how could we possibly know that *went* is the past of *go* were it not for their common meaning? The morphemic differences, therefore, constitute a major clue as to the underlying content systems, but they are ultimately unreliable because the relationship between an expression system and its related content system is not necessarily fully coherent. Compare the following paradigms:

(a)	(b)
je parle	je veux
tu parles	tu veux
il parle	il veut
nous parlons	nous voulons
vous parlez	vous voulez
ils parlent	ils veulent

We normally describe (a) as a regular and (b) as an irregular paradigm. The latter is divergent in two respects:

(i) the personal endings, in their written form, do not belong to an 'open' set, that may be utilized in the formation of new verbs, and
(ii) there are three divergent stems: /vɸ/, /vul/, and /vœl/. No one would declare, however, that these three stems cover three different meanings: they are three different morphs, variant forms (allomorphs) with a common unitary meaning, that of the verb *vouloir*.

The lack of congruence between sign and significate in French is typical of a language of the Indo-European type. We know, in fact, that the three present stems of *vouloir* are all the result of historically conditioned sound change, and that many verbs in French had similar differences which have been analogically levelled with the passage of time.

Nevertheless the mechanical structure of the content system is only to be observed through the medium of the morphosyntax. Or to use Firth's succinct call to arms: "No semantics without morphology!" Systemic differences of meaning, in short, are always morphosyntactically marked. We must remember, however, that a morphological difference does not necessarily require a semantic difference. Likewise a semantic difference does not require a morphological difference everywhere in the paradigm, as we see when we compare *sing, sang, sung*, with *put, put, put*.

9.2 *Arbitrariness and the law of coherence*

Guillaume is also fond of repeating that content (his *psychisme*) and expression (his *sémiologie*) operate under different laws. The law that governs the relationships of content systems is a law of 'coherence' (see 1.3), whereas that which governs semiology is a law of 'simple expressive adequacy' which he calls the *loi de simple suffisance* (1971:70–71, et passim). A past tense in English, for example, always has the same basic underlying meaning; that is the Law of Coherence. But the past tense is marked in many ways: suffix, ablaut, etc., each of which is sufficient to convey the meaning "past"; that is the Law of Expressive Adequacy, or Law of Simple Sufficiency.

Very often, however, as well as carrying the basic meaning, a particular morph may also bring a peculiar nuance of meaning. This happens in a variety of circumstances:

(a) an historical accident may produce two variant forms, each of which will adopt slight variations of nuance. Since /n/ and /l/ do not always assimilatively determine the voicing of a following consonant in English, we find variant preterit forms of several verbs: *burned, burnt*; *spilled, spilt*; *spelled, spelt*; *smelled, smelt*; *penned (i.e. put in a pen or enclosure), pent*. Some of these would be classified as quite different by native speakers (e.g. *penned in* but *pent up*), others would convey nuances to some that they do not have for others (e.g. *burnt* for some is determinate, *burned* indeterminate)

(b) a wide divergence of meaning may cause speakers to create a distinguishably different morph. The past tense of *hang*, for example, is *hung*; but capital punishment requires *hanged*.

(c) a paradigm may historically produce, by regular sound change, two different stems. If divergent meanings attach themselves to these stems, two new paradigms may be formed by an amoeba like split, new forms being created analogically as required. The Latin verb *disjejunare* "to break fast", for example, because of historical sound change, should have given the following irregular paradigm in modern French:

> je déjeune
> tu déjeunes
> il déjeune
> nous dînons
> vous dînez
> ils déjeunent

The infinitive would have been *dîner*. The verb took on two different senses, however, and split into two, forming two new verbs: *déjeuner* "to breakfast" and *dîner* "to dine".

(d) Analogical levelling may produce a new form, and the old form may still linger on, but carrying a different nuance from the new regularized form. The English *get, got, gotten*, for example, was subject to the pressure, common to all dialects, to reduce preterit and past participle to a single form. The change was effective in British English, which today has only *get, got, got*. American English, on the other hand, acquired the new participial form *got*, but also kept the old form *gotten*. The new *got* carries the nuance of possession (static), whereas the old *gotten* now carries overtones of action, of change of state (dynamic):

(1) He's just got a small suitcase
Il n'a qu'une petite valise
(2) He's just gotten a small suitcase
Il vient d'acheter une petite valise

A typical example of the survival of an old irregularity in French is the variation *je peux/je puis*. The etymological form is actually *je puis*, and *je peux* is the analogically reshaped form which is used for all normal expression meaning "I can, I am able, I may". The form *je puis* is used only in the special sense of "I may, I am in a position to", and is most commonly found in the interrogative form *puis-je*, since it is rare for a speaker to enquire if he himself is able to do something, but common enough to ask for permission. In the affirmative *je peux vous dire* would mean "I'm capable of telling you", whereas *je puis vous dire* means "I'm allowed to tell you, I'm in a position to tell you".

There is also what appears to be an alternate indicative form of *je sais*, namely *je sache*, as found in the usage of (3) and (4).

(3) Je ne sache personne mieux indiqué pour faire ce travail
"I know of no one better suited for doing this job"
(4) Je ne sache pas si le commis est là
"I don't know whether or not the clerk is there"
(5) Pas que je sache
"Not that I know of"

The main clause usage in (3) and (4) is found only in the first person singular. In (4) the speaker here is indicating a twofold lack of knowledge: whether the clerk is there, whether the clerk is not there, and it is this double uncertainty (maybe, maybe not) that seemingly triggers the form *sache*. In (3) *sache* likewise indicates a complete lack of any alternative: it is not just a question of not knowing, but of being totally at a loss to make a suggestion. Since the form *sache* in (5) is a subjunctive (being in a subordinate clause with an *idée regardante* in the negative), the forms in (3) and (4) have normally also been treated as subjunctives. But the usage in (5) is also found in other persons (e.g. *Pas que l'on sache*), and it is more likely that *sache* in (3) and (4) is an alternative indicative, since it is the etymological form, *je sais* being an analogically reshaped form. The justification for this analysis is to be found in three items of supporting evidence: (a) the verb in (3) and (4) is in a main clause, with no *que*, (b) the usage is found only in the first person singular, exactly as with *je puis*, and (c) both *puis* and *sache* are the expected historical forms for the first person, *peux*, *sais* having been analogically reshaped.

9.3 *Allomorphs of* aller

Guillaume points out several interesting irregularities in the semiological paradigms of French verbal sets. One is the division of the morphs *all-*, *v-*, and *ir-* in the verb *to go* (which, as in English, and indeed, in many other languages, is suppletive), showing the results of intrusion of morphs from other sets and other paradigms. In French the *all-* morph even intrudes into the paradigm of the *v-* morph:

je vais	nous allons
tu vas	vous allez
il va	ils vont

Guillaume claims (1971:75–76) that the justification of this irregularity lies ultimately in the different nature of the grammatical content of the first and second person pronouns in the plural. These latter are semantically complex (you and I, he and I, etc.), containing different persons, whereas the third person plural is merely compound (e.g. 3 and 3) and never contains any grammatical person other than third. The singular forms, by their very nature, are semantically simple, but the *nous* is particularly complex (1 + 2, or 1 + 3, or 1 + 2 + 3), and *vous* is necessarily 2 + 3.

9.4 *The* 'verbes de puissance'

An even more interesting category is a set of verbs that Guillaume calls the *verbes de puissance* (1990:216) and which may be identified by a common feature: the number of morphological forms that either use a subjunctive stem or show subjunctive-type alternates (1971:235–9). The six verbs are as follows:

(i) existence	être	"be"		
	avoir	"have"		
(ii) capacity	pouvoir	"be able to"	"(can, may)"	
	savoir	"know"	"(can)"	
(iii) volition	vouloir	"wish"	"(will)"	
	devoir	"be obliged to"	"(must, ought to, shall)"	

All other verbs in French use the indicative stem for the imperative forms of the verb, but with these verbs we find subjunctive stems: *soyez, ayez, sachez, veuillez*. Present participles show some variation; *être* has *étant*, *avoir* has *ayant*, and there are several pairs: *puissant/ pouvant*; *sachant/savant*; *voulant/-veillant* (in compounds). In each of these latter cases, one of the two forms has become the regular participle, the other form is used as a simple adjective.

A point of particular interest is that these six verbs, whose paradigms show a common morphological trait of the intrusion of subjunctive stems into the regular indicative sets (a feature we have called turbulence) largely correspond to the English modal auxiliaries. The main feature of the modals, it must be remembered, is that they are to be found only in the morphology of the subjunctive, and are not found in either infinitive or indicative forms.

The intrusion of subjunctive forms into these paradigms is a clear indicator that this group forms a semantic subset, and that Guillaume's label of *verbes de puissance*, verbs of potentiality, is appropriate. All other actions, events and states are contingent on existence, capacity and volition. Imperatives of these typically cannot have the same force as a normal verb. One cannot command a person to know, or to be able, with the same authority as one can command them to speak, stand, or sit, and the actual resultant knowledge or ability, if any, can only be observed indirectly whereas the resultant speaking can be observed directly. Consequently, imperatives of this subset can express little more than a wish, and it is not surprising that French has here come to make use of subjunctive type stems, by which recognition is given, in the morphology, of the different lexical status of these verbs. Nor is it surprising that alternate forms such as *je peux/je puis, je sais/je sache, pouvant/puissant*, and *savant/sachant* have survived with different nuances of meaning.

9.5 *The morphology of the imperative*

In Chapter Seven we did not deal with the imperative as a separate mood, since the morphology of the imperative is borrowed from the paradigms of the indicative and the subjunctive. Guillaume comments (1992:157):

> ... en français il n'y a pas, dans une théorie du mode, à traiter particulièrement du mode impératif. Le mode impératif est un mode d'expressivité, un mode de parole. Ce n'est pas un mode de pensée. Du point de vue de la pensée, il relève ordinairement de l'indicatif, et pour quelques verbes seulement, qui sont les verbes les plus subductifs, du mode subjontif: *sois, aie, veuille, sache*.

The most comprehensive overview of the imperative, as I have already pointed out is in Curat (1991:151–170), and Curat demonstrates that even the *verbes de puissance* do not always use subjunctive forms, but that there is a certain amount of interplay between subjunctive and indicative forms in the imperative of these verbs. If, for example, the imperative of *vouloir* shows an indicative inflection on a subjunctive stem (e.g. *veuillez*), this is not the only form to be found. With the idiom *en vouloir à quelqu'un*, "to have it in for someone", the indicative stem may be found, and Curat quotes the following (1991:159):

> Ne m'en voulez pas, monsieur, ce n'est pas moi qui fait les règlements
> "Don't take it out on me, sir, I'm not the one who makes the rules"

Many of Curat's examples are from comic strips, and in one of these illustrations a confident and expansive boat owner is saying to a timorous boarding passenger "*As pas peur...*" The force of this seems to be "No need to be afraid" rather than the "Don't be afraid" which would be the sense of the normal "*Aie pas peur*".

There has been, unfortunately, an orthographic tradition to delete the final -*s* in the spelling of the imperative, the argument being that since Latin did not have a final -*s* on the imperative singular, it was illogical for a Romance language such as French to have even an orthographic -*s* in this position. The confusion here arises from the fact that Latin had a distinctive morphology of the imperative, whereas French, as Guillaume points out above, simply exploits the morpology of the indicative and subjunctive.

It is quite easy to demonstrate, in fact, that the second person singular imperative form of Modern French is in fact the corresponding indicative form, since the -*s* that is traditionally deleted in the spelling shows up as a liaison consonant in forms such as the following:

(6) vas-y   "go ahead"
(7) verses-y de l'eau "pour some water into it"
(8) cueilles-en   "pick some"

Such usage shows quite clearly that this is the morphology of the indicative, and that the deleting of the final -*s* stems from a confusion of Latin grammar and French grammar.

9.6 *Conclusion*

In order to establish the categories of content, we necessarily rely on the evidence of the morphosyntax, the only directly observable evidence that we have for such categories. We have to be careful, however, not to treat the morphosyntax as the ultimate arbiter of semantic categories, because of the variations created by irregularities in the morphology. These irregularities then become an object of study on their own because of the opportunities that they allow for marking semantic subsets, which may be distinguished either morphologically (as the verbs of potentiality) or syntactically (as the verbs of resultant state), and much work remains to be done in this kind of analysis: in delineating the functioning of meaning that lies behind the morphological or syntactic fact.

CHAPTER TEN
VERBAL PARADIGMS

10. *Introduction: Regular and irregular verbs*
The irregular verbs of our languages are historical remains a little bit like old houses or antique buildings from long ago. Sometimes, they are the products of phonetic change, as in the English *send/sent* or the contrasts *dois/devons* and *bois/buvons* in French. Sometimes they are the traces of a long-past morphology, now out of date, like the 'strong' verbs of German and English, which still carry vocalic distinctions that go back to the ablaut system of Indo-European.

There are morphological descriptions, in Martinet 1967 and Dubois 1967, repeated in Matte 1989, that classify the verbs of French according to the number of different (or allomorphic) bases or stems, starting with *être*, next with verbs having 6 or 5 bases, ending with verbs with a single base. Speakers tend, as we have seen (9.1), to regularize this morphological turmoil, so that the expression system tends to become a faithful reflection of the corresponding content system.

Consequently, when it comes to creating a new verb, it is normal to employ the morphology of the regular verbs, the paradigm considered 'alive', and not those of the irregular verbs which have a variety of paradigms which are all considered 'dead'. In similar fashion German and English produce new verbs according to the 'weak' paradigm of verbs classified as regular, and are slowly abandoning the 'strong' paradigms.

10.1 *Verbal paradigms of French*
As we know, Classical Latin had four verbal paradigms which, through regular phonological change, gave the following infinitive suffixes in Modern French:

(1) -āre > -er, (2) -ēre > -oir, (3) -ĕre > -re, (4) -īre > -ir.

But French, like other Romance languages, reduced the four conjugations of Latin to three. (Romance languages differ in the manner of making this reduction). The three French patterns are as follows: (1) verbs of the *aimer* pattern (2) verbs of the *finir* pattern (3) verbs of the *vendre* pattern. These are the three regular paradigms of Modern French; the verbs with the infinitive in *-oir* are all irregular.

One could ask why the Romance languages retained three verb conjugations when they kept very little from the five noun declensions of Latin. For most verbs in the Romance languages, it is simply a matter of thematic vowel difference, variation without any observable meaning, and normally neologisms take their morphology from a single paradigm.

For French, however, things are not quite that simple. We know that neologisms (*stopper, téléphoner, téléviser*) follow the morphology of the *aimer* pattern. But this is only partially true: there are also neologisms, such as *amerrir*, "to land on the water, the sea (*la mer*)", *alunir* "to land on the moon (*la lune*)", after the model of *atterrir* "to land (*la terre*)", which take their morphology from the pattern of *finir*. Thus, there are two verbal paradigms in Modern French which can be considered 'living'.

If, in fact, we admit the existence of two living paradigms, we should expect that there will be a difference of meaning, between the two. It is not surprising then, that one of the two paradigms serves one kind of verb, while the other serves all the rest. This amounts to admitting the existence of a special, marked paradigm, called the inchoative, and an ordinary, unmarked paradigm, both 'living'. As Kobayashi (1988) has shown, not all verbs of the *-ir* conjugation have the inchoative meaning, because some of them are morphological relics, but the majority do, and as we have seen, new inchoative verbs are still added to the paradigm.

We know that the morphology of the *finir* paradigm is not at all what one would expect historically and that the evolution of this paradigm is quite different in French from the evolution which one could call normal, which the same Latin paradigm has given in Spanish and in Portuguese. In Italian and Romanian certain changes have been made in the same direction as in French, but French has gone much farther than other languages in establishing a new morphology by means of the /-sk-/ suffix of Classical Latin.

10.2 *Derivational verb suffixes of Latin*

Latin, following the common pattern of IndoEuropean languages, used verb suffixes which followed the radical, and preceded the flexional ending. The purpose of these suffixes was to express differences of lexical aspect, or *Aktionsart*. The suffix /-it-/, for example, (Ernout 1953:140–141) gives the verb a 'frequentative' or 'iterative' sense: based on *crepare* "to make noise", we have *crepitare* "to make a continuous noise"; on *rogare* "to ask", we have *rogitare* "to keep asking". The suffix /-sk-/ has an inchoative meaning, marking the entry into a state, as in the following examples (Ernout 1953: 133, here translated):

This suffix has served among other things to form the numerous group of inchoatives of form -asco, -esco, -isco, derived from verbs, from adjectives or from nouns, as in the following:

ama-sco	"I begin to like (amo)"
cale-sco	"I overheat (caleo)"
compe-sco	"I contain, I repress"
obdormi-sco	"I go to sleep (dormio)"
dure-sco	"I become hard (durus)"
igne-sco	"I ignite (ignis)"
ira-scor	"I get angry (ira)"
vespera-scit	"evening is falling (vesper)"
invetera-sco	"I age (vetus)"

This formation with -sco had good fortune in Latin. The suffix continued to survive in the Romance languages, particularly in Italian and in French where it spread into the present of most verbs from -īre: French *je finis, nous finissons* "I finish, we finish"; Italian *finisco, finiscono* "I finish, they finish".

10.3 *The French suffix /-i(s)-/*

Thus French has created, in adding the Latin suffix /-sk-/ in a regular way to verbs of Latin's fourth conjugation /-īre/, a systematic morphology of the inchoative. Added to the thematic vowel /-ī-/ (a suffix itself originally) to give /-īsk-/, this suffix, through normal evolution, has become /-is-/ in French before a vowel, /-i-/ when in the final position and before a consonant. Thus, verbs of conjugation *finir* present the suffix /-i(s)-/ between the root and the inflexional ending, a suffix which seems to confer an inchoative meaning.

In the participle *finissant*, for example, one can find the radical /fin-/, the suffix /-i(s)-/ and the inflectional ending /-ã/, the unique mark of the present participle in French. If one does not admit that the suffix /-i(s)-/ is a word formative, a derivation marker, it is necessary to show, as is done in traditional grammars, that the morph of the present participle is *-issant* for verbs of the *finir* pattern, confusing the suffix, in stem final position, and the real inflexion.

Nevertheless, in the paradigm of the present indicative of *finir*, in the singular, we find the suffix /-i(s)-/ under the form of its shortened allomorph (without the /s/) because of the historical loss of the /s/ (a) in the final position (1st and 2nd person) and (b) before a consonant (3rd person):

Latin	Old French	Modern French
finisco	je finis	/fin-i/
finiscis	tu finis	/fin-i/
finiscit	il finist	/fin-i/

In the plural of the same paradigm we find the same suffix /-i(s)-/ under the form of its extended form which includes an /s/ curiously in position of axial consonant (see next section), and the plural endings:

Latin	Old French	Modern French
finiscimus	nous finissons	/fin-is-õ/
finiscitis	vous finissez	/fin-is-e/
finiscunt	ils finissent	/fin-is-(ə)/

Throughout the present of verbs of the *finir* conjugation, consequently, one finds a suffix /-i(s)-/, which was used in the Latin era to indicate an inchoative sense, that is the entry into a new state. For *finir* this would be without doubt the state of completion: for *rougir, jaunir, noircir*, etc., a change of colour, for *atterrir, amérir, alunir*, the arrival at the surface and so on. Historically this suffix has been used to make inchoative verbs derived from substantives: *aigrir, chérir, brunir, grossir, blêmir, mûrir*; sometimes with the prefix *a-: affaiblir, attendrir, abrutir, amincir, assainir, assourdir*; sometimes with *en-: enrichir, enhardir*, and so on.

Because of neologisms such as *alunir* in Modern French, it is proper to insist that the suffix is still alive, and that it must be treated as a formative element, a suffix which is part of the stem, not part of the inflexions.

Once the real difference between theme and inflexion is seen for the *finir* conjugation, striking similarities become apparent between the three verbal paradigms of French:

	AIMER	FINIR	VENDRE
je	—	(-i)-	—
tu	—	(-i)-	—
il/elle	—	(-i)-	—
nous	õ	(-is)õ	(-C)õ
vous	e	(-is)e	(-C)e
ils/elles	—	(-is)-	(-C)-

FIGURE 1

As far as concerns the paradigm of present tense, it is obvious that in French the three different paradigms that are typical of Romance languages have been effectively reduced to a single pattern.

10.4 *The axial consonant*

The only difference between the present of *finir* pattern verbs and those of the *vendre* pattern, for example, is the presence in the former of the inchoative suffix; these two paradigms have in common that which G. Guillaume called (1984:40) "the axial consonant, which intervenes between the stem theme and the audible inflection". The /s/ of *finir* and the /d/ of *vendre*, are not pronounced when in final position, but are always pronounced when in inter-vocalic position, when followed by audible inflections.

For historical reasons, most axial consonants of the verbs of the *aimer* conjuguation do not occur in the final position. For verbs such as *vider, inviter, prouver*, etc., for example, there is always a consonant before the audible flexions, but this consonant is pronounced in the singular, having been historically protected by the schwa (representing the unaccented /a/ of Latin), which later was lost. Thus, for the thousands of verbs of this paradigm, the axial consonant at the end of the root is also pronounced in the singular. But there is also a small group of verbs: *lier, jouer, créer, évoluer*, etc., which do not have an axial consonant. It is interesting to note that popular French has tried to fill this gap: one hears *ils lisent (= lient), ils jousent (= jouent)*. (If this tentative regularisation had succeeded, it would have completely regularised the whole morphology of the present in French!)

10.5 *Other correspondences in the paradigms*

Besides the present of the indicative, there are many other verb forms where there is identity between the three main paradigms of French, in spellings (Figure 2) as well as in pronunciation:

	AIMER	FINIR	VENDRE
present part.	-ant	-(iss)ant	-ant
imperfect	-ais	-(iss)ais	-ais
pres. subj.	-e	-(iss)e	-e

FIGURE 2

We should be able to add, to these paradigms, the future and the conditional, but one troublesome little detail hinders us: *vendre* keeps its axial consonant before the /-r-/ which marks these tenses, whereas in the infinitive *finir* and in the forms *finirai* and *finirais*, which historically arise from the infinitive, there is no trace of the axial consonant.

We know, certainly, that *s* was lost throughout Old French before a consonant, but this is not the final explanation of this divergence, which is found in the fact that the infinitive of the Latin *finire* stayed true to its morphology of the fourth conjugation (-ire), and never added the suffix /-sk-/, which would have made it a verb of the third conjugation:

* *finiskere*, which would then have given
* *finisre* in Old French which would have led to
* *finire* in Modern French (just like *lire, rire, dire, écrire*).

There are, however, certain unusual infinitives such as *noircir, éclaircir* "to blacken, to clear/clarify", where the *-c-* element has been thought to represent Latin *-sk-*. The evidence is dubious, however, since this would indicate that in *éclaircissement* the suffix occurs twice. Kobayashi (1988:400) quotes Meyer-Lübke as indicating that a completely convincing explanation of this *-c-* suffix is still wanting.

There are, nevertheless, facts which suggest that one should analyse the infinitive of the pattern *finir* in Modern French as /fin-i-r/ with the inchoative suffix: this would mean that this form has undergone an historical re-analysis.

Historically, in fact, the final /-r/ was lost in infinitives of the *finir* conjugation just as it was in the infinitives of the *aimer* conjugation. But, whereas the vowel /-e/ of *aimer* has remained as a sufficient marker of the infinitive (and the past participle) of *-er* verbs, the vowel /-i/ of the infinitive /fini/ (18th century) must have been analysed as representing the suffix /-i(s)-/, with the result that the /r/ of the infinitive was restored (Bourciez 1958:179). From this restoration, there are two results: (1) infinitives of the patterns *finir* and *vendre* now have the same phonological mark /-r/, (2) *finir* now distiguishes the infinitive /finir/ from the past participle /fini/, which otherwise (like those of the pattern *aimer* where one has only /eme/ for both) would not have been distinguished.

To analyse the infinitive of the pattern *finir* as /fin-i-r/, where the vowel /-i-/ represents the suffix /-i(s)-, and /-r/ the unique mark of the infinitive, also resolves the problem of the difference between *finir* and *vendre* in the infinitive, the future and the conditional. For those verbs of the *vendre* conjugation, in fact, only the verbs of which the axial consonant is of the plosive type (e.g. *vendre, vaincre*) keep this consonant in the forms of the infinitive, future and conditional. The verbs which have an axial consonant of the fricative type lose the axial consonant in these forms, just as is done with *finir*:

verb:	ECRIRE	LIRE	FINIR
axial consonant:	/v/	/z/	/s/
present:	ekri	li	fini
infinitive:	ekrir	lir	finir
future:	ekrire	lire	finire
conditional:	ekrirɛ	lirɛ	finirɛ

FIGURE 3

(Other verbs of the same type: *nuire, luire, conduire, plaire, taire*. There are two exceptions: *vivre* and *suivre*).

10.6 The forms of the Latin perfect

So far, we have shown all forms of the *finir* conjugation as belonging to a pattern common to the other conjugations, except the passé simple, the imperfect of the subjunctive, and the past participle.

In the passé simple and the imperfect of the subjunctive one immediately notes the identity of the paradigm of *finir* with that of *vendre*, but this time without there being question of a suffix /-i(s)-/ to maintain the identity: the two paradigms are simply identical, and there is no suffix /-i(s)/ in the passé simple, nor, which is more surprising, in the imperfect of the subjunctive:

>   que je finisse, vendisse   que nous finissions, vendissions
>   que tu finisses, vendisses   que vous finissiez, vendissiez
>   qu'il finît, vendît   qu'ils finissent, vendissent

Everywhere, in fact, in the Passé simple and the imperfect subjunctive, we find a single identical morphology in the paradigms of both the *finir* conjugation and the *vendre* conjugation. In *français populaire* this morphology was extended even to the *aimer* conjugation. It was only in the nineteenth century, according to Dauzat (1935:202) that the passé simple of the *je tombis* type disappeared from the popular speech of Paris. Such forms may still be heard in certain remote rural areas of Atlantic Canada in the Acadian dialect made famous by Antonine Maillet in *La Sagouine* (1974).

We do not have to look far for an explanation of the lack of the suffix /-i(s)/ in the passé simple and imperfect subjunctive: Latin never used the /-sk/ suffix with the perfect forms of the verbal paradigm. Inchoatives represent actions: the idea of a progression towards a new state, the movement of entry into a new state. Once the action is complete, the inchoative element is no longer relevant.

Thus we see an explanation for the identity of the paradigms of the passé simple and the imperfect subjunctive in the *finir* and *vendre* conjugations. The morphology of the passé simple simply comes from either /-*ivī*, -*ivistī*, -*ivit*/ or /-*īvī*, -*īvistī*, -*īvit*/ with loss of the intervocalic *v* and the fusion of the two vowels, be they short or long. The same is true for the imperfect subjunctive, where one finds the following historical evolution of the inflexions:

>   -ivissem   >   -isse   >   /is/
>   -ivisses   >   -isses   >   /is/
>   -ivisset   >   -ist   >   ît > /i/

In Old French the -s- was lost before following consonant, resulting in the lengthening of the preceding vowel; this vowel length was marked by a circumflex accent in the orthography of Old French. In the plural forms of the subjunctive the element /-is-/ also comes from the combination of the thematic vowel with the Latin subjunctive inflexions, not the suffix /-isk/.

10.7 *The past participle*

The past participle /fini/, being also a retrospective element, which finds its historical origin in the Latin perfect paradigms, has not adopted the suffix /sk/. Consequently, this participle is a regular reflex of Latin *finitu(m)*.

But there is, yet again, an interesting parallel between the paradigm of the verbs of the *perdre* conjugation and that of the *finir* conjugation. It is normal, for example, for the verbs of the *perdre* conjugation which have a plosive axial consonant (and which keep (see 10.5 above) this axial consonant in the infinitive, in the future, and in the conditional) to adopt the flexion /-y/ for the past participle: *perdu, convaincu*. But the verbs which have a fricative axial consonant (e.g. *écrire, dire, conduire, luire, nuire* — the exception is *lire*) have a past participle in /-i/ like the verbs of the *finir* conjugation. Here there is a clear parallelism (phonological, it goes without saying) between *écrit, dit, conduit, nui, lui* and the participles of the *fini* pattern.

It is this same parallelism which leads us to suggest that the participle *fini*, also, has been re-analysed as /fin-i/, and that, for modern speakers, the final vowel of this form is the normal allomorph of the suffix /-i(s)-/ of the verbs of this pattern. A paradigmatic comparison between *finir* and *écrire*, for example reveals that throughout the paradigm (except in the passé simple and in the imperfect subjunctive — which have disappeared, it should be noted, from spoken French), the final vowel of the stem of the verb *écrire*, to which the axial consonant /-v-/ is added before an audible inflexion, corresponds exactly to the vowel /i/ of the suffix /-i(s)-/ of the verbs of the pattern *finir*.

10.8 *Conclusion*

The fact that there are two 'living' conjugations in French indicates that there are two morphological sets which are still meaningful. The analysis shows that the suffix /-i(s)/ has an inchoative meaning in all the forms of the paradigm of *finir* which are still living in modern spoken French, morphology which is used in the formation of verbs with an inchoative meaning, whereas the regular morphology of the pattern *aimer* completes the paradigmatic model of other verbal neologisms.

Tobin has reported (1993:344–348) that research in the French lexicon shows that whereas the vast majority of verbs are of the -*er* type:

-er:	6448
-oir:	42
-re:	304
-ir:	413

there are in fact a dozen minimal pairs contrasting the -*er* morphology with the -*ir* morphology, of which the following are some of the most interesting.

atterrer	"to overwhelm, knock down [to the ground]"
atterrir	"to land, alight, run ashore"
éclairer	"to light, brighten"
éclaircir	"to clarify, clear up"
forcer	"to force, compel [use strength]"
forcir	"to broaden out, fill out [become stronger]"

The existence of such minimal pairs is a further indication of the meaningful nature of this derivational contrast.

Our survey of the morphology of the paradigms of the French verb reveals that there is a certain pressure to level the morphological differences when they convey no meaning difference, and equally to exploit and expand morphological differences that may be used as vehicles for making new meaning distinctions, as in the development of the Latin *īre* conjugation into a new morphology for inchoative verbs.

Nothing could better illustrate the necessity of a close examination and study of both content system and expression system. In such studies it is important to keep in mind the priority of content over expression, as expounded by Guillaume's two laws, 'the Law of Coherence', and 'the Law of Simple Sufficiency' (1.3, 9.2). It is in content that systemic coherence is found; expression is not equally coherent, irregularities and turbulence being frequent phenomena. The coherence in expression (in the paradigmatic morphology, for example) will always be sufficient, however, to delineate the cognitive structure of the corresponding content system.

It is also important to take into account the fact that the linguistic sign, although arbitrary in the limited and specific sense intended by Saussure, may nevertheless be motivated (as Saussure himself pointed out: 1916:131), and that such motivation may be an important factor in linguistic change. In fact it is the very arbitrary nature of the linguistic sign that permits linguistic change: because the sign (morpheme) has no *necessary* relation with the significate (sememe), it may well undergo on the one hand the effects of regular sound change, or on the other hand the constant pressure to regularize by analogy.

BIBLIOGRAPHY OF WORKS REFERRED TO OR CONSULTED

Ayres-Bennett, Wendy, & Janice Carruthers. 1992. "Une regrettable et fort disgracieuse faute de français? The description and analysis of the French *surcomposés* from 1530 to the present day." *Transactions of the Philological Society* 90.187-218.
Barral, Marcel. *1980. L'imparfait du subjonctif: Etude sur l'emploi et la concordance des temps du subjonctif.* Paris: Picard.
Benveniste, Emile. 1950. "Actif et moyen dans le verbe". *Journal de Psychologie* 43.121-129.
——. 1966. *Problèmes de linguistique générale*. Paris: Gallimard.
——. 1966a. "Les relations de temps dans le verbe. Benveniste 1966.235-50.
Binnick, Robert I. 1991. *Time and the Verb*. Oxford: Oxford University Press.
Black, James R. 1975. *Middle Voice in French*. Unpublished M.A. Thesis, Memorial University of Newfoundland.
Blanche-Benveniste, Claire. 1984. "Commentaires sur le passif en français". *Travaux du cercle linguistique d'Aix-en-Provence* 2.1-23.
Bloch, Bernard. 1947. "English verb inflection". *Language* 23.399-418. (Repr. in Joos 1957.243-54.)
——. & George L. Trager. 1942. *Outline of Linguistic Analysis*. Baltimore, Md: Linguistic Society of America.
Bloomfield, Leonard. 1926. "A Set of Postulates for the Science of Language". *Language* 2.153-64. (Repr. in Joos 1957/1966.26-31.)
——. 1933. *Language*. New York: Holt.
Bondy, Léon. 1958. "En marge des discussions sur les modes et les temps". *Le français moderne* 26.93-100.
Bonnard, Henri. 1964. "Avec Arne Klum vers une théorie scientifique des marques temporelles". *Le français moderne* 32.85-100.
——. 1974. "Les axiomes *temps* et *mode*". *Le français moderne* 42.72-89.
——. 1988. "Verbe et temps". *L'information grammaticale* 36.3-6.
Bourciez, Edouard. 1958. *Phonétique française*. Paris: Klincksieck.
Brogyanyi, Bela. 1983. "A Few Remarks on the Origin of the Phrase 'où tout se tient'". *Historiographia Linguistica* 10.143-47.

Bull, W.E. 1963. *Time, tense, and the verb: A study in theoretical and applied linguistics, with particular attention to Spanish*. University of California Publications in Linguistics 19. Berkeley: University of California Press.

Burston, J.L. 1979. "The pronominal verb construction in French. An argument against the fortuitous homonomy hypothesis". *Lingua* 48.147-176.

———. 1982. "French reflexive clitics and argument binding". *Australian Journal of Linguistics* 2.213-221.

Chevalier, Jean-Claude. 1969. "Remarques comparées sur l'infinitif espagnol et l'infinitif français". *Bulletin hispanique* 71, 1-2.140-73.

———. 1978. *Verbe et phrase: les problèmes de la voix en espagnol et en français*. Paris: Editions hispaniques.

Clarke, Herbert H. 1973. "Space, time, semantics, and the child". *Cognitive development and the acquisition of language*, ed. by T. Moore. New York: Academic Press.

Claudé, Pierre. 1985. *Grammaire du verbe français*. Strasbourg: Annales du Centre Régional de Documentation Pédagogique de Strasbourg.

Clédat, L. 1903. "Le participe passé, le passé composé et les deux auxiliaires". *Révue de philologie française et de littérature* 17.19-62.

Coates, Jennifer. 1983. *The semantics of the modal auxiliaries*. London: Oxford University Press.

Cohen, Marcel. 1965. *Le subjonctif en français contemporain*. Paris: Société d'Edition d'Enseignement Supérieur.

Comrie, Bernard. 1976. *Aspect*. Cambridge: Cambridge University Press.

———. 1981. *Language Universals and Linguistic Typology*. Chicago: University of Chicago Press.

———. 1981a. "On Reichenbach's approach to tense". *Papers from the Seventeenth Regional Meeting*, ed. by Roberta A. Hendrick, Carrie S. Masek & Mary Frances Miller. Chicago: Chicago Linguistic Society.

———. 1985. *Tense*. Cambridge Text books in Linguistics. Cambridge: Cambridge University Press.

Cornu, Maurice. 1953. *Les formes surcomposées du français*. Bern: Francke.

Curat, Hervé. 1982. *La locution verbale en français moderne*. *Cahiers de psychomécanique de langage*. Québec: Presses de l'Université Laval.

———. 1991. *Morphologie verbale et référence temporelle en français moderne*. Genève & Paris: Droz.

———. & Lionel Meney. 1983. Gustave Guillaume et la psycho-systématique du langage. Québec: Presses de l'Université Laval.

Dahl, Östen. 1985. *Tense and aspect systems*. Oxford: Blackwell.

Damourette, Jacques & Edouard Pichon. 1911-1940. *Des mots à la pensée: Essai de grammaire de la langue française*. (7 vols). Paris: d'Autrey.
Dauzat, A. 1935. *Où en sont les études de français*. Paris: d'Autrey.
———. 1937. "Le fléchissement du passé simple et de l'imparfait du subjonctif". *Français moderne* 5.97-112.
Deane, Paul. 1992. *Grammar in Mind and Brain*. Berlin: Mouton de Gruyter.
Dolbec, Jean & Daniel LeFlem. 1981. "Le subjonctif avec *après que*: faute ou variation significative?" *Langues et linguistique* 7.124-54.
Donaldson, W.D. 1973. *French Reflexive Verbs: A Case Grammar Description*. The Hague: Mouton.
Dowty, David. 1991. "Thematic proto-roles and argument selection". *Language* 67.574-619.
Dubois, Jean. 1967. *Grammaire structurale du français: le verbe*. Paris: Larousse.
Duffley, Patrick J. 1985. *Les emplois du participe présent en français et en anglais*. Québec: Centre International de Recherche sur le Bilinguisme, Publication B-147, Université Laval.
Ernout, Alfred. 1953. *Morphologie historique du latin*. 3e édition. Paris: Klincksieck.
Fleischmann, Suzanne. 1982a. *The future in thought and language. Diachronic evidence from Romance*. Cambridge: Cambridge University Press.
———. 1982b. "The past and the future? Are they 'coming' or 'going'?", *Proceedings of the Eighth Annual Meeting of the Berkeley Linguistics Society* 8.322-34.
Florea, Ligia-Stela. 1986. "Approche contrastive du subjonctif dans la perspective guillaumienne. Domaine français-roumain". *Revue roumaine de linguistique* 31, 6.557-567.
Foley, William A. & Robert D. Van Valin Jr. 1984. *Functional Syntax and Universal Grammar*. Cambridge: University Press.
Foulet, L. 1925. "Le développement des formes surcomposées". *Romania* 51. 203-252.
Frei, Henri. 1971. *La Grammaire des fautes*. Genève: Slatkine Reprints. (Réimpression de l'édition de Paris-Genève, 1929).
Fuchs, Catherine & Anne-Marie Léonard. 1979. *Vers une théorie des aspects: Les systèmes du français et de l'anglais*. The Hague: Mouton.
Garcia, Erica. 1975. *The Role of Theory in Linguistic Analysis: the Spanish Pronoun System*. Amsterdam: North-Holland.
Garey, Howard B. 1957. "Verbal aspect in French". *Language* 33, 2. 91-110.

Garnier, Georges. 1984. "L'aspect verbal en français et en anglais". *La traduction. De la théorie à la didactique*, ed. by M. Ballard. Lille: Presses Universitaires de Lille.
———. 1985. *Linguistique et Traduction. Éléments de systématique verbale comparée du français et de l'anglais*. Caen: Paradigme.
Geneste, Philippe. 1987. *Gustave Guillaume et Jean Piaget: contribution à la pensée génétique*. Paris: Klincksieck.
Geniušiené, E. 1987. *The typology of reflexives*. Berlin: Mouton de Gruyter.
Givón, T. 1973. "The time-axis phenomenon". *Language* 49.890-925.
Glatigny, Michel. 1981. "Psychomécanique et enseignement des temps verbaux en français". Joly & Hirtle 1981.445-456.
Glättli, Hugo. 1970. "A propos du mode régi par *après que*". *Vox Romanica* 29, 1.264-72
———. 1970a. "Encore des observations sur *après que* suivi du subjonctif". *Vox Romanica* 29, 2.279-82.
———. 1974. "Sur le mode régi par *jusqu'à ce que*". *Revue de linguistique romane* 38.210-22.
Golian, Milan. 1979. *L'aspect verbal en français*. Hamburg: Helmut Buske Verlag.
Gougenheim, Georges. 1939. *Système grammatical de la langue française*. Paris: d'Artrey.
Grevisse, Maurice. 1969. *Le bon usage*. 9th ed. Gembloux: Duculot.
——— & A. Goosse. 1986. *Le bon usage*. 12th edn. Gembloux: Duculot.
Guillaume, Gustave. 1919. *Le Problème de l'article et sa solution dans la langue française*. Paris: Hachette.
———. 1929. *Temps et Verbe*. (Reprinted 1965). Paris: Champion.
———. 1933. "Immanence et transcendance dans la catégorie du verbe: esquisse d'une théorie psychologique du verbe". [*Journal de Psychologie 1933*]. Guillaume 1964.46-58.
———. 1943. "Existe-t-il un déponent en français?". *Le français moderne* 11.9-30. Guillaume 1964.127-142.
———. 1945. *L'architectonique du temps dans les langues classiques*. Copenhagen: Munksgaard.
———. 1951. "La représentation du temps dans la langue française". [*Le français moderne* 1951]. Guillaume 1964.184-207.
———. 1952. *La langue est-elle ou n'est-elle pas un système?* Cahiers de Psychomécanique, 1.). Quebec: Presses de l'Université Laval. Guillaume 1964.220-240.

Guillaume, Gustave. 1964. *Langage et science du langage*. Paris: Nizet; Québec: Presses de l'Université Laval.
———. 1971. *Leçons de Linguistique 1: Structure sémiologique et structure psychique de la langue française I*. Paris: Klincksieck; Québec: Presses de l'Université Laval.
———. 1971a. *Leçons de Linguistique 2: Psycho-systématique du langage. Principes, méthodes et applications*. Paris: Klincksieck; Québec: Presses de l'Université Laval.
———. 1973. *Principes de linguistique théorique*. Paris: Klincksieck; Québec: Presses de l'Université Laval.
———. 1974. *Leçons de linguistique 4: Structure sémiologique et structure psychique de la langue française II*. Québec: Presses de l'Université Laval; Paris: Klincksieck.
———. 1982. *Leçons de linguistique 5. Systèmes linguistiques et successivité des systèmes*. Québec: Presses de l'Université Laval; Lille: Presses Universitaires.
———. 1984. *Foundations for a Science of Language*. (Translation by Walter Hirtle and John Hewson of Guillaume 1973). Amsterdam & Philadelphia: John Benjamins.
———. 1986. *Leçons de linguistique 7: Esquisse d'une grammaire descriptive de la langue française II*. Quebec: Presses de l'Université Laval; Lille: Presses Universitaires.
———. 1989. *Leçons de linguistique 9: Grammaire particulière du français et grammaire générale*. Québec: Presses de l'Université Laval; Lille: Presses Universitaires.
———. 1990. *Leçons de linguistique 10: Esquisse d'une grammaire descriptive de la langue française (II)*. Québec: Presses de l'Université Laval; Lille: Presses Universitaires.
———. 1991. *Leçons de linguistique 11: Esquisse d'une grammaire descriptive de la langue française (III)*. Québec: Presses de l'Université Laval; Lille: Presses Universitaires.
———. 1992. *Leçons de linguistique 12: Leçons de l'année 1938-1939*. Québec: Presses de l'Université Laval; Lille: Presses Universitaires.
Guimier, Claude. 1985. *Syntaxe de l'adverbe anglais*. Lille: Presses de l'Université de Lille.
Haltus, G. 1986. "L'emploi des formes surcomposées dans les variétés linguistiques du français et l'attitude des grammairiens". *Actes du XVIIième congrés international de linguistique et philologie romane* IV. 423-437. Aix-en-Provence: Université; Marseilles: Lafitte.

Hatcher, Anna.G. 1942. *Reflexive Verbs: Latin, Old French, Modern French*. Baltimore: John Hopkins Press.
Havet, Louis. 1919. Review of Guillaume 1919. *Journal des savants* 5.158.
Hewson, John. 1972. "The Essential Guillaume: An Explicative Survey". *Linguistics* 92.13-27.
____. 1976. "La voix moyenne des langues romanes" *Atti del 14 Congresso Internazionale di Linguistica e Filologia romanza* V.325-330. Napoli Macchiaroli; Amsterdam & Philadelphia: John Benjamins.
____. 1984. "Notes for the reader". In Introduction to Guillaume 1984.
____. 1987. "Translating *langue* and *langage*". *Papers from the Tenth Annual Meeting of the Atlantic Provinces Linguistic Association*, ed. by A.M. Kinloch et al, 64-73. Fredericton, NB: University of New Brunswick.
____. 1988. "Voice in French: Active, Middle and Passive". *Actes de langue française et de linguistique* 1.39-57.
____. 1988a. "Le suffixe aspectuel /-i(s)/ et les paradigmes verbaux du français". *Papers from the Eleventh Annual Conference of the Atlantic Provinces Linguistic Association*, ed. Rosemary Babitch,75-88. Shippagan, New Brunswick: Centre Universitaire de Shippagan.
____. 1989. "Tense vs. Aspect in the French Verb". *Actes de langue française et de linguistique* 2.117-127.
____. 1990. "The Auxiliary *DO* in English". *Journal of the Atlantic Provinces Linguistic Association* 12.39-52.
____. 1990a. "What is a present?" *Papers from the Thirteenth Annual Meeting of the Atlantic Provinces Linguistic Association*, ed. by David H. Jory,50-56. Saint John, NB: University of New Brunswick.
____. 1990b. "What is a Subjunctive?" *Actes de langue française et de linguistique* 3.157-168.
____. 1990c. "'Un système où tout se tient': Origin and evolution of an idea". *History and Historiography of Linguistics. Proceedings of the Fourth International Conference on the History of the Language Sciences, Vol. 2*, ed. by H-J Niederehe and E.F.K.Koerner,787-794. Amsterdam & Philadelphia: John Benjamins.
Hirschbühler, Paul. 1986. "The middle and the pseudo-middle in French". *Advances in Romance Linguistics* ed. by J.-P. Montreuil & David Birdsong. Dordrecht: Foris.
Hirtle, Walter H. 1964. "The English Present Subjunctive". *Canadian Journal of Linguistics* 9.75-82.
____. 1967. *The Simple and Progressive Forms*. Québec: Presses de l'Université Laval.

Hirtle, Walter H. 1975. *Time, Aspect and the Verb*. Québec: Presses de l'Université Laval.
Hjelmslev, Louis. 1935. *La Catégorie des cas*. Aarhus: Universitetsforlaget. (Reprint Munich: Wilhelm Fink, 1972).
_____. 1959. *Essais linguistiques*. Copenhagen: Nordisk Sprog og Kulturforlag. (New edn., Paris: Ed. de Minuit, 1971).
Hockett, Charles F. 1967. "Where the Tongue Slips, there Slip I". *To Honor Roman Jakobson*. The Hague: Mouton.
Imbs, Paul. 1953. *Le subjonctif en français moderne*. Strasbourg: Université de Strasbourg.
_____. 1960. *L'emploi des temps verbaux en français moderne: essai de grammaire descriptive*. Bibliothèque Française et Romane publiée par le Centre de Philologie Romane de la Faculté des Lettres de Strasbourg, série A: Manuels et Études Linguistiques, I. Paris: Klincksieck.
Jakobson, Roman. 1932. "Zur Struktur des russischen Verbums", *Charisteria G. Mathesio quiquagenario*.74ff. (Reprinted in *Readings in Linguistics II*, ed. by Eric P. Hamp et al. Chicago: University Press, 1966).
_____. 1936. "Beitrag zur allgemeinen Kasuslehre". *TCLP* 6.240-88. (Reprinted in *Readings in Linguistics II*, ed. by Eric P. Hamp et al. Chicago: Univ. of Chicago Press, 1966; translated and reprinted in Jakobson 1990).
_____. 1957. "Shifters, verbal categories and the Russian verb." (Repr. in Jakobson 1971)
_____. 1971. *Selected writings II*. The Hague: Mouton.
_____. 1971b. *Studies in Child Language and Aphasia*. The Hague: Mouton.
_____. 1990. *On Language*. Ed. by Linda Waugh & Monique Monville-Burston. Cambridge, MA: Harvard University Press.
Jespersen, Otto. 1922. *Language: Its Nature, Development and Origin*. London: Allen and Unwin.
_____. 1924. *The Philosophy of Grammar*. London: Allen & Unwin. (Paperback version, New York: Norton, 1965).
Johnson, Mark. 1987. *The Body in the Mind: The Bodily Basis of Meaning, Imagination, and Reason*. Chicago: Univ. of Chicago Press.
_____. 1992. "Philosophical implications of cognitive semantics". *Cognitive Linguistics* 3-4.345-366.
Joly, André. 1977. "Les auxiliaires *avoir* et *être*, approche psycho-systématique". *Le français dans le monde* 17.22-8.
Joly, André & Marie-José Lerouge. 1980. "Problèmes de l'analyse du temps en psychomécanique". *La psychomécanique et les théories de l'énonciation* ed. by André Joly, 7-35. Lille: Presses Universitaires de Lille.

Joly, André & Walter Hirtle, eds. 1981. *Langage et psychomécanique du langage. Etudes dédiées à Roch Valin.* Lille: Presses Universitaires; Québec: Presses de l'Université Laval.
Joos, Martin. 1957/1966. *Readings in Linguistics I: The Development of Descriptive Linguistics in America.* 4th ed. Chicago: Univ. of Chicago Press.
Kemmer, Suzanne. 1993. *The Middle Voice.* Amsterdam & Philadelphia: John Benjamins.
Klaiman, M.H. 1991. *Grammatical Voice.* Cambridge: Cambridge University Press.
Kobayashi, Kozue. 1988. "On the Formation of the Romance Inchoative Conjugation — A New Theory". *Romance Philology* 41.394-408.
de Kock, Josse. 1969-70. "Avoir et être, auxiliaires des formes actives, passives et pronominales". *Travaux de Linguistique* (Ghent) 1.13-69.
Koerner, E. F. Konrad. 1984. "French Influence on Saussure". *Canadian Journal of Linguistics/Revue Canadienne de Linguistique* 29.20-41.
Korrel, Lia. 1991. *Duration in English.* Berlin: Mouton de Gruyter.
Labelle, Marie. 1992. "Change of state and valency". *Journal of Linguistics* 28.375-414.
Laflèche, Guy. 1973. "Étude de psycho-systématique sur les valeurs aspectives des temps du passé en français". *Revue des langues romanes,* 80.365-389
Lakoff, G. 1987. *Women, Fire and Dangerous Things.* Chicago: Univ. of Chicago Press.
Lanc, Michèle. 1981. "A propos de quelques problèmes relevant de la relation entre aspect et voix". Joly & Hirtle 1981.195-200.
Langacker, Ronald. W. 1978. "The form and meaning of the English auxiliary". *Language* 54.853-82.
———. 1986. "An Introduction to Cognitive Grammar". *Cognitive Science* 10.1-40.
———. 1987. *Foundations of Cognitive Grammar I. Theoretical Prerequisites.* Stanford: Stanford Univ. Press.
Lazar, Gilbert. 1994. *L'actance.* Paris: Presses Universitaires de France.
LeBidois, Georges & Robert. 1968. *Syntaxe du français moderne* (vol. 1). Paris: Éditions Auguste Picard.
LeFlem, Daniel C. 1984. "Des faits à une théorie du système verbal: le problème du sens". *Langues et Linguistique* 10.123-50.
Lesage, René. 1981. "La chronogénèse peut-elle servir à l'enseignement?" Joly & Hirtle 1981.457-64.
Maillet, Antonine. 1974. *La Sagouine.* Ottawa: Lémeac.
Mansion, J.E. 1959. *A Grammar of Present Day French.* London: Harrap.

Martin, Robert. 1963. "Quelques refléxions sur l'ambiguité du passif et de la 'voix mixte' en français moderne". *Bulletin des jeunes romanistes* 7.32-8.

———. 1971. *Temps et aspect. Essai sur l'emploi des temps narratifs en moyen français*. Bibliothèque Française et Romane, Série A: Manuels et Études Linguistiques, no. 20. Paris: Klincksieck.

Martinet, André. 1967. *Le français sans fard*. Paris: Presses Universitaires de France.

Matte, Edward J. 1989. *French and English Verbal Systems: A Descriptive and Contrastive Synthesis*. New York, Bern, Frankfurt am Main, Paris: Peter Lang.

Meillet, Antoine. 1937. *Introduction à l'étude comparative des langues indo-européennes, 8th.* ed. Paris: Hachette. (First ed., 1903.)

Mélis, L. 1990b. *La voie pronominale*. Paris, Louvain: Duculot.

Mellet, Sylvie. 1981. "L'aspect verbal chez G. Guillaume et ses disciples". *L'information grammaticale*, 9.6-12.

Moignet, Gérard. 1974. *Études de psycho-systématique française*. Paris: Klincksieck.

———. 1980. "La théorie psycho-systématique de l'aspect verbal". *Actes du colloque sur la notion d'aspect*.41-49. Metz: Centre d'Analyse Syntaxique de l'Université de Metz.

———. 1981. *Systématique de la langue française*. Paris: Klincksieck.

Molho, Maurice. 1959. "Impératif, indicatif et subjonctif". *Le français moderne* 27,3.199-203.

Ouellet, Jacques. 1987. "Sémantique grammaticale du verbe I". *Langues et Linguistique* 13.183-230

———. 1988. "Sémantique grammaticale du verbe II". *Langues et Linguistique* 14.199-249.

Palmer, Frank R. 1990. *Modality and the English modals*. 2nd. edn. London and New York: Longman.

Peeters, Bert. 1991. "Encore une fois 'où tout se tient'". *Historiographia Linguistica* 17.427-436.

Penfield, Wilder, & Lamar Roberts. 1959. *Speech and Brain Mechanisms*. Princeton: Princeton University Press.

Perkins, M.R. 1983. *Modal expressions in English*. London: Frances Pinter.

Perrot, Jean. 1956. "Autour des passés. Réflexions sur les systèmes verbaux du latin et du français". *Revue des langues romanes*, 72.137-69.

Pfister, Max. 1974. "L'imparfait, le passé simple et le passé composé en français moderne". *Revue de linguistique romane* 38.400-417.

Pichon, E. 1934. "L'auxiliaire *être* dans le français d'aujourd'hui". *Le français moderne* 2.317-30.
Pohl, Jacques. 1974. "Le constituant verbal". *Le français moderne* 42.341-344.
Posner, Rebecca. 1972. "Aspects of Aspect and Tense in French" *Romance Philology* 26.94-111.
Pottier, Bernard. 1978. "Les voix du français. Sémantique et syntaxe". *Cahiers de lexicologie* 33,2.3-39.
──. 1980. "Temps et espace". *Hommage à la mémoire de Gérard Moignet. Travaux de linguistique et de littérature* 18,1.31-42.
──. 1980a. "Essai de syntèse sur l'aspect". *La notion d'aspect*, ed. by J. David & R. Martin, 239-46. Metz-Paris.
Quirk, Randolph, Sidney Greenbaum, Geoffrey Leech, & Jan Svartik. 1972. *A Grammar of Contemporary English*. London: Longman.
Reichenbach, Hans. 1947. *Elements of symbolic logic*. New York: Harcourt, Collier-Macmillan.
Reid, T.B.W. 1955. "On the analysis of the tense system of French". *Revue de linguistique romane* 19.23-38.
──. 1970. "Verbal aspect in Modern French". *The French Language: Studies presented to L.C. Harmer* ed. by T.G.S. Combe & Peter Rickard,146-71. London: Harrap.
Rocchetti, Alvaro. 1981. "De l'indo-européen aux langues romanes: une hypothèse sur l'évolution du système verbal". Joly & Hirtle 1981.254-66.
Rosch, Eleanor, Carolyn Mervis, Wayne Gray, Davis Johnson & Penny Boyes-Braem. 1976. "Basic Objects in Natural Categories". *Cognitive Psychology* 7.573-605.
Rothemberg, Mira. 1974. *Les verbes à la fois transitifs et intransitifs en français contemporain*. The Hague: Mouton.
Roulland, D. 1989. "La notion de *verbe auxiliaire* chez G. Guillaume". *La question de l'auxiliaire*. Travaux linguistique du CERLICO. Rennes: Presses Universitaires de Rennes.
Ruwet, Nicolas. 1972. "Les constructions pronominales en français". *Le français moderne* 40.102-5.
Sapir, Edward. 1921. *Language: an introduction to the study of speech*. New York: Harcourt, Brace & World.
──. 1933. "La Réalité psychologique des phonèmes", *Journal de Psychologie Normale et Pathologique* 30.247-65. (English translation published in *Selected Writings of Edward Sapir* 46-60. Berkeley: Univ. of California Press, 1949.)

Saussure, Ferdinand de. 1879. *Mémoire sur le système primitif des voyelles dans les langues indo-européennes*. Leipzig: B.A.Teubner. (Repr. Hildesheim: G. Olms, 1968.)
———. 1916. *Cours de linguistique générale*. Ed. by Charles Bally & Albert Sechehaye with the collaboration of Albert Riedlinger. Lausanne & Paris: Payot.
Schogt, Henry G. 1968. *Le système verbale du français contemporain*. The Hague: Mouton.
Stefanini, Jean. 1954. "La Tradition grammaticale française et les temps surcomposés". *Annales de la Faculté des Lettres* (Aix/Marseille) 28.67-108.
———. 1962. *La Voix pronominale en ancien et en moyen français*. Aix-en-Provence: Éditions Ophrys.
———. 1971. "A propos des verbes pronominaux". *Langue française* 11.110-125.
Tesnière, Lucien. 1959. *Eléments de syntaxe structurale*. Paris: Klincksieck.
Tobin, Yishai. 1993. *Aspect in the English Verb: Process and Result in Language*. London and New York: Longman.
Toman, Jindrich. 1987. "Not from 1903, not from Meillet." *Historiographia Linguistica* 14.403
Valin, Roch. *1964. La méthode comparative en linguistique historique et en psychomécanique du langage*. Québec: Presses de l'Université Laval.
———. 1965. "Les aspects du verbe français". *Omagiu lui Alexandru Rosetti*.967-975. (Repr. In 1944.37-52).
———. 1966. "Le présent français". *Mélanges de linguistique et de philologie romanes offerts à Mgr Pierre Gardette*. Paris: Klincksieck.
———. 1968. "Des conditions d'existence d'une science du mentalisme linguistique". *Les langues modernes* 62.297-309. (Repr. in 1994.101-121).
———. 1981. *Perspectives psychomécaniques sur la syntaxe*. Québec: Presses de l'Université Laval.
———. 1994. *L'envers des mots*. Québec: Presses de l'Université Laval; Paris:Klincksieck.
Van Voorst, Jan. 1988. *Event Structure*. Amsterdam & Philadelphia: John Benjamins.
Vassant, Annette. 1980. "Lexique, sémantique et grammaire dans la voix verbale en français". *Travaux de linguistique et de littérature* 18.143-163.
———. 1981. "Incidence et décadence dans la voix verbale en français". Joly & Hirtle 1981.284-309.
———. 1988. "Passé simple et passé composé chez E. Benveniste et G. Guillaume". *Modèles linguistiques* 19.113-129.

Vet, Co. 1980. *Temps, aspects et adverbes de temps en français contemporain.* Genève: Droz.
Vincent, Nigel. 1982. "The development of the auxiliaries *habere* and *esse* in Romance". Vincent and Harris 1982.71-89.
——. & M. Harris (eds.). 1982. *Studies in the Romance verb.* London: Croom Helm.
von Wartburg, Walther. & P. Zumthor. 1958. *Précis de syntaxe du français contemporain.* (2e éd). Berne: Francke.
Wagner, Robert L. & Jaqueline Pinchon. 1962. *Grammaire du français classique et moderne.* Paris: Hachette.
Walter, Henriette. 1988. *Le francais dans tous les sens.* Paris: Robert Lafont.
Waugh, Linda R. 1975. "A semantic analysis of the French tense system". *Orbis* 24.436-85.
Wierzbicka, Anna. 1988. *The Semantics of Grammar.* Amsterdam & Philadelphia: John Benjamins.
Wilmet, Marc. 1969. "'Après que' suivi du subjonctif". *La Linguistique* 2.27-39.
——. 1970. *Le système de l'indicatif en moyen français.* Genève: Droz.
——. 1976. *Etudes de morphosyntaxe verbale.* Paris: Klincksieck.
——. 1976a. "Le subjonctif suivant 'après que'". Wilmet 1976.129-152.
Winters, Margaret E. 1989. "Diachronic prototype theory: on the evolution of the French subjunctive". *Linguistics* 27.703-730.
——. 1993. "On the Semantic Structure of the French Subjunctive". *Linguistic Perspectives on the Romance Languages,* ed. by W.J.Ashby, 271-279. Amsterdam & Philadelphia: John Benjamins.
Wunderli, Peter. 1970. "Der Konjunctiv nach 'après que'". *Vox Romanica* 29.230-263.
——. 1970a. "Nochmals zum Konjunktiv in vorzeitigen Temporalsatz". *Vox Romanica* 29.273-278.
Zribi-Hertz, A. 1978. "«Le poulet a cuit», «le poulet s'est cuit»: une opposition aspectuelle parmi les verbes neutres du français", *Studies in French Linguistics* 1.75-94.
——. 1982. "La construction «se-moyen» du français et son statut dans le triangle: moyen — passif — réfléchi", *Linguisticae Investigationes* 6.345-401.
——. 1987. "La réflexivité ergative en français moderne". *Le français moderne* 55.23-54.

GENERAL INDEX

ablaut, 6, 142, 148
abstractions, 14, 39, 42
  analytic abstractions, 8
Acadian dialect, 154
accompli, 39, 98, 101, 102, 103, 105, 106, 134, 135
accomplissement, 39, 98, 101, 135
  virtuel, 98, 101, 103
act of language, 2, 3,10
active sentence, 65
activity, 8, 91, 105, 129, 134
  cognitive activity, 129, 130
activity of language, 8
adjectival relationship, 25
adjective(s), 36, 40, 113, 145, 150
adverb(s), 59, 129, 136, 137
adverbial, 60, 97, 134
affirmation, 116
affirmative, 116
agent, 33, 63, 64, 65, 67, 68, 76, 77, 78, 79, 80
  prototypical agent, 68
agreement, 71
  participial agreement, 64
  verbal agreement, 64
agreement of tense, 54
Aktionsart, 76, 149
Algonkian, 80
allomorphs, 141, 144, 150, 155
allophone(s) 2, 3, 11, 95
alloseme, 124
  grammatical allosemes, 95
alpha chronotype, 22, 44, 91, 92, 95
alpha moment, 44, 88, 89, 90, 91, 93, 94, 95, 96, 107, 129, 130, 131, 133, 134, 136, 137
alpha quantum, 44
American English, 140, 143
American pronunciation, 4
analogical levelling, 140, 142
Ancient Greek, 68, 84

animate gender, 81
antecedent, 116, 117, 122, 123, 124
anteriority, 56, 57, 58, 60, 61
anti-mentalism, 14
aorist, 77
aphasia, 46
après que, 118, 119
arbitraire du signe, 7, 139
arguments, 63
Ascending Time, 20, 21, 27, 37, 41, 42, 44, 99, 100, 110, 125, 126, 127, 128
aspect, 11, 12, 13, 15, 16, 18, 19, 20, 23, 27, 33, 36, 38, 48, 49, 54, 56, 59, 85, 86, 98, 131
  imperfective, 39, 100
  perfective, 39, 87
  performative, 39, 100
  Progressive Aspect, 27, 87
  Prospective Aspect, 27, 85, 87
  Retrospective Aspect, 27, 86, 87
  transcendent aspect, 20, 33, 48, 49, 50, 87
assiette, 59
assimilation, 2
Atlantic Canada, 154
auxiliary, 11, 12, 18, 29, 30, 31, 32, 33, 34, 49, 50, 51, 52, 53, 54, 59, 60, 70, 73, 74, 75, 76, 77, 82, 85, 96, 137
  grammatical auxiliaries, 28, 29, 30
  modal auxiliaries, 28, 29, 34, 145
  passive auxiliary, 76
avant que, 118
avoir, 73, 76, 77, 82
axial consonant, 151, 152, 155
Ayres-Bennet & Carruthers, 49
Bantu, 80
Barral, 18-19
base of verb, 6
be, 23, 25, 28, 30, 31, 32, 33, 70, 74, 75
become, 71
Benveniste, 1, 13, 49

bi-transcendent, 48, 49, 50, 62
binary features, 8
binary relationship, 44
Binnick, 12
Bishop Bossuet, 50
Bloch, 6
Bloch & Trager 4
Bloomfield, 2,5
Bloomfieldian(s), 6, 86
Boileau, 97
Bourciez, 153
brinkmanship, 101
British English, 120, 140, 142
British pronunciation, 4
Brogyanyi, 1
Bruneau, 86
Brunot, F., 86
Bull, 12
Burston, 63, 82
Canada, 117, 121, 154
Canon of Exhaustiveness, 123
Canon of Coherence, 124
card, 4
cardinal system, 3
case systems, 6
categories, 11, 13
   descriptive categories, 11
   linguistic categories, 13, 85, 88, 1 2 6, 127
   morphological categories, 46
   morphosyntactic category, 74
   natural categories, 100
   non-linguistic categories, 11, 12
   semantic categories, 146
causative element, 79
ce, 117
Celtic, 100
champ du possible, 115
champ du probable, 115
chess pieces, 4,6,
chess moves, 4,6,
child language, 126
choice of words, 10
Christmann, 86
chronogenesis, 35, 36, 41, 43, 47, 92, 112, 125, 127
chronogenetic stages, 36

chronotype, 22, 130
Clark, 99
Classical Latin, 148, 149
clause(s)
   clauses of time, 54
   conditional clauses, 103, 108
   dependent clause, 25, 58, 122, 123
   main clause, 54, 57, 60, 115, 116, 143, 144
   noun clause, 63
   relative clause, 58, 116, 123, 124
   subordinate clauses, 42, 54, 56, 57, 58, 59, 60, 115, 116, 117, 119, 112, 123
   when-clauses, 119
clitic pronoun, 70
closed syllables, 3
Coates, 29
cognitive faculty, 125
cognitive processes, 88
cognitive staging, 46
cognitive universal, 26, 110
Cohen, 111
colloquial, 45, 50, 57
communicative goal, 10
compact-diffuse, 3
comparative method, 7
comparative reconstruction, 1
complete performance, 20
completion (of event), 26, 41
composé, 55, 57
compound preposition, 117
compounding, 18, 33
Comrie, 12, 63, 86
conceivability, 6
condition, 9, 103, 108, 109
conditional, 37, 42, 45, 48, 59, 93, 99, 105, 106, 107, 108, 109, 128, 152, 153, 155
   compound conditional, 102, 106
   conditional of probability, 109
conjugations, 148, 150, 153, 154, 155
conjunctions, 117, 118
   compound conjunctions, 117
conscious, 9, 135
consciousness, 23, 44, 88, 94, 107, 125, 126, 127, 129
consequence, 9, 108, 109
container, 26, 36, 41, 42, 46, 93, 94, 125

content, 4, 7, 26, 30 , 36, 41, 42, 63, 93, 94, 110, 125, 140, 141, 146, 156
  conceptual content, 5
  grammatical content, 30, 144
  internal content, 100
  lexical content, 31, 33
  semantic content, 20, 41, 96
  temporal content, 42
content side of language, 5, 6
context, 11, 47, 54, 56, 59, 60, 102, 106, 117, 124
  linguistic context, 11
contrast(s), 11, 17, 18, 23, 26, 33, 44, 45, 86, 99, 105, 110, 111, 114, 120
  aspectual contrasts, 10, 86, 99, 100
  binary contrasts, 14, 18, 26, 32, 110, 123, 124, 131
  cognitive contrasts, 91, 111, 112, 131
  contrasts of staging, 5
  distinctive contrasts, 3
  functional contrast, 115
  grammatical contrasts, 35, 112
  horizontal contrast, 45
  lexical contrasts, 111
  meaning contrasts, 140
  meaningful contrasts, 17, 31, 111
  mechanical contrasts, 114, 115
  mental contrasts, 16
  morphological contrast, 25, 78
  notional contrast, 6
  syntactic contrasts, 78
  systemic contrasts, 5, 90, 129
  temporal contrasts, 87
  underlying contrast, 18
  vertical contrast, 45
contrastive positions, 101
conventional symbolisation, 5
Cornu, 49
cortex, 3, 88, 129
Curat, Hervé, 15, 92, 95, 145, 146
Dahl, 12
Damourette & Pichon, 49, 50, 69
dare, 28, 29
Dauzat, 86, 154
de Boer, 111
Deane, 112

Decadence, 19, 22, 23, 37, 44, 92, 93, 96, 97, 98, 105, 106, 107, 108, 110, 113, 114, 125, 131, 134, 135
demonstrative, 117, 118
derivational suffixes, 149
Descending Time, 19, 20, 27, 37, 40, 41, 42, 44, 99, 100, 110, 125, 126, 127, 128
determination, 29
dialectic, 15
dimension, 21
diphthongs, 3
directly observable, 5, 8, 14, 17, 50
discours, 8, 9
discourse, vi, 7, 8, 9, 10, 17, 94, 111, 112, 115, 124, 140
distinctions
  aspectual distinctions, 38, 39, 51
  cognitive distinctions, 89
  horizontal distinction, 94
  linguistic distinctions, 89, 130
  qualitative distinctions, 94
  quantitative distinctions, 94
  tense distinctions, 38, 51, 94
distinctive features, 13
do, 24, 28, 30, 31, 32, 34
Dolbec & LeFlem, 119, 120
Donaldson, 69
Dowty, 65
Dubois, 148
Dutch, 129, 136
Eastern Europe, 117
Ecole des Hautes Etudes, vi,
egocentricity, 112
Einstein, 89, 90
Einsteinian model of universe, 23, 89
elements
  contrastive elements, 18
  elements of content, 4
  elements of expression, 4
  grammatical elements, 15
  linguistic element(s), 13
  regular systemic element, 7
  surface elements, 124
  systemic elements, 2, 7, 8, 14
  underlying elements, 124
Eliot, 75
empirical data, 14

empiricism, 14
endings, 45
energeia, 9, 10
English, 17, 19, 20, 21, 22, 23, 25, 28, 29, 32, 34, 40, 41, 44, 45, 54, 55, 56, 58, 59, 60, 63, 64, 68, 75, 82, 85, 86, 87, 88, 89, 91, 95, 100, 103, 108, 120, 129, 131, 132, 133, 134, 135, 136, 139, 142, 144, 148
ephemeral, 8, 9
ergon, 9, 10
Ernout, 149
Erector set, 7
Eskimo, 3
Esprit, 119
essence, 32
eternal truths, 95
être, 66, 70, 73, 74, 75, 76, 77, 82
event(s), 12, 19, 20, 22, 23, 24, 25, 27, 32, 33, 36, 37, 40, 41, 42, 43, 44, 46, 49, 53, 56, 57, 58, 61, 74, 85, 87, 88, 94, 95, 97, 98, 100, 101, 102, 104, 105, 107, 112, 113, 118, 120, 121, 124, 125, 126, 127, 128, 131, 132, 134
   complete (event), 39, 40, 85, 96, 97, 100, 104, 105, 106, 128, 137
   experiential event, 11, 32, 33, 42, 106, 120, 125
   future (event), 12, 52, 95, 106, 112
   material event, 25, 106
   non-past event(s), 42
   past (event), 12, 45, 52, 53, 96, 97, 108, 112, 137
   potential event, 25, 101, 113, 120
   present event, 52, 112
   subordinate event, 124
   verbal events, 5
   virtual event, 101
existence, 32, 116
experience, 11, 18, 37, 88, 89, 91, 93, 110, 123, 124, 125, 126, 127, 129, 130, 131
   cognitive experience, 129, 130, 131, 132
experiential world, 11, 42, 112
expression, 4, 7, 124, 140, 141, 156
   surface expression, 44

Fables, 122
fact, 123
fait accompli, 61
fiction, 11
field of possibility, 115
filing system, 9
Firth, 141
Fleischman, 99
Foley, 63
form, 139, 140, 142, 143
   active form, 66, 82, 83, 84
   aspectual forms, 27, 28, 33, 36, 39, 54, 56, 61, 71, 85
   compound forms, 17, 18, 27, 33, 36, 48, 49, 50, 52, 55, 56, 61, 62, 66, 70, 71, 82, 86, 103
   double compound forms, 52
   finite (forms), 9, 32, 63, 64
   grammatical forms, 11, 31, 47
   indicative forms, 145
   literary forms, 75, 91
   marked forms, 40
   middle voice forms, 76, 77, 81, 82, 83, 100
   morphological form(s), 17, 41, 99, 144
   paradigmatic forms, 99
   passive forms, 77
   periphrastic form(s), 54
   quasi-nominal forms, 26, 112
   simple forms, 17, 32, 33, 35, 36, 44, 48, 51, 62, 66, 87, 88
   subjunctive forms, 23, 36
   unmarked forms(s), 18, 40
   verb forms, 11, 12, 29, 30, 32, 36, 50, 56, 112
formes simples, 38, 50
formes surcomposées, 57, 58, 61
formes composées, 39, 50, 52
Foulet, 49
fount of type, 2, 9
français populaire, 154
français moderne, 68
France, 14, 60
French Constitution, 118
French, 11, 13, 14, 15, 17, 21, 22, 25, 34, 36, 37, 38, 40, 41, 44, 50, 52, 54,

56, 60, 63, 64, 65, 68, 69, 74, 77, 78,
79, 81, 82, 84, 86, 87, 88, 89, 90, 91,
92, 93, 95, 97, 99, 100, 104, 107,
110, 111, 113, 115, 116, 120, 121,
125, 126, 129, 131, 133, 134, 135,
136, 137, 139, 140, 141, 146, 148,
150, 152, 155
frequentative, 149
Fuchs, 13, 14
functional school, 13
functions, 4, 85, 86
future in the past, 107, 108
game of chess, 4, 139
Garcia, 78
Garnier, 15
Geniušiené, 69
geometrical line, 21
German, 74, 148
Germanic, 4, 100, 112
gerund, 136
Gesamtbedeutung, 96
get, 71
Glättli, 119
Golian, 13, 14, 86
grammar, 5
grammatical adaptation (of words), 10
grammatical analyses, 15
grammatical support, 112
grammaticalisation, 26
grave-acute, 3
Greek, 77, 87
Grevisse, 50, 66, 74, 76, 78, 97, 118
ground plan, 10
Guillaume, v, 1, 5, 6, 8, 10, 11, 12, 13, 14,
   15, 19, 27, 31, 35, 36, 37, 38, 39, 41,
   42, 43, 44, 47, 50, 64, 68, 77, 82, 86,
   92, 93, 94, 96, 98, 99, 100, 102, 104,
   105, 110, 113, 115, 123, 124, 125,
   130, 139, 140, 144, 145, 146
Guimier, Claude, 10
habitual action, 103
Haltus, 49
Hatcher, 69
have to , 29
have, 28, 30, 31, 32, 33, 60, 75
hearer, 44, 87
Hewson, 1, 81

high front vowel, 3
high-mid vowels, 3
Hirschbühler, 63
Hirtle, 20, 24
Historic Present, 94
historical reconstruction, vi
historical linguistics, 4, 111, 140
Hjelmslev, v,4, 5, 6, 63, 139
Hockett, 1, 7
hour glass, 19, 92, 96
idée critique, 121
idée regardée, 42, 115, 116, 120
idée regardante, 42, 115, 116, 120, 143
idée regardante critique, 120
imagination, 62, 125, 126, 127, 128, 129,
   130
Imbs, 14, 98, 111
Immanence, 26, 33
Immanent, 48, 49, 50, 52, 62, 100
imparfait , 15
imparfait modal, 102
Imperative, 15, 23, 30, 145, 146
imperfect, 25, 42, 45, 46, 48, 59, 93, 96,
   97, 98, 99, 100, 101, 102, 103, 104,
   105, 106, 107, 109, 128, 134
imperfective, 10, 20, 38, 98
inaccompli, 39
inceptive, 87, 97, 98, 104
inchoative, 149, 150, 154, 155, 156
Incidence, 19, 37, 44, 92, 93, 96, 97, 105,
   106, 107, 108, 110, 113, 125, 131,
   135
incorporation of words, 9/10
Indic, 4
indicative, 18,19, 23, 24, 25, 34, 42, 43, 44,
   49, 50, 51, 66, 87, 88, 92, 110, 112,
   113, 114, 115, 116, 118, 120, 122,
   124, 140, 143, 145
indicative inflection, 146
individual, 9
Indo-European, 46, 63, 64, 68, 84, 88, 128,
   141, 148, 149
infectum , 11, 39
infinite, 9
infinitive, 23, 25, 26, 28, 29, 30, 32, 37, 38,
   39, 40, 41, 48, 112, 113, 125, 126,
   136, 145, 148, 152, 153, 155

GENERAL INDEX

content infinitive, 30
transcendent infinitive, 28, 29
infinitive mood, 51
inflection(s), 31, 93, 146, 150, 151, 152, 154
intended message, 10
internal predication, 39
interrogation, 32, 117
intransitive, 32, 63, 65, 67, 76, 77, 78, 81, 82, 83
Inuktitut, 3,4,
invariant(s), v, 11, 78, 95
Italian, 74, 75, 81, 88, 149, 150
iterative, 149
Jakobson, v, 1, 3, 5, 6, 8, 11, 12, 13, 14, 23, 46, 92, 96, 139
Jespersen, 23, 64, 125
Johnson, 8, 89, 130
jusqu'à ce que, 117
Kahn, 86
Kemmer, 69
King James Bible, 75
Klaiman, 83
Kobayashi, 149, 153
Koerner, 1
Korrel, 129, 135, 136
La Sagouine, 154
La Fontaine, 122
Labelle, 63, 82, 83
Langacker, 5
langage, 7
language, 8, 11, 13, 14, 15, 17, 63, 110
langue, 7, 8
laryngeals, 1
Latin, 10, 11, 36, 39, 68, 77, 84, 90, 91, 94, 114, 119, 146, 149, 150, 151, 152, 154, 155
Law of Coherence, 141, 156
Law of Expressive Adequacy, 141
Law of Simple Sufficiency, 141, 156
Lazard, 63
LeFlem, 92
Lerch, 86
lexical dematerialisation, 31
lexical relationship, 32
limit, 18
line of time, 12

linguistic method, 12
linguistics, 14, 15, 86, 139
loi de cohérence, 6, 141, 156
loi de simple suffisance, 7, 141, 142, 156
long vowels, 3
Maillet, Antonine, 154
main verb, 51
Mansion, 50, 54, 55, 56, 57, 58, 101, 104, 105, 108
markers, 4
Martin, Robert, 15, 98, 102
Martinet, 13, 14, 148
Matte, 118, 148
may, 28, 29
Meyer-Lübke, 153
meaning relationships, 4
meaning(s), 4, 5, 6, 11, 13, 17, 39, 99, 120, 123, 124, 130, 139, 141, 142
  basic meanings, 5, 142
  epistemic meaning, 29
  grammatical meaning(s), 35, 63, 83, 92, 123
  invariant meaning, 95, 96
  lexical meaning, 31, 64, 81, 83, 112
  permanent meaning, 11
  potential meanings, 17
  prototypical meaning, 69
  referential meaning, 11
  surface meaning(s), 11, 140
  underlying meaning(s), 11, 17, 70, 123
means of representation, 12
Meccano set, 7
mechanism(s)
  cognitive mechanisms, 61
  grammatical mechanism, 16
  mental mechanisms, 6, 14
  operative mechanisms, 110
  representational mechanisms, 23
  underlying mechanism, 124
Medio-active, 84
Meillet, 1, 50, 86
Melis, 69, 70
même, 120
Mémoir sur les voyelles, 1
memory, 8, 18, 19, 62, 88, 97, 99, 110, 125, 126, 127, 128, 129

memory cells, 88, 107
mental entity, 3
mental faculty, 8
mental operation, 47
mental processing, vi
Mervis, 65
mid vowels, 3
mid-front vowels, 3, 4
Middle French, 15
Midsummer Night's Dream, 91
minimal pairs, 31, 117, 121, 122, 123, 156
modal(s), 29, 30, 145
modern linguistics, 5
Modern English, 25, 31, 75, 84
Modern French, 115, 128, 146, 148, 149, 151, 153
Modern German, 140
Modern Italian, 75
Modern Romance, 11
Moignet, 15, 111
mood, 16, 23, 36, 11, 115, 125
   indicative mood, 43, 111, 113
   quasi-nominal mood, 23, 27, 36, 41, 112, 113, 115
   subjunctive mood, 41, 111, 113, 145
morph, 140, 142
morpheme, 139, 140, 157
morphemic differences, 139, 140
morphological predication, 26, 29, 39
morphology, 6, 12, 13, 15, 17, 35, 36, 45, 70, 77, 79, 93, 105, 140, 141, 145, 146, 148, 149, 152, 154, 155, 156
   paradigmatic morphology, 12
   passive morphology, 77
   regular morphology, 6
   systemic morphology, 150
   verbal morphology, 12, 13
morphosyntactic shape, 12
morphosyntactic types, 35
morphosyntax, 4, 6, 7, 13, 35, 48, 49, 63, 68, 70, 77, 80, 84, 141, 146
mother tongue, 8, 9
motivation, 139, 140, 156
motor mechanism of speech, 3
movement, 19, 99, 105, 106, 112, 113
   qualitative movement, 110
   quantitative movement, 110
MOVING-EGO, 99

MOVING-TIME, 99
MOVING-WORLD, 99
must, 28
native speakers, 18, 54, 58, 102, 111, 124
ne... que, 120
need, 28, 29
negation, 32, 118
negative, 24, 116
nomenclature, 11
nominal(s), 38, 39, 63, 113
non-passive, 72
notional chronology, 115
noun, 26, 36, 39, 42, 63, 94, 113, 150
   mass noun, 27
noun declension, 149
object, 63, 64, 67, 70, 117
   direct object, 64, 65, 67, 75, 76
   grammatical object, 67
   indirect object, 64, 70,
object pronoun, 71, 78
obligation, 102
observation, 8
occurrence, 32, 42, 44, 46, 113, 120, 121
Old French, 75, 140, 151, 152, 154, 155
Old High German, 140
omega chronotype, 22, 45, 91, 92, 95
omega moment, 22, 44, 45, 88, 89, 91, 93, 94, 95, 96, 103, 107, 129, 130, 131, 132, 133, 134, 136, 137
omega quantum, 44
onomasiology, 11
open syllables, 3
ought, 28, 29
Palmer, 29
paradigms, 6, 17, 24, 49, 99, 140, 141, 142, 148, 149, 150, 151, 152, 154, 155, 156
   regular paradigms, 148
   unmarked paradigm, 149
   verbal paradigms, 17, 23, 34, 148, 149, 151, 154
parallelism of forms, 57, 58
parallelism of tenses, 56, 57, 59
parameters of tense, 92
parole, 8
participle(s), 23, 25, 26, 30, 36, 150
   imperfective participle, 26

past participle, 20, 22, 23, 37, 38, 39, 40, 41, 51, 53, 64, 66, 71, 113, 125, 126, 137, 154, 155
perfective participle, 26
present participle, 20, 23, 37, 38, 39, 40, 41, 113, 125, 126, 145
parts of speech, 9
passé antérieur, 58, 59, 60
passé composé, 42, 49, 55, 57, 59, 60, 61, 74, 76, 85, 86, 97, 128, 129, 136, 137
passé défini, 45
passé simple, 15, 34, 42, 45, 48, 55, 57, 61, 85, 96, 97, 98, 99, 100, 107, 154, 155
passion, 78
passive, 26, 33, 34, 63, 64, 65, 66, 70, 71, 72, 74, 77, 78, 79, 81, 84, 126
past perfect, 134
patient, 63, 64, 65, 67, 68, 70, 76, 77, 78, 80, 84
prototypical patient, 68
Peeters, 1
Penfield, 47, 88, 97
perceivability, 6
perception, 125, 126
perfect, 11, 39, 48, 86, 87, 154
perfective, 11, 38, 98, 103
perfectum, 11, 39
performative, 31
Perkins, 29
permanency, 18
permanent, 9, 17
person, 35
phoneme, 2, 3, 4, 11, 12, 86
phonemic overlapping, 2, 12
phonemic shape, 6
phonetics, 9, 12
phonic, 2
phonology, 8, 9, 11, 13, 14
physical correlate, 3
physiology, 13
pluperfect, 59
plural marker, 2
point de repère, 127
point of articulation, 13
point of event, 12
point of reference, 12

point of speech, 12
Portuguese, 88, 149
position in a system, 112
positivism, 13, 14
possible (realm of), 115, 116, 122, 124
potentiality, 29, 42, 102
Prague School, 1
predicate, 42
predication, 26
present perfect, 22, 45, 55, 60, 85, 89, 91, 95, 129, 133, 134, 135, 136, 137
preterit, 20, 25, 45, 89, 93, 97, 107, 127, 128, 136
probable (realm of), 115, 116, 112, 124
processing
    cognitive processing, 125
progressive, 20, 98, 100, 131
pronoun, 36, 42, 78, 113, 126
proto-languages, 14
prototypical exemplars, 78
prototypical role, 70
psychisme, 141
psychomechanics, v, vi
Puck, 91
quantum, 77, 92, 93, 131
quantum of time, 44
quasi active, 78
quasi passive, 78
quasi-nominal(s), 66, 125
que, 117
Quirk, 17
real world, 11
reality, 14
reciprocity, 68, 80
reference, 11, 12, 97, 106
    future reference, 49, 50
    non-past reference, 25
    past reference, 28, 117, 135
    present reference, 137
    temporal reference, 119
reference points, 12
reflexive(s), 67, 68, 69, 70, 77, 79, 80, 82
reflexive pronoun, 70, 77, 78
reflexive type pronouns, 78, 79
Reichenbach, 11, 12, 13, 15
relativity of time, 89
reported speech, 45, 46

representation, 5, 11, 12, 32, 38, 41, 45, 46, 85, 93, 100, 101, 107, 112, 124, 126, 131, 132, 133, 134, 137
  cognitive representation, 129
  dynamic representation, 36
  external representation, 26
  grammatical representation, 32, 64
  intermediary representation, 11?
  internal representation, 26
  linguistic representation, 19
  nominal representation, 43
  static representation, 39
  tense representations, 23
  underlying representation, 11, 44
representation of time, 37, 45, 87, 92, 114
reshaping, 11
result, 40
resultant state, 72, 74, 76
retrospective, 21, 48, 103, 155
Richelet, 119
Romance, 4, 10, 11, 36, 43, 77, 78, 84, 87, 100, 112, 146, 148, 149, 150, 151
Romanian, 149
Rosch, 65, 112
Rothemberg, 63, 69, 82
rules, 10, 11
Russian, 39, 117, 139
Ruwet, 63
Sanskrit, 84
Sapir, 2, 12
Saussure, 1, 2, 4, 5, 7, 139, 140, 156
Sauvageot, 86
Schogt, 13, 85, 111
second language interference, 122
secondary development, 18
semantic roles, 63
semantics, 5, 141
sememe, 139, 140, 157
  grammatical sememe, 96
sémiologie, 141
semiology, 139, 142
sentence, 8, 9, 10, 11
sentence adverbs, 10
sentence grammar, 4
sentence planning, 10
sequence of tenses, 24, 42, 59, 103
set of contrasts, 11
Shakespeare, 31, 91

shall, 28, 29, 95
shifters, 23, 125
shifts, 114
should, 28
sign, 139, 141, 157
  linguistic sign, 139, 156, 157
signifiant, 4
significate, 139, 141, 157
signifié, 4
signifié de puissance, 96
signifié d'effet, 124
signifier, 139
Simenon, 104
Simon, Pierre-Henri, 119
simple future, 37
simple non-past, 20, 21, 22, 28, 32, 91
simple past, 20, 22, 28, 32, 53, 61, 98
simple present, 44, 91, 134
singular, 93
situation, 124
Slavic, 4, 87, 100
sound, 4
space, 21, 23, 38, 89, 90
Spanish, 81, 88, 149
spastic vowel sound, 3
speaker(s), 13, 23, 44, 87, 97, 110, 114, 115, 120
static event, 36
Stefanini, 1, 49, 69
stem: indicative stem, 144, 146
  simple stem, 39
  subjunctive stem, 144, 145, 146
  unmarked stems, 90
Sten, 86
strategic goal, 10
structuralist approach, 5
structuralists, 4
structure, 8, 35
  cognitive structure, 35, 156
  grammatical structure, 4, 5,
  mental structure, 35
  morphosyntactic structure, 35
  phonological structure, 7
  semiological structure, 35
  stratified structure, 44
  SV structure, 76, 77
  SVO structure, 76

GENERAL INDEX 179

syntactic structure, 10
style, 55, 57, 101
subconscious, 8, 9, 14, 135
subject, 23, 26, 27, 33, 36, 41, 42, 43, 51, 52, 63, 64, 65, 67, 68, 70, 72, 76, 77, 78, 79, 80, 81, 82, 83, 84, 97,100, 102, 105, 107, 112, 113, 121
   agentive subject, 77, 78, 79, 80, 82, 83, 84
   animate subject, 82
   grammatical subject, 64, 65, 67, 113
   inanimate subject, 63, 64, 81, 82
   patientive subject, 78, 79, 80, 83
   transitive subject(s), 65, 100
subjunctive, 23, 24, 25, 28, 30, 35, 36, 37, 41, 44, 51, 66, 112, 113, 114, 115, 116, 117, 118, 119, 120, 121, 122, 123, 124, 125, 143
   imperfect subjunctive, 41, 42, 49, 113, 125,127, 128, 154, 155
   present sunjunctive, 41, 42, 113, 114, 125, 127
   second subjunctive, 25
   simple subjunctive, 23
subjunctive inflexions, 155
subsystems, 16, 112
superlatives, 122
suppletive, 144
suppletive preterit, 25
support, 36, 42, 112
surcomposé, 48, 50 , 53, 57, 59, 60, 61, 66
surface description, 11
syllables, 3
synchronic linguistics, 4
syntactic collusion, 29, 36
syntactic predication, 29
syntactic sequences, 24
syntax, 5, 79
system, v, 1,2, 23, 4, 5, 7, 9, 10, 13, 14, 15, 17, 35, 86, 92, 95, 102
   aspect system, 15, 34, 61, 99
   binary system, 6, 10
   cognitive systems, 7, 16, 49, 138
   content system(s), 1, 6, 7, 11, 17, 24, 35, 36, 47, 51, 61, 92, 99, 110, 113, 123, 124, 139, 140, 141, 148, 156
   descriptive systems, 11

expression system, 7, 35, 139, 140, 141, 148, 156
formal system, 5
grammatical system, 5, 6, 8, 47, 111
indicative system, 10/11, 87
linguistic system, 2/3, 10, 110, 129
mental system(s), 35
morphosyntactic system, 35
phonemic system, 1, 2
phonological system, 7, 8, 46
representational system, 12, 94, 110
semiological systems, 139
tense system, 15, 18, 20, 23, 34, 47, 87, 88, 92, 99, 110, 129
underlying system, 12, 13, 14, 49, 114, 123, 124, 129, 138, 140
underlying verbal system, 12
verbal system, vi, 1, 5, 12, 13, 16, 17, 46, 47, 89, 94, 107, 112
voice system, 99
systèmes de valeurs, 6
system of aspect, 29, 94
system of contrasts, v
system of meaning, 5, 92
system of representation, 12
system of signs, 139
system of systems, 1, 13
system of tenses, 18, 94, 110, 131
systemic change, 1, 111
systemic coherence, 6, 156
systemic differences, 45, 11, 129, 138, 141
systemic factor, 22
systemic nature, 15
systemic relationship, 36
temporal terms, 90
temps expliqué, 27, 51
temps impliqué, 27, 51
tense, 10, 11, 12, 13, 15, 16, 17, 18, 20, 22, 27, 29, 36, 38, 39, 49, 50, 52, 56, 59, 66, 85, 86, 88, 89, 131, 140
   future (tense), 11, 15, 34, 45, 48, 49, 50, 54, 59, 77, 86, 90, 93, 94, 99, 100, 105, 107, 108, 109, 113, 128, 131, 137, 152, 153, 155
   non-past tense, 6, 17, 18, 27, 50, 54, 55, 85, 91, 133, 137

past (tense), 11, 12, 17, 18, 22, 25, 27, 34, 45, 49, 85, 86, 90, 91, 96, 113, 127, 129, 131, 132, 134, 142
present (tense), 11, 12, 18, 21, 22, 23, 44, 49, 50, 54, 55, 85, 89, 90, 91, 94, 95, 96, 108, 113, 129, 132, 133, 151, 152
simple tense(s), 30, 100
tense mark, 12
tense marking, 18
terminology, 18
Tesnière, 64
thematic roles, 65
thematic vowel, 150, 154
theoretical method, 14
theory, 14, 15
third person, 24, 28
three vowel system, 3
threshold, 18, 21, 23, 37, 44, 89, 90, 91, 92, 29, 130, 132, 135
time, 12, 18, 19, 23, 24, 37, 38, 41, 46, 89, 90, 93, 113, 126, 129
  egocentric time, 112
  Event Time, 27, 36, 39, 42, 51, 52, 53, 86, 87, 98, 110, 113, 114
  experiential time, 44, 90, 112, 113, 114, 125, 127
  future (time), 18, 19, 21, 23, 34, 37, 41, 43, 46, 49, 50, 54, 85, 90, 92, 94, 95, 99, 106, 108, 110, 114, 125, 126, 130, 131, 133
  imaginary time, 18
  memorial time, 18, 22, 87, 89, 91, 95, 97, 118, 130
  Mental Time, 112, 125, 126, 127
  non-memorial time, 18, 87, 89, 91, 95, 130
  non-past (time), 6, 17, 18, 29, 41, 44, 87, 89, 130, 132
  past (time), 6, 17, 18, 19, 20, 21, 23, 29, 37, 41, 43, 46, 49, 53, 85, 86, 87, 89, 90, 92, 93, 94, 95, 99, 100, 108, 110, 114, 125, 129, 130, 132, 133
  present (time), 19, 20, 21, 43, 44, 46, 51, 53, 85, 88, 89, 92, 93, 99, 100, 103, 106, 108, 114, 125, 126, 129, 130, 131, 133

Universe Time, 18, 19, 25, 27, 37, 39, 43, 44, 51, 86, 87, 98, 99, 110, 112, 113, 114, 125, 126, 127, 128
time image, 36, 37, 43, 47, 92, 125
time spheres, 19, 20, 23, 24, 36, 38, 42, 44, 45, 46, 87, 99, 114, 125
time zones, 112
to, 26, 29, 30
Tobin, 156
Toman, 1
tongue, 7, 8, 9, 10
transcendence, 33
transcendent non-past, 22
transcendent position, 26
transitivity, 63, 69, 78, 83
translation, 17
triangular vowel system, 3
turbulence, 82, 145, 156
underlying reality, 14
unit of discourse, 9/10
usage(s), 11, 12, 13, 23, 29, 54, 60, 95, 101, 102, 108, 111, 114, 118, 119, 120, 121, 122, 123, 124, 128, 129, 134, 135, 144
  aspectual usage, 32
  contrastive usage, 1, 91, 132, 133, 135, 136
  modal usage, 119
  peripheral usages, 65, 80
  prototypical usages, 65, 80
  verb usage, 11
use of system, 9
valency, 64
valeur, 5, 11, 124
Valin, vi, 8, 10, 39, 51, 140
value, 5, 12, 18
  contrastive values, 12
  surface values, 77
  tense value, 18
  underlying value, 78
value judgements, 120, 121, 122, 123
Van Voorst, 63
Van Valin, 63
variable usage, 122
variant usage, 78
Vassant, 11, 49
vast present, 114
vectors, 96
velar consonant, 2

verb, 11, 12, 63, 64
   active verbs, 63, 64, 71, 76, 77, 78, 79, 82
   base of verb, 6
   deponent(s), 68, 77, 79
   irregular verbs, 148
   pronominal verbs, 53, 63, 68, 69, 70, 71, 77, 78, 79, 80, 82
   reciprocal (verbs), 70, 77, 79, 80
   regular verbs, 148
   resultative verbs, 74
   stative verbs, 31
   strong verbs, 148
   transitive (verbs), 32, 63, 65, 67, 70, 75, 76, 78, 83
verbs of motion, 72, 82
verbs of resultant state, 71, 74, 82, 147
verb phrase, 12
verbal(s), 30, 32
verbal piece, 12
verbes de puissance, 144, 145
vertical hierarchy, 92
Vet, 13
via media, 68
view
   exterior view, 32, 41, 96, 97, 100, 105
   external view, 26, 27, 29, 39, 107
   immanent view, 19, 32
   interior view, 32, 39, 41, 96, 97, 98, 105, 128
   internal view, 26, 29, 39, 100, 107
   operational view, 8
   systemic view, 1, 111
visée de discours, 10
visée phrastique, 10
voice, 16, 33, 63, 67, 69, 81, 82, 83
   active voice, 33, 34, 63, 65, 67, 68, 70, 76, 77, 84, 99
   fourth, 82
   medio-passive voice, 84
   middle voice, 63, 67, 68, 69, 70, 76, 77, 78, 79, 80, 81, 82, 83, 84
   passive voice, 65, 66, 67, 68, 70, 77, 79, 99, 126
volition, 78, 79
von Wartburg & Zumthor, 111
vowel grid, 4

vowel systems, 3, 15
vowels, 3, 4, 46
Wagner & Pinchon, 50
Walter, 49, 60, 61
Waugh, 96
will, 28, 29
Wilmet, 15, 119
Woisetschlaeger, 29
word, 7, 8, 9
would, 28, 60
Wunderli, 119
zero suffix, 6
Zribi-Herz, 63

LIST OF FRENCH VERB FORMS

a, 120
a acheté, 111, 121
a battu, 65, 67
a brisé, 83
a cassé, 63, 64, 83
a commencé à/de, 135
a dîné, 57
a dit, 58, 107, 108
a entré, 76
a été battu, 65, 67
a été parti, 53
a eu coupé, 61
a eu mangé, 61
a eu dîné, 57
a fait beau, 54
a parlé, 52, 53
a promis, 57
a proposé, 109
a raison, 116
a répondu, 103
a resté, 73
a réussi, 102
a rougi, 64
a sorti, 76
a subi, 65
a tombé, 76
a vaincu, 76
abrutir, 151
acheter, 22
adjourn, 24
affaiblir, 151
ai aimé, 11
ai attendu, 117
ai battu, 66
ai demandé, 40
ai dormi, 74
ai entendu, 40
ai été, 74
ai été battu, 66
ai eu battu, 66
ai eu parlé, 48

ai faim, 46
ai monté, 76
ai parlé, 48, 49, 50
ai vu, 55, 85, 136, 137
ai vus, 64
aie battu (que je), 66
aie été battu (que je), 66
aie eu battu, 66
aie eu parlé, 48
aie parlé, 48
aie pas peur, 146
aigrir, 151
aimai, 11, 90
aimais, 11, 90
aime, 11, 90
aimer, 140 148, 149, 152, 154, 155
aimerai, 11, 31, 90
aimerais, 11, 90
aimez, 140
aimons, 140
ait acheté, 111, 121
ait été investi, 118
ait raison, 116
ait su, 42
ait vaincu, 123, 124
aller, 72, 81, 82, 144
allez, 144
allons, 81, 144
alunir, 149, 151
amerrir, 149, 151
amez, 140
amincir, 151
amons, 140
appelle, 113
approuve, 121
arrivait, 104
arrive, 91, 95
arriver, 72
arrives, 132
as pas peur, 146
assainir, 151

LIST OF FRENCH VERB FORMS

assemble, 80
assourdir, 151
attendiez, 117
attendrai, 117
attendrir, 151
attends, 95
atterrir, 74, 149, 151, 156
atterrer, 156
aura dîné, 57
aura eu dîné, 57
aura fait beau, 55
aurai aimé, 11
aurai battu, 66
aurai été battu, 66
aurai eu parlé, 48
aurai parlé, 48
auraient eu fini, 59
auraient fini, 59, 107
auraient inventé, 109
auraient perdu, 58
aurais aimé, 11
aurais battu, 66
aurais commis, 102
aurais été battu, 66
aurais eu parlé , 48
aurais parlé, 48
aurait dîné, 57
aurait été, 103, 103
aurait eu dîné, 57
aurait fait beau, 55
aurait payé, 108
auront eu fini, 59
auront fini, 58, 59, 107
auront payé, 58
auront perdu, 58
avaient eu fini, 59
avaient fini, 58
avaient payé, 58
avaient perdu, 58
avais aimé, 11
avais battu, 66
avais été battu, 66
avais eu parlé, 48
avais parlé, 48
avait dîné, 57, 59
avait eu dîné, 57
avait faim, 46
avait fait beau, 55

avait perdu, 108
avoir, 144, 145
avoir battu, 66
avoir été battu, 66
avoir eu parlé, 48
avoir parlé, 48
avons, 122
ayant, 145
ayant battu, 66
ayant été battu, 66
ayant eu parlé, 48
ayant parlé, 48
ayez, 144
ayons, 122
batisse (que je)
bats, 66
battais, 66
battant, 66
batte (que je), 66
battis, 66
battrai, 66
battrais, 66
battre, 66
blêmir, 151
bois, 148
bout, 95
briser, 82, 83
brunir, 151
buvons, 148
casser, 82, 83
change d'avis, 136
changeais, 102
chanter, 40
cherche, 117
chérir, 151
commencer, 136
commettais, 101
comprenais, 113
comprendra, 113
comprends, 113, 121
compreniez, 118
comprenne, 118
conduire, 153
conduit, 155
connaisse, 116
connaît, 116
connaître, 111, 131
continué, 135, 136

continuer, 136
convaincu, 155
courir, 72
créer, 152
crois, 40, 116
croître, 74
découvrait, 104
déjeune, 142
déjeunent, 142
déjeuner, 142
déjeunes, 142
demanda, 103, 104
demeurer, 73
deraillait, 102
descendre, 72, 74
devais, 102
devenir, 72, 73
devoir, 144
devons, 148
diminuer, 74
dîner, 142
dînez, 142
dînons, 142
dire, 131, 153, 155
dis, 116
dises, 117
dit, 155
dois, 148
dois faire, 96
éclaircir, 153, 156
éclairer, 156
écrire, 153, 155
écrit, 155
employer, 113
enhardir, 151
enrichir, 151
entrer, 72
es entré, 122
espère, 116
est blessé, 74, 100
est blessée, 71, 72
est décidé, 71
est eu réveillé, 54
est mort, 74
est morte, 72
est née, 72
est parti, 53, 72, 100
est resté, 73

est ronde, 95
est sorti, 55, 57, 59, 74, 118
est sortie, 76
est vaincu, 76
est venu, 117
étaient partis, 59
étais, 103
étais battu, 66
étais sorti, 55
était, 98, 103, 106, 107
était sorti, 57
étant, 145
étant battu, 66
été battu, 66
été prononcées, 119
étions, 104
être, 73, 144, 145, 148
être battu, 66
étudiante, 40
eu battu, 66
eu été battu, 66
eurent fini, 58
eus aimé, 11
eus battu, 66
eus été battu, 66
eus parlé, 48
eusse battu (que je), 66
eusse été battu (que je), 66
eusse eu parlé, 48, 49
eusse parlé, 48
eut dîné, 56
eut mangé, 61
eut peur, 87, 97
évoluer, 152
faire, 131
fais, 96
faisait beau, 54
fait beau, 54
faites, 108
fallait, 102
fera beau, 54
ferais, 108
ferait beau, 54
ferez, 108
fiancé, 40
fini, 155
finir, 140, 148,149,150,151,152,153, 154, 155

LIST OF FRENCH VERB FORMS

finirai, 152
finirais, 152
finis, 150
finissant, 150
finissent, 151
finissez, 151
finissons, 150, 151
finist, 151
fis, 104
fit beau, 54
fit noir, 97
forcer, 156
forcir, 156
fu, 98
fus battu, 66
fusse (que je), 42
fusse battu (que je), 66
grossir, 151
habita, 97
habitait, 134
habite, 133, 134
habitez, 45
horses, 6
inviter, 152
irai, 95
jaunir, 151
jouent, 152
jouer, 140, 152
jousent, 152
j'arrivé!, 44
levait, 103
lient, 152
lier, 152
lire, 153, 155
lisent, 152
luire, 153, 155
mange, 104, 134, 135
mangeais, 104, 135
mangez, 118
marcher, 72
me brûle, 89
me lave, 78
me suis dit, 71
me vient, 89, 136
me vois, 68
monter, 72
morts, 40
mot juste, 47

mourir, 72
mûrir, 151
m'avait vu
m'en suis souvenu, 71
naître, 72
nier, 122
noircir, 151, 153
nui, 155
nuire, 153, 155
n'attends, 95
n'avait, 102
ont eu fini, 59
ont fini, 58
ont payé, 58
ont perdu, 58
paient, 58
parlai, 34, 36, 37, 43, 45, 48, 92, 97
parlaient, 105
parlais, 34, 36, 37, 43, 45, 48 92, 105
parlait, 51, 103, 105
parlant, 35, 36, 38, 43, 48, 51
parlasse, 35, 43, 48
parle, 34, 36, 37, 43, 45, 48, 52, 118,141
parle (que je), 35, 43, 48
parlé, 35, 36, 38, 43, 48, 51, 52
parlent, 141
parler, 35, 36, 38, 43, 48, 51, 140
parlera, 52
parlerai, 34, 36, 37, 43, 45, 48, 92
parleraient, 105
parlerais, 34, 36, 37, 43, 45, 48, 92, 97, 105
parlerait, 105
parleriez, 105
parlerions, 105
parlez, 118, 141
parliez, 105
parlions, 105
parlons, 141
pars, 44, 91, 95
part, 53, 94
partaient, 58
partent, 58
partir, 72, 77
partira, 95
partirent, 58
passant, 40
passé, 40
passé défini, 45

payaient, 58
payera, 108
payeraient, 58, 107
payerait, 108
payèrent, 58
payeront, 58, 107
pendu(e), 104
perd, 108
perdaient, 58
perdait, 108
perdent, 58
perdirent, 58
perdraient, 58, 107
perdre, 155
perdront, 58, 107
perdu, 155
peut, 120
peuvent, 118
peux, 143, 145
plaire, 153
pleut, 45
portait, 103
pourraient, 107
pourront, 107
pouvait, 102
pouvant, 145
pouvoir, 144
prêche, 122
prendrais, 103
presenter, 113
prouver, 152
puis, 143, 145
puissant, 145
recommencé, 135, 136
recommencer, 136
reçut, 98, 107
refusa, 108
regrette, 120, 121
relierait, 109
rencontrai, 104
rentrait, 104
rentrer, 72, 73
require , 24
rester, 72
retourner, 72
revenir, 72
rire, 153
rougir, 151

rougit, 82
sachant, 145
sache, 42, 116, 117, 143, 145
sachent, 117
sachez, 144
sachiez, 118
sais, 143, 145
sait, 98, 116, 117
savait, 103
savant, 145
savent, 117
savoir, 98, 111, 131, 144
savons, 119
se bat, 67
se battre, 80
se cache, 68
se coucher, 71
se débattre avec, 80
se débattre, 77
se déshabiller, 71
se (être) réfugiées, 120
se fâcher, 71, 78
se fiancer, 80
se jettent, 81
se lamenter, 77, 78
se lancer, 70
se lasser, 71
se lave, 67, 70
se laver, 71, 77
se lever, 71
se mange, 79
se marier, 71, 80
se meurt, 100
se noyer, 78
se passait, 103
se ressembler, 80
se rétablir, 71
se réveiller, 78
se rougir, 82
se sont eu levées, 54
se sont regardé(e)s, 70, 80
se souvenir (de), 77
se souvenir, 70
se tromper, 78
se vende, 79
se vend, 68
sera, 106, 109
sera sorti, 55, 57

LIST OF FRENCH VERB FORMS 187

serai battu, 66
seraient, 109
seraient partis, 59
serais battu, 66
serais tombé, 102
serait, 55, 103, 106, 108, 109, 122
serait sorti, 57
seront partis, 59
signifiant, 113
signifié, 113
signifier, 113
soient, 117
sois, 117, 145
sois (que je), 42
sois battu (que je), 66
sois entré, 122
sois marié, 113
soit, 116
soit venu, 120
sommes, 104
sont partis, 59
sort, 54, 57, 91
sortait, 54, 57, 104
sortir, 72
sortira, 57
sortirai, 54
sortirait, 54, 57
sortit, 54, 56
soyez, 117, 144
stopper, 149
suis allé, 82
suis battu, 66
suis d'avis, 121
suis entré, 103
suis monté, 75
suis resté, 73, 74
suis rentré, 82
suis tombé, 74
suivre, 153
sut, 98
sût, 42
s'abstenir (de), 77
s'assembler, 80
s'en aller, 70, 81
s'endormir, 78
s'ennuyer, 78
s'est bâtie, 70
s'est blessée, 71

s'est brisée, 83
s'est cassé, 63, 64, 83
s'est coupé, 80
s'est décidé, 71
s'est regardé, 70, 80
s'est retrouvée, 70
s'est rougi, 64
s'établir, 71
s'évader, 70, 71
s'habiller, 71
s'ouvrait, 103
taire, 153
téléphoner, 149
téléviser, 149
tombais, 101
tomber, 72, 73
travailla, 97
va, 144
vaincre, 153
vais, 94, 144
vas, 144
-veillant, 145
veille, 145
vendre, 140, 148, 151, 152, 153, 154
venir, 72, 73
veuillez, 145, 146
veulent, 141
veut, 113, 141
veux, 141
vider, 152
viendra, 115
vienne, 115, 116, 117, 118
viens, 22, 91, 132, 133
vient, 22
vient de, 143
vis, 85
vit, 82
vivre, 153
vont, 144
voudrais, 108
voudrez, 108
voulait, 113
voulant, 145
voulez, 146
voulez, 141
vouloir, 141, 144, 146
voulons, 141
voyait, 103

In the CURRENT ISSUES IN LINGUISTIC THEORY (CILT) series (edited by: E.F. Konrad Koerner, University of Ottawa) the following volumes have been published thus far or are scheduled for publication:

1. KOERNER, Konrad (ed.): *The Transformational-Generative Paradigm and Modern Linguistic Theory.* 1975.
2. WEIDERT, Alfons: *Componential Analysis of Lushai Phonology.* 1975.
3. MAHER, J. Peter: *Papers on Language Theory and History I: Creation and Tradition in Language.* Foreword by Raimo Anttila. 1979.
4. HOPPER, Paul J. (ed.): *Studies in Descriptive and Historical Linguistics. Festschrift for Winfred P. Lehmann.* 1977.
5. ITKONEN, Esa: *Grammatical Theory and Metascience: A critical investigation into the methodological and philosophical foundations of 'autonomous' linguistics.* 1978.
6. ANTTILA, Raimo: *Historical and Comparative Linguistics.* 1989.
7. MEISEL, Jürgen M. & Martin D. PAM (eds): *Linear Order and Generative Theory.* 1979.
8. WILBUR, Terence H.: *Prolegomena to a Grammar of Basque.* 1979.
9. HOLLIEN, Harry & Patricia (eds): *Current Issues in the Phonetic Sciences. Proceedings of the IPS-77 Congress, Miami Beach, Florida, 17-19 December 1977.* 1979.
10. PRIDEAUX, Gary D. (ed.): *Perspectives in Experimental Linguistics. Papers from the University of Alberta Conference on Experimental Linguistics, Edmonton, 13-14 Oct. 1978.* 1979.
11. BROGYANYI, Bela (ed.): *Studies in Diachronic, Synchronic, and Typological Linguistics: Festschrift for Oswald Szemerényi on the Occasion of his 65th Birthday.* 1979.
12. FISIAK, Jacek (ed.): *Theoretical Issues in Contrastive Linguistics.* 1981. Out of print
13. MAHER, J. Peter, Allan R. BOMHARD & Konrad KOERNER (eds): *Papers from the Third International Conference on Historical Linguistics, Hamburg, August 22-26 1977.* 1982.
14. TRAUGOTT, Elizabeth C., Rebecca LaBRUM & Susan SHEPHERD (eds): *Papers from the Fourth International Conference on Historical Linguistics, Stanford, March 26-30 1979.* 1980.
15. ANDERSON, John (ed.): *Language Form and Linguistic Variation. Papers dedicated to Angus McIntosh.* 1982.
16. ARBEITMAN, Yoël L. & Allan R. BOMHARD (eds): *Bono Homini Donum: Essays in Historical Linguistics, in Memory of J.Alexander Kerns.* 1981.
17. LIEB, Hans-Heinrich: *Integrational Linguistics. 6 volumes. Vol. II-VI n.y.p.* 1984/93.
18. IZZO, Herbert J. (ed.): *Italic and Romance. Linguistic Studies in Honor of Ernst Pulgram.* 1980.
19. RAMAT, Paolo et al. (eds): *Linguistic Reconstruction and Indo-European Syntax. Proceedings of the Colloquium of the 'Indogermanischhe Gesellschaft'. University of Pavia, 6-7 September 1979.* 1980.
20. NORRICK, Neal R.: *Semiotic Principles in Semantic Theory.* 1981.
21. AHLQVIST, Anders (ed.): *Papers from the Fifth International Conference on Historical Linguistics, Galway, April 6-10 1981.* 1982.
22. UNTERMANN, Jürgen & Bela BROGYANYI (eds): *Das Germanische und die Rekonstruktion der Indogermanischen Grundsprache. Akten des Freiburger Kolloquiums der Indogermanischen Gesellschaft, Freiburg, 26-27 Februar 1981.* 1984.
23. DANIELSEN, Niels: *Papers in Theoretical Linguistics.* Edited by Per Baerentzen. 1992.
24. LEHMANN, Winfred P. & Yakov MALKIEL (eds): *Perspectives on Historical Linguistics. Papers from a conference held at the meeting of the Language Theory Division, Modern Language Assn., San Francisco, 27-30 December 1979.* 1982.
25. ANDERSEN, Paul Kent: *Word Order Typology and Comparative Constructions.* 1983.
26. BALDI, Philip (ed.): *Papers from the XIIth Linguistic Symposium on Romance Languages, Univ. Park, April 1-3, 1982.* 1984.

27. BOMHARD, Alan R.: *Toward Proto-Nostratic. A New Approach to the Comparison of Proto-Indo-European and Proto-Afroasiatic.* Foreword by Paul J. Hopper. 1984.
28. BYNON, James (ed.): *Current Progress in Afro-Asiatic Linguistics: Papers of the Third International Hamito-Semitic Congress, London, 1978.* 1984.
29. PAPROTTÉ, Wolf & René DIRVEN (eds): *The Ubiquity of Metaphor: Metaphor in language and thought.* 1985 (publ. 1986).
30. HALL, Robert A. Jr.: *Proto-Romance Morphology.* = Comparative Romance Grammar, vol. III. 1984.
31. GUILLAUME, Gustave: *Foundations for a Science of Language.*
32. COPELAND, James E. (ed.): *New Directions in Linguistics and Semiotics.* Co-edition with Rice University Press who hold exclusive rights for US and Canada. 1984.
33. VERSTEEGH, Kees: *Pidginization and Creolization. The Case of Arabic.* 1984.
34. FISIAK, Jacek (ed.): *Papers from the VIth International Conference on Historical Linguistics, Poznan, 22-26 August. 1983.* 1985.
35. COLLINGE, N.E.: *The Laws of Indo-European.* 1985.
36. KING, Larry D. & Catherine A. MALEY (eds): *Selected papers from the XIIIth Linguistic Symposium on Romance Languages, Chapel Hill, N.C., 24-26 March 1983.* 1985.
37. GRIFFEN, T.D.: *Aspects of Dynamic Phonology.* 1985.
38. BROGYANYI, Bela & Thomas KRÖMMELBEIN (eds): *Germanic Dialects:Linguistic and Philological Investigations.* 1986.
39. BENSON, James D., Michael J. CUMMINGS, & William S. GREAVES (eds): *Linguistics in a Systemic Perspective.* 1988.
40. FRIES, Peter Howard (ed.) in collaboration with Nancy M. Fries: *Toward an Understanding of Language: Charles C. Fries in Perspective.* 1985.
41. EATON, Roger, et al. (eds): *Papers from the 4th International Conference on English Historical Linguistics, April 10-13, 1985.* 1985.
42. MAKKAI, Adam & Alan K. MELBY (eds): *Linguistics and Philosophy. Festschrift for Rulon S. Wells.* 1985 (publ. 1986).
43. AKAMATSU, Tsutomu: *The Theory of Neutralization and the Archiphoneme in Functional Phonology.* 1988.
44. JUNGRAITHMAYR, Herrmann & Walter W. MUELLER (eds): *Proceedings of the Fourth International Hamito-Semitic Congress.* 1987.
45. KOOPMAN, W.F., F.C. Van der LEEK, O. FISCHER & R. EATON (eds): *Explanation and Linguistic Change.* 1986
46. PRIDEAUX, Gary D. & William J. BAKER: *Strategies and Structures: The processing of relative clauses.* 1987.
47. LEHMANN, Winfred P. (ed.): *Language Typology 1985. Papers from the Linguistic Typology Symposium, Moscow, 9-13 Dec. 1985.* 1986.
48. RAMAT, Anna G., Onofrio CARRUBA and Giuliano BERNINI (eds): *Papers from the 7th International Conference on Historical Linguistics.* 1987.
49. WAUGH, Linda R. and Stephen RUDY (eds): *New Vistas in Grammar: Invariance and Variation. Proceedings of the Second International Roman Jakobson Conference, New York University, Nov.5-8, 1985.* 1991.
50. RUDZKA-OSTYN, Brygida (ed.): *Topics in Cognitive Linguistics.* 1988.
51. CHATTERJEE, Ranjit: *Aspect and Meaning in Slavic and Indic. With a foreword by Paul Friedrich.* 1989.
52. FASOLD, Ralph W. & Deborah SCHIFFRIN (eds): *Language Change and Variation.* 1989.
53. SANKOFF, David: *Diversity and Diachrony.* 1986.
54. WEIDERT, Alfons: *Tibeto-Burman Tonology. A comparative analysis.* 1987
55. HALL, Robert A. Jr.: *Linguistics and Pseudo-Linguistics.* 1987.

56. HOCKETT, Charles F.: *Refurbishing our Foundations. Elementary linguistics from an advanced point of view.* 1987.
57. BUBENIK, Vít: *Hellenistic and Roman Greece as a Sociolinguistic Area.* 1989.
58. ARBEITMAN, Yoël. L. (ed.): *Fucus: A Semitic/Afrasian Gathering in Remembrance of Albert Ehrman.* 1988.
59. VAN VOORST, Jan: *Event Structure.* 1988.
60. KIRSCHNER, Carl & Janet DECESARIS (eds): *Studies in Romance Linguistics. Selected Proceedings from the XVII Linguistic Symposium on Romance Languages.* 1989.
61. CORRIGAN, Roberta L., Fred ECKMAN & Michael NOONAN (eds): *Linguistic Categorization. Proceedings of an International Symposium in Milwaukee, Wisconsin, April 10-11, 1987.* 1989.
62. FRAJZYNGIER, Zygmunt (ed.): *Current Progress in Chadic Linguistics. Proceedings of the International Symposium on Chadic Linguistics, Boulder, Colorado, 1-2 May 1987.* 1989.
63. EID, Mushira (ed.): *Perspectives on Arabic Linguistics I. Papers from the First Annual Symposium on Arabic Linguistics.* 1990.
64. BROGYANYI, Bela (ed.): *Prehistory, History and Historiography of Language, Speech, and Linguistic Theory. Papers in honor of Oswald Szemérenyi I.* 1992.
65. ADAMSON, Sylvia, Vivien A. LAW, Nigel VINCENT and Susan WRIGHT (eds): *Papers from the 5th International Conference on English Historical Linguistics.* 1990.
66. ANDERSEN, Henning and Konrad KOERNER (eds): *Historical Linguistics 1987. Papers from the 8th International Conference on Historical Linguistics, Lille, August 30-Sept., 1987.* 1990.
67. LEHMANN, Winfred P. (ed.): *Language Typology 1987. Systematic Balance in Language. Papers from the Linguistic Typology Symposium, Berkeley, 1-3 Dec 1987.* 1990.
68. BALL, Martin, James FIFE, Erich POPPE &Jenny ROWLAND (eds): *Celtic Linguistics/ Ieithyddiaeth Geltaidd. Readings in the Brythonic Languages. Festschrift for T. Arwyn Watkins.* 1990.
69. WANNER, Dieter and Douglas A. KIBBEE (eds): *New Analyses in Romance Linguistics. Selected papers from the Linguistic Symposium on Romance Languages XVIIII, Urbana-Champaign, April 7-9, 1988.* 1991.
70. JENSEN, John T.: *Morphology. Word structure in generative grammar.* 1990.
71. O'GRADY, William: *Categories and Case. The sentence structure of Korean.* 1991.
72. EID, Mushira and John MCCARTHY (eds): *Perspectives on Arabic Linguistics II. Papers from the Second Annual Symposium on Arabic Linguistics.* 1990.
73. STAMENOV, Maxim (ed.): *Current Advances in Semantic Theory.* 1991.
74. LAEUFER, Christiane and Terrell A. MORGAN (eds): *Theoretical Analyses in Romance Linguistics.* 1991.
75. DROSTE, Flip G. and John E. JOSEPH (eds): *Linguistic Theory and Grammatical Description. Nine Current Approaches.* 1991.
76. WICKENS, Mark A.: *Grammatical Number in English Nouns. An empirical and theoretical account.* 1992.
77. BOLTZ, William G. and Michael C. SHAPIRO (eds): *Studies in the Historical Phonology of Asian Languages.* 1991.
78. KAC, Michael: *Grammars and Grammaticality.* 1992.
79. ANTONSEN, Elmer H. and Hans Henrich HOCK (eds): *STAEF-CRAEFT: Studies in Germanic Linguistics. Select papers from the First and Second Symposium on Germanic Linguistics, University of Chicago, 24 April 1985, and Univ. of Illinois at Urbana-Champaign, 3-4 Oct. 1986.* 1991.
80. COMRIE, Bernard and Mushira EID (eds): *Perspectives on Arabic Linguistics III. Papers from the Third Annual Symposium on Arabic Linguistics.* 1991.
81. LEHMANN, Winfred P. and H.J. HEWITT (eds): *Language Typology 1988. Typological Models in the Service of Reconstruction.* 1991.

82. VAN VALIN, Robert D. (ed.): *Advances in Role and Reference Grammar.* 1992.
83. FIFE, James and Erich POPPE (eds): *Studies in Brythonic Word Order.* 1991.
84. DAVIS, Garry W. and Gregory K. IVERSON (eds): *Explanation in Historical Linguistics.* 1992.
85. BROSELOW, Ellen, Mushira EID and John McCARTHY (eds): *Perspectives on Arabic Linguistics IV. Papers from the Annual Symposium on Arabic Linguistics.* 1992.
86. KESS, Joseph F.: *Psycholinguistics. Psychology, linguistics, and the study of natural language.* 1992.
87. BROGYANYI, Bela and Reiner LIPP (eds): *Historical Philology: Greek, Latin, and Romance. Papers in honor of Oswald Szemerényi II.* 1992.
88. SHIELDS, Kenneth: *A History of Indo-European Verb Morphology.* 1992.
89. BURRIDGE, Kate: *Syntactic Change in Germanic. A study of some aspects of language change in Germanic with particular reference to Middle Dutch.* 1992.
90. KING, Larry D.: *The Semantic Structure of Spanish. Meaning and grammatical form.* 1992.
91. HIRSCHBÜHLER, Paul and Konrad KOERNER (eds): *Romance Languages and Modern Linguistic Theory. Selected papers from the XX Linguistic Symposium on Romance Languages, University of Ottawa, April 10-14, 1990.* 1992.
92. POYATOS, Fernando: *Paralanguage: A linguistic and interdisciplinary approach to interactive speech and sounds.* 1992.
93. LIPPI-GREEN, Rosina (ed.): *Recent Developments in Germanic Linguistics.* 1992.
94. HAGÈGE, Claude: *The Language Builder. An essay on the human signature in linguistic morphogenesis.* 1992.
95. MILLER, D. Gary: *Complex Verb Formation.* 1992.
96. LIEB, Hans-Heinrich (ed.): *Prospects for a New Structuralism.* 1992.
97. BROGYANYI, Bela & Reiner LIPP (eds): *Comparative-Historical Linguistics: Indo-European and Finno-Ugric. Papers in honor of Oswald Szemerényi III.* 1992.
98. EID, Mushira & Gregory K. IVERSON: *Principles and Prediction: The analysis of natural language.* 1993.
99. JENSEN, John T.: *English Phonology.* 1993.
100. MUFWENE, Salikoko S. and Lioba MOSHI (eds): *Topics in African Linguistics. Papers from the XXI Annual Conference on African Linguistics, University of Georgia, April 1990.* 1993.
101. EID, Mushira & Clive HOLES (eds): *Perspectives on Arabic Linguistics V. Papers from the Fifth Annual Symposium on Arabic Linguistics.* 1993.
102. DAVIS, Philip W. (ed.): *Alternative Linguistics. Descriptive and theoretical Modes.* 1995.
103. ASHBY, William J., Marianne MITHUN, Giorgio PERISSINOTTO and Eduardo RAPOSO: *Linguistic Perspectives on Romance Languages. Selected papers from the XXI Linguistic Symposium on Romance Languages, Santa Barbara, February 21-24, 1991.* 1993.
104. KURZOVÁ, Helena: *From Indo-European to Latin. The evolution of a morphosyntactic type.* 1993.
105. HUALDE, José Ignacio and Jon ORTIZ DE URBANA (eds): *Generative Studies in Basque Linguistics.* 1993.
106. AERTSEN, Henk and Robert J. JEFFERS (eds): *Historical Linguistics 1989. Papers from the 9th International Conference on Historical Linguistics, New Brunswick, 14-18 August 1989.* 1993.
107. MARLE, Jaap van (ed.): *Historical Linguistics 1991. Papers from the 10th International Conference on Historical Linguistics, Amsterdam, August 12-16, 1991.* 1993.
108. LIEB, Hans-Heinrich: *Linguistic Variables. Towards a unified theory of linguistic variation.* 1993.
109. PAGLIUCA, William (ed.): *Perspectives on Grammaticalization.* 1994.
110. SIMONE, Raffaele (ed.): *Iconicity in Language.* 1995.

111. TOBIN, Yishai: *Invariance, Markedness and Distinctive Feature Analysis. A contrastive study of sign systems in English and Hebrew.* 1994.
112. CULIOLI, Antoine: *Cognition and Representation in Linguistic Theory.* Translated, edited and introduced by Michel Liddle. 1995.
113. FERNÁNDEZ, Francisco, Miguel FUSTER and Juan Jose CALVO (eds): *English Historical Linguistics 1992. Papers from the 7th International Conference on English Historical Linguistics, Valencia, 22-26 September 1992.* 1994.
114. EGLI, U., P. PAUSE, Chr. SCHWARZE, A. von STECHOW, G. WIENOLD (eds): *Lexical Knowledge in the Organisation of Language.* 1995.
115. EID, Mushira, Vincente CANTARINO and Keith WALTERS (eds): *Perspectives on Arabic Linguistics. Vol. VI. Papers from the Sixth Annual Symposium on Arabic Linguistics.* 1994.
116. MILLER, D. Gary: *Ancient Scripts and Phonological Knowledge.* 1994.
117. PHILIPPAKI-WARBURTON, I., K. NICOLAIDIS and M. SIFIANOU (eds): *Themes in Greek Linguistics. Papers from the first International Conference on Greek Linguistics, Reading, September 1993.* 1994.
118. HASAN, Ruqaiya and Peter H. FRIES (eds): *On Subject and Theme. A discourse functional perspective.* 1995.
119. LIPPI-GREEN, Rosina: *Language Ideology and Language Change in Early Modern German. A sociolinguistic study of the consonantal system of Nuremberg.* 1994.
120. STONHAM, John T. : *Combinatorial Morphology.* 1994.
121. HASAN, Ruqaiya, Carmel CLORAN and David BUTT (eds): *Functional Descriptions. Theorie in practice.* 1996.
122. SMITH, John Charles and Martin MAIDEN (eds): *Linguistic Theory and the Romance Languages.* 1995.
123. AMASTAE, Jon, Grant GOODALL, Mario MONTALBETTI and Marianne PHINNEY: *Contemporary Research in Romance Linguistics. Papers from the XXII Linguistic Symposium on Romance Languages, El Paso//Juárez, February 22-24, 1994.* 1995.
124. ANDERSEN, Henning: *Historical Linguistics 1993. Selected papers from the 11th International Conference on Historical Linguistics, Los Angeles, 16-20 August 1993.* 1995.
125. SINGH, Rajendra (ed.): *Towards a Critical Sociolinguistics.* 1996.
126. MATRAS, Yaron (ed.): *Romani in Contact. The history, structure and sociology of a language.* 1995.
127. GUY, Gregory R., Crawford FEAGIN, Deborah SCHIFFRIN and John BAUGH (eds): *Towards a Social Science of Language. Papers in honor of William Labov. Volume 1: Variation and change in language and society.* 1996.
128. GUY, Gregory R., Crawford FEAGIN, Deborah SCHIFFRIN and John BAUGH (eds): *Towards a Social Science of Language. Papers in honor of William Labov. Volume 2: Social interaction and discourse structures.* n.y.p.
129. LEVIN, Saul: *Semitic and Indo-European: The Principal Etymologies. With observations on Afro-Asiatic.* 1995.
130. EID, Mushira (ed.) *Perspectives on Arabic Linguistics. Vol. VII. Papers from the Seventh Annual Symposium on Arabic Linguistics.* 1995.
131. HUALDE, Jose Ignacio, Joseba A. LAKARRA and R.L. Trask (eds): *Towards a History of the Basque Language.* 1995.
132. HERSCHENSOHN, Julia: *Case Suspension and Binary Complement Structure in French.* 1996.
133. ZAGONA, Karen (ed.): *Grammatical Theory and Romance Languages. Selected papers from the 25th Linguistic Symposium on Romance Languages (LSRL XXV) Seattle, 2-4 March 1995.* 1996.
134. EID, Mushira (ed.): *Perspectives on Arabic Linguistics Vol. VIII. Papers from the Eighth Annual Symposium on Arabic Linguistics.* 1996.

135. BRITTON Derek (ed.): *Papers from the 8th International Conference on English Historical Linguistics.* 1996.
136. MITKOV, Ruslan and Nicolas NICOLOV (eds): *Recent Advances in Natural Language Processing.* n.y.p.
137. LIPPI-GREEN, Rosina and Joseph C. SALMONS (eds): *Germanic Linguistics. Syntactic and diachronic.* 1996.
138. SACKMANN, Robin (ed.): *Theoretical Linguistics and Grammatical Description.* 1996.
139. BLACK, James R. and Virginia MOTAPANYANE (eds): *Microparametric Syntax and Dialect Variation.* 1996.
140. BLACK, James R. and Virginia MOTAPANYANE (eds): *Clitics, Pronouns and Movement.* n.y.p.
141. EID, Mushira and Dilworth PARKINSON (eds): *Perspectives on Arabic Linguistics Vol. IX. Papers from the Ninth Annual Symposium on Arabic Linguistics, Georgetown University, Washington D.C., 1995.* 1996.
142. JOSEPH, Brian D. and Joseph C. SALMONS (eds): *Nostratic. Sifting the Evidence.* n.y.p.
143. ATHANASIADOU, Angeliki and René DIRVEN (eds): *On Conditionals Again.* n.y.p.
144. SINGH, Rajendra (ed): *Trubetzkoy's Orphan. Proceedings of the Montréal Roundtable "Morphophonology: contemporary responses (Montréal, October 1994).* 1996.
145. HEWSON, John and Vit BUBENIK: *Tense and Aspect in Indo-European Languages. Theory, typology, diachrony.* 1997.
146. HINSKENS, Frans, Roeland VAN HOUT and Leo WETZELS (eds): *Variation, Change, and Phonological Theory.* n.y.p.
147. HEWSON, John: *The Cognitive System of the French Verb.* 1997.
148. WOLF, George and Nigel LOVE (eds): *Linguistics Inside Out. Roy Harris and his critics.* 1997.
149. HALL, T. Alan: *The Phonology of Coronals.* n.y.p.